Although the author has made every effort to ensure that the information in this book was correct at the time of print, the author does not assume and hereby disclaim any liability to any party for any loss, damage, or disruption caused by errors or omissions, whether such errors or omissions result from negligence, accident, or any other cause.

978-0-473-68844-8

© 2023 Taryn Dryfhout. All Rights Reserved.
www.TarynDryfhout.com

No part of this book may be reproduced or transmitted in any form or by any means, electronic or mechanical, including photocopying or recording, or by any information storage and retrieval system, without permission in writing from the publisher.

All photos and/or copyrighted material appearing in this book remains the work of its owners. Every effort has been made to give credit. No infringement is intended in this work. The title of this work, "But I'm a Gilmore!", is a phrase from *Gilmore Girls* and is not owned by the author. This book is not official, authorised by, or affiliated with The CW, Warner Brothers, Dorothy Parker Drank Here Productions or their representatives.

Contents

Introduction

Part One: Cast and Crew
It's a Show

(In order of appearance):

- Copper Boom!: Conflict and Controversy
- Emily Kuroda (1.1) Mrs. Kim
- Shelly Cole (1.2) Madeline Lynn
- Dakin Matthews (1.2) Hanlin Charleston
- Ted Rooney (1.2) Morey Dell
- Carla McCloskey (1.3) First Assistant Director
- Robert Lee (1.5) Background
- Michael Winters (1.7) Taylor Doose
- Valerie Campbell (1.11) Costumer / Costume Supervisor
- Joe Fria (1.12) Joe Mastoni / Waiter
- Albert Coleman (1.13) Editor
- David Sutcliffe (1.14) Christopher Hayden
- Grant Lee Phillips (1.16) Town Troubadour
- Stephen Clancy (1.20) Director / Steadicam Operator
- Jon Wellner (1.21) Mikey
- Biff Yeager (2.2) Tom
- Dave Berthiaume (2.2) Location Manager
- Sheila Lawrence (2.2) Writer / Co-Executive Producer
- Adam Wylie (2.9) Brad Langford
- Evie Peck (2.20) Karen
- Jessica 'Sugar' Kiper (3.1) Shane
- George Bell (3.11) Professor Bell / Dialogue Coach
- Aris Alvarado (3.20) Caesar
- David Bertman (4.2) Editor

- Ethan Cohn (4.3) Glen Babble / Josh
- Patty Malcolm (4.4) Stand-in for Lauren Graham / Woman #1 / Mrs. Harris / Leanne / Secretary
- Peter Klausner (4.5) William
- Rini Bell (4.6) Lulu Kuschner
- Lynda Scarlino (4.7) Buff Otis
- Julie Dolan (4.13) Anna / Customer / Passing Woman
- A.J. Tesler (4.17) Rob
- Tara Platt (4.19) Shelly
- Chris Flanders (4.20) Shel
- Alan Loayza (5.3) Colin Mcrae
- Lee Shallat Chemel (5.4) Director
- Nick Holmes (5.7) Robert Grimaldi
- Artie O'Daly (5.7) Seth
- Elisabeth Abbott (5.15) Rosemary
- Devon Sorvari (5.19) Honor Huntzberger
- Dave Shalansky (5.20) Harry
- John Kapelos (6.2) Orientation Leader
- Yuri Lowenthal (6.10) Sous Chef / Carl
- Devon Michaels (6.12) Bill
- David Greenman (6.15) Fred
- Tahmus Rounds (6.15) Buzu Barnes
- Ryen Herrmann (6.16) Alexandra
- Ronnie Alvarez (7.3) Connor / Tutor
- Lou Saliba (7.6) Ronald
- Austin Tichenor (7.13) Doctor Goldstein

Part Two: Creators
It's a Lifestyle

- Jennie and Marcus Whitaker (The Fan Fest Society)
- Kristi Carlson (Eat Like a Gilmore Cookbooks)

- Kristine Eckart (The Gilmore Book Club)
- Larisa Kliman (Eating Gilmore)
- Ariane Lariviere (GG Inspired Lifestyle)
- Megan Craig (Stars Lorelai Crafts)
- Jackie and Candice Amundson (Candies Crafties)
- Julianne Buonocore (The Literary Lifestyle)
- A S Berman (The Gilmore Girls Companion)
- Jess Fellows-Miliner (Oy with the cups already)
- Chas Demster (itsfilmedthere.com)
- DeAnn Stansbury (Clover Furniture Shack)
- Kendra Westphalen (Kendra Westphalen Designs)

Part Three: Cult Fans
It's a Religion

- Nicole Gallucci (Connecticut, USA)
- Laura Sanderfer (Atlanta, USA)
- Jennifer Wood (Colorado, USA)
- Teresa Beracci (Naples, Italy)
- Amanda Ranay Griffey (Georgia, USA)
- Claudia Schoder (Dresden, Germany).
- Maria Cristina Locuratolo (Rome, Italy)
- Krista Callahan (Pennsylvania, USA)
- Nikki Ella Thomas (Derbyshire, UK)
- Ruth and Ellen Bustin (Northamptonshire, UK)
- Ella Spice (Maryland, USA)
- Sarah Putnam (Washington, USA)
- Nicole Robinson (Arizona, USA)
- Ashley Tate (California, USA)
- Trista McMorrow (Florida, USA)
- April Richer (Ontario, Canada)
- Clarissa Jones (Ohio, USA)

- Erica Andrews (West Virginia, USA)
- Shelly Barnhart (Ohio, USA)
- Nicole Marreiros (Connecticut, USA)
- Zoe Ronchi (Victoria, Australia)
- Alicia Reichert (Michigan, USA)
- Jamie Lee Marie Naragon (Ohio, USA)
- Katie Wagner (New Hampshire, USA)
- Jessica Weiss (California, USA)
- Datha Caler Curtis (Georgia, USA)
- Shelby Parker (California, USA)
- Cora Farrish (Michigan, USA)
- Valerie Johnston (Ontario, Canada)
- Karine Michaud (Bron, France)
- Britany Smith (Wisconsin, USA)
- Samantha Lloyd (Victoria, Australia)
- Olivia Roth (New York, USA)

Appendix One: Trista McMorrow's Fan Fest Entry
Appendix Two: Brooke Criswell and Rachel Renbarger's Research
Acknowledgements
Photo Credits
About the Author

Introduction

This book has been the product of a long process, which began in 2017 when I started writing my first book about the television show *Gilmore Girls—You've Been Gilmored!: The Unofficial Encyclopedia and Comprehensive Guide to Gilmore Girls and Stars Hollow.* After the publication and success of this book, I announced my intentions to write another book, which would focus on the experiences of the fans of the show. Having joined several social media groups for fans of the show, and chatting to fans from all over the globe, it quickly became apparent to me that every *Gilmore Girls* fan has a story. I shared this view in my first book, along with my own 'Gilmore story'—how the show led me to university, the college newspaper, and ultimately to writing, and the creation of my first *Gilmore Girls* book.

While my story has been shared in the introduction to *You've Been Gilmored!*, I came to learn of many stories that had not been shared, and which were much more interesting and meaningful than my own. These stories included a daughter who spent the final days of her mother's life watching the show together, a soldier who found solace from the sounds of war by watching *Gilmore Girls,* a woman who watched *Gilmore Girls* while she recovered from a vicious dog attack, and an Australian woman who found comfort in *Gilmore Girls* while she came to terms with a life-changing diagnosis. What all of these fan stories have in common is community—relationships. *Gilmore Girls* is a show that people share. The fans in this book watched the show with family, friends, or found family and friends in the characters that inhabit Stars Hollow. Many of these fans also found a home in the vibrant online fan community, cemented friendships at the Gilmore inspired fan festivals, or have resonated with the relationships on the show. For these fans—and I would argue all fans—people are at the heart of our Gilmore story. These stories, and so much more, came to shape the original inception for this book.

This project however, like all good works of art, changed shape and grew over time. A good friend of mine, who eventually came onboard the book as a creative consultant encouraged me to reach out to cast and crew to see if they would be willing to share their experiences as well. While I didn't have high hopes that many of them would be interested in speaking with a writer that they didn't know—who lived at the bottom of the world—about a show they worked on some 20 years ago, I will be forever indebted to the over 50 cast and crew members who graciously shared their time and memories with me for the creation of this book.

Initially I wasn't sure what the cast and crew interviews would draw out, or what shape the interview material would take. Would it be a 'tell all', or simply an account of how the show was behind the scenes? As the interviews took place, I started to realise that the cast and crew also, had 'Gilmore stories' of their very own. The cast stories that are contained in this book are not transcripts of my interviews with them. Rather, I have done my best to take each cast member's stories and tell them using a single voice, in a way that accurately reflects their Gilmore story.

To add to the magic of speaking with the cast, and getting to hear their experiences firsthand, something beautiful happened that I couldn't have anticipated. Where the fan stories were centred around relationships and community, so too were the cast and crew stories. While this was pleasantly surprising, it probably shouldn't have been a surprise. Because whether you were in *Gilmore Girls*, or watched it, we all have a Gilmore Story. We are all Gilmores at heart.

This unplanned marriage of themes is the real heart of this book. At one point in this journey, when the amount of cast, crew, and fans who so generously donated their time and stories to this project exceeded 100, I very seriously considered splitting the book into two - one which covered the experiences of the cast and crew, and one which would relay the fan experiences. However, the natural unity that existed within the book was too serendipitous, and I felt that the work would not be what it is, if this separation occurred. And so, this book took its final form.

This book takes shape in three main sections: the three 'C's:

- Cast and Crew: It's a Show
- Creators: It's a Lifestyle
- Cult Followers: It's a Religion

The first section opens with a chapter called 'Copper Boom!'. This chapter offers a brief handling of all of the negative stories and material that came out of my interview work, and research about the show. I initially shied away from this material, and planned to avoid it at all costs. When a negative memory or experience came up during interviews, I tried my best to work with the cast or crew member to navigate the material so that it would highlight the positives of the show, and would largely gloss over details which might portray the show from a darker angle. However, as the interviews continued, the sheer amount of this material continued to grow and it was difficult to deny its significance. My decision to include it culminated in a conversation with a cast member who was disappointed that I would be 'fluffing' over the reality of the show, and was not interested in faithfully, and accurately representing how the show was. In his perspective, holding back this information was a misrepresentation of the show, and robbed him of validation. He had a particularly difficult time on set, and he did not want his truth to be smoothed over or avoided. Since my original intention was not to create a 'tell all' book of 'dirty little secrets' about the show, I finally made the decision to deal with this material in the first chapter, after which the book will move on to memoirs of the good times, and happy memories of the show for those who worked on it.

Following this, the rest of the 'Cast and Crew: It's a Show' section will recount the experiences of the cast and crew who worked on the show. This section contains the Gilmore stories of producers, editors, directors, cameramen, costumers, dialogue coaches, and of course, actors. The latter of these range in character density from series regulars to recurring roles, to guest stars and co-stars. What I hope will become clear as you read, is that the smaller roles are some of the most significant ones in *Gilmore Girls*, and I would argue that these small, significant characters are what make the show so unique. The peculiar, eccentric, and sometimes outright bizarre characters that inhabit the world of Stars Hollow and the Gilmore-verse breathe life into the show and illuminate the scenes, episodes, and story arcs. Whilst some of the stories from actors who played more major characters on the show have been told through books, interviews, and appearances, the actors who played more minor parts have memories and stories that have never been expressed before this book. In this sense, the book takes you on a journey through the memories of those whose role on the show was integral, but who have previously been overlooked. This is especially true for crew members, some of whom were present full-time over many years, but who have not shared their experiences of working on the show until now. While I enjoyed putting together all of the stories in this section, my two favourite are those of Ryen Herrmann, and Peter Klausner, whose touching stories about the connection that *Gilmore Girls* gave them with their parents, are truly heartwarming.

The second section, 'Creators: It's a Lifestyle' is the first section that recounts the experiences of fans but is focused on those fans whose love for *Gilmore Girls* has been so profound that they have turned their interest in the show into some kind of work, hobby, or passion project—into a lifestyle. While I resonated with most of the fan stories that were submitted, I felt a special affinity to the stories within this section, as I include myself among these creators. Many of the stories in this section have been penned by the creators themselves and have been edited into their final form. In this section you will read about how the Fan Fest Society (formerly Gilmore Girls Fan Fest) came together, how one man decided to compile a list of every location on the show, how one woman opened a *Gilmore Girls* themed furniture store, and how fans became merchants of *Gilmore Girls* inspired items. These creators are not only artistic and enterprising, but they show how people with a passion for something can take it and make it so much more than a television show. They can mould it into their work, and their life.

The third and final section, 'Cult Fans: It's a Religion' explores the Gilmore stories of those who watch the show. The memoirs found in this section range from the deeply personal, to the fun and funky. You will hear how *Gilmore Girls* got fans through college, divorce, family deaths, depression, accidents, and illness. You will read about a fan who had a *Gilmore Girls* wedding, a soldier who discovered the show while deployed in Iraq, and a high school teacher who recreated the Festival of Living Arts in her history classroom. The stories in this section represent a diverse age and geographical spread, with fans from all over the world sharing what the show means to them.

None of the stories in any part of this book are intended to be exhaustive. Since space did not allow for over 100 biographies to be published within this book, each story serves as a snapshot. The cast and crew stories offer a snapshot of what led them to *Gilmore Girls*, what their time on the show was like, and what their life has looked like since *Gilmore Girls*. Likewise, the creators and cult fans sections show a snapshot of how *Gilmore Girls* has richly affected those who have watched it, while not being able to present an exhaustive account of their lives. In addition, each section contains the stories from merely a sample of people. IMDB lists more than 1600 cast and crew members in *Gilmore Girls*, so the 50 that this book contains represents a fraction of those who worked on the show. The same is true of the creators, and of course, fans.

The span of time during which I worked on my last *Gilmore Girls* book, and this one, has been some of the most enjoyable work I have done in my life. I have endeavoured with all my heart to tell these stories well, recognising the vulnerability, honesty, and beauty, with which I have been entrusted. It was only near the end of the project that I became aware of how much the experiences of telling these stories had shaped my own. The stories in this book remain precious to me, and I hope that they will be treasured by all who read them.

While the chapters can be read in any order, I strongly encourage readers to work from cover to cover. The marriage of the themes from cast to fans is best appreciated in this order. As you read these collected stories from cast and crew, creators, and cult fans, I hope that you will find within their stories the inherent oneness that unifies all those who touch, or are touched by, the show. Those whose lives have intersected with *Gilmore Girls* appear to be all cut from the same cloth and are part of a wider community that has been shaped by the unique character of the show. They are the global citizens of *Gilmore Girls,* who each have a story to tell, and a life that has developed in some way through their exposure to the show, and their love for it. For these inhabitants of the Gilmore verse, it is so much more than a television show. It's a lifestyle, it's a religion, it's a family.

Taryn

PART ONE
CAST & CREW

It's a Show

Copper Boom!

"I found it to be a very unhappy set to work on. The lead actors were very self-absorbed and had an unjustifiable sense of entitlement—egos flourishing and conflict everywhere. I chose not to return, life is too short."

- Cast member

While most of the cast and crew on the show had nothing but lovely things to say about the atmosphere on set—including their co-stars, and the working conditions they experienced during their time on *Gilmore Girls,* there was a significant amount of negative material that arose during my interview work for this book. In addition to the cast and crew stories that are featured in this book, I also spoke with cast and crew members whose experiences on the show were so negative that they were not even prepared to be named in this book. This is largely due to their ongoing presence in the television and film industry, and their understandable hesitance to damage any of their working relationships or jeopardise roles on other projects. Many of these actors and crew members were happy for me, however, to discuss their experiences, without their names.

At this point I would like to issue a warning: things are going to get a bit difficult. This is the only chapter in this book, in which this negative material will be addressed. If you don't want to ruin the magic of Stars Hollow or feel that knowing how things really were behind the cameras would negatively impact your experience of *Gilmore Girls,* then make your way to chapter two and start this book with Emily Kuroda's cheerful recount of her time on the show.

I was initially ambivalent about including this material, in what would otherwise be a warm, positive collection of stories about the show. It was a long, difficult process, wading through the negative material and deciding how to handle it, and deciding whether it should be incorporated fully, partially, or be omitted entirely. After speaking at length with my creative consultant, and with several cast and crew members who did share their more difficult experiences of working on this show, I came to the decision that this book wouldn't be an authentic account of how the show was, without this material. While most of the stories are heartwarming, and uplifting, I don't want to misrepresent, or smooth over the difficulties that existed, just because they are uncomfortable. What made up my mind to include it, was a conversation with one actor, who had agreed to be interviewed. This actor was upset when I discussed the possibility of excluding any negative material from the book, as he felt that his experience was going to be misrepresented, and that I would be concealing the hardships that he suffered professionally whilst on this show, by choosing not to reveal the problematic, and at times painful, aspects of *Gilmore Girls* that we have not heard much of until now. To honour the sensitive stories and memories that were so bravely shared with me, I feel it is only right to address some of these issues, before this book moves forward.

I was obviously not on set with any of the cast and crew and cannot confirm any of the information in this chapter. This chapter merely reflects information given to me through interviews with members of the cast and crew.

Whilst it is not my intention to name specific people, one common theme amongst the cast and crew was difficulties working with some of the actors. It was common knowledge that some of the *Gilmore Girls* actors made a habit of screaming at people—often the directors—and more often, each other. Other common complaints included refusing to make eye contact or speak with other cast and crew on the set, acting cold towards people, and at times going as far as pretending that people weren't there—even when they were clearly being spoken to, or looked at. The reputation of some actors was so ubiquitous, that several cast members reported being warned by fellow actors to stay away from the show, and not to even audition for it, and warned again by staff when they arrived on set. Allegedly, crew members would try to prepare guest actors and extras for rude, diva behaviour before they got on to the set, in an attempt to help them get through their day of shooting. The hope was that by shifting their expectations, the actors might be more likely to stay on. It is no secret that many cast members chose not to stay, and that there was a high turn around of both cast and crew on the show. One background actor made a rather public post on his Facebook page about his difficult time on the show. What followed was a large thread of comments, with a litany of eye-opening experiences, mainly from background actors, about their time in Stars Hollow. These memories included being treated with condescension, verbal abuse (some extras reported being called "maggots" and "cockroaches" by an actor), and ultimately being fired for expressing their hurt feelings over the humiliating and alarming conditions under which they had to work with others. One cast member said that the poor attitudes of some began to "infect" everyone, and by the end of the day, it was like a "virus" that had spread through the set.

Some cast members were so difficult to work with that unbeknownst to fans, they were recast and their episodes were re-shot. The original footage for these cast members has never been released to the public. One actor I spoke with, left acting because of his experience on *Gilmore Girls*. To date, he has not returned to the industry.

> "Just an unhappy tense set, with the leads acting out like Hollywood royalty. I have no patience for that

kind of behavior. It just makes life difficult for a lot of good, hard working people."

- Cast member

Tension between some of the actors has also been heavily rumoured on the internet, and this was confirmed in multiple cast and crew interviews. Cast members not getting along led to problems filming romantic scenes, fights breaking out on set, and regular meltdowns. Of course, in any setting where different personalities are working together, there is a certain amount of tension. David Sutcliffe said, as you will read later in this book, that he experienced similar in-house fighting in other television shows he was involved in such as *Will and Grace* and argues that this in-house fighting contributes to the quality of a production. In the case of *Gilmore Girls*, cast and crew members were passionately "fighting for the show". At times on *Gilmore Girls*, this tension led to more than just fights—scenarios such as trying to get certain characters written out, and playing disturbing pranks, were used in an attempt to run people off the show.

Guest actors, extras and crew members also had frequent problems with the same few cast members. The labels "primadonna," "diva," "monster," and several others that I won't repeat here, were used to describe some of the cast members' personalities, as well as criticism over how they conducted themselves professionally. One cast member is said to have consistently overstepped their role by doing things like giving directive notes to other actors. Another is said to have not bothered to learn their lines and had to be consistently fed them from a prompt, word for word. One crew member recalled an awkward moment where he was standing, watching a 'walk and talk' scene between two characters. The filming was taking place, when the actor who was delivering their lines stopped, staring straight ahead.

"What is that?", the actor said, pointing to the crew member.

"THAT!" the actor said, pointing again.

"I can't act with THAT in my view".

It was soon realised that the "that" the actor was referring to, was the crew member watching the scene being filmed. Since this was his workplace, the crew member obviously felt embarrassed and uncomfortable by what he felt was unnecessary rudeness and was reluctant to return to the set again. A guest actor also recounted his time on the show as very upsetting, because a series regular expressed disappointment at his racial identity. According to the guest actor, the series regular had different ideas about what race the actor in this role should be, and verbally attacked him. He left the set feeling uncomfortable and hurt. Despite starring in award winning movies since, he has not forgotten this unfortunate experience.

One actor's name came up time and time again during the research for this book. Stories of drug use, temper tantrums, and abusive behaviour surround this actor, and most cast and crew members who worked with them agreed that the difficulty in managing the moods and behaviour of this actor was one of the more draining demands on set. One actor who worked closely with this person, was given the job of managing the scenes they shot together, in order to try and minimise any upsets. This included managing background actors, who were not allowed to make noise (even whispering was prohibited), get in the actors eyeline, or make any noise with props. If these things were not adequately managed, the actor in question would become vocally upset, and become increasingly abusive towards the cast and crew. This difficult cast member also, allegedly, struggled with not being the highest paid actor on the show.

One factor that contributed to the show's success was the demanding schedule, and gruelling hours that went into putting together each expertly crafted episode. However, this came at a cost. Working conditions were a common discussion point during the interviews—for both cast and crew. The working hours on *Gilmore Girls* appear to have been demanding—over and above anything that is considered normal in the industry. Being tired and overwhelmed on set came with the territory, and unfortunately led to a high turnaround of crew. Crew members often fell asleep from exhaustion on set, and cast members were known to faint from filming outside in the California summer heat over long periods of time.

While one would hope that these demanding conditions were well rewarded, it is well known that the crew were not treated well financially either. There was also a discrepancy in the contracts for the crew and cast members, which paved the way for some issues in this area. According to union rules at the time, cast members had to be away from the set for a minimum amount of hours to account for transport and sleep. This window for transport and sleep was lower for crew members, meaning they could not get a full night's sleep before having to be back on set. As a result, their medical and dental health was not taken care of and declined as a result. One crew member said that the demands of the *Gilmore Girls* schedule contributed to the decision not to bring children into their relationship.

While there may be both truth and fiction in these accounts, there is some proof to be found in the relationships that have stood the test of time. Many of the cast and crew members in this book attest to the long-standing friendships they have maintained from the show—some of which carried into other professional settings. Melissa McCarthy was one name that came up over and over. Cast and crew members couldn't say enough about how kindhearted and helpful she was towards them on set. As we will explore later in the book, Valerie Campbell was also beloved by many. She is credited by multiple cast and crew members as being the social 'glue' that kept the *Gilmore Girls* family together. These attestations not only speak to the great people that worked on the show, but they indicate something else. In the silence, we see what might be the truth in some of these anecdotes. The truth may also lie in lighter Internet Movie Database (IMDB) resumes. Actors who are notoriously difficult to deal with are blacklisted in the industry, and typically have less busy careers than rising icons such as Melissa McCarthy.

In defence of these negative stories, I think most fans will appreciate that some of these experiences were contributing factors to the quality of the show. The intensified stress of the environment is a witness to how people change and react when they are working on something they really care about. People feeling comfortable enough to fight like passionate lovers behind the camera says something about the emotional loads that these actors and members of the crew were carrying for the show. It was important to them that the show was good, and so as Sutcliffe points out, they were "fighting" for it. In addition, the actors in this show were under constant scrutiny—as most Hollywood actors are. When you add in the ups and downs of personal life, the stress must be very difficult to manage. And, people handle that differently. What is clear, is that *Gilmore Girls* would not have been the show that it is without these people, and without their passionate love for the final product.

Emily Kuroda

Mrs Kim

  I got my start on *Gilmore Girls* the usual way, with an audition for the role of Mrs. Kim. It's always hard to know what you are going to do at these auditions, but it was a success and I got to go to Toronto to shoot the pilot. I remember hanging out with Keiko Agena, and Liz Torres in that first episode and having a great time.

  I didn't really have an initial impression of the show, because it was a pilot, so it was not an established show. I couldn't really tell from the script what Amy Sherman-Palladino was going to do with it. For instance, some of those hallmarks of the show weren't immediately apparent to me - how fast the dialogue was, how smart it was. The casting of course turned out to be wonderful—it was perfect. It wasn't until I saw everybody together and I saw how everybody gelled that I really understood what *Gilmore Girls* was.

I was taken on in a recurring role, but in this industry, that is no guarantee that you will be called back. In fact, whenever I get a recurring role, I always assume I will not be called back. After the shooting of the pilot, I took a part in a play in Washington DC, when I was called back to do another episode of *Gilmore Girls*. I didn't want to leave the play for a one-episode job, and so my manager negotiated a three-episode deal. So, I quit the play and returned to the show. Of course, my part of the show ended up being 43 episodes, plus the revival.

Anytime I walked onto the set, I was always pleasantly surprised with what the set and prop people had come up with, because each of the settings were magical. The snow, The 'A-Tisket-A Tasket' episode, the knitting episode—everything! Stars Hollow was so much fun. It was like really living in the town, because we all knew everybody. Everyone was consistent throughout the show—the sound people, the props department—the show had a lot of long-time people on it, and so we became a family. It was always lovely to step onto the Warner Bros lot and have that moment when you show up to work and see the town, and all of your family in it. I always liked that.

My role on *Gilmore Girls* was different from my other roles, mainly because of the length of time I got to be on the show. Being on one project for seven years makes it easy. When I do guest spots, it's more difficult. It's always awkward because when I walk onto a new set I am not sure how everybody works, or sure about the character. I have to work with the director, or the writers a lot, about what they see the character as. Being on a show for so long, allows an actor to start understanding the character so it becomes less work and more natural. For instance, the scenes where Lane got married. By that time I didn't really have to work anymore. If I just said the lines, the past history of this character—the journey that I had already gone through with this character, in this town, it just came out of me. I just said the lines, and it just came naturally. I didn't really have to think anymore. Until that day that I had to speak Korean…that was bad.

We didn't get the scripts for the episodes until the last minute because people were stealing them and putting them on the internet. I didn't get it until the last minute, so I read it, and had a bit of a panic when I saw all of the Korean language that was going to be required of me for the episode. I voiced my concerns, and was told by the producer - Helen Pai, that her mother would be able to work with me on it. Her mother offered to coach me in my Korean. But it just wasn't enough. I tried—I didn't sleep all that night before. I was laying there trying to speak Korean, but it just wasn't sinking in. Luckily, the woman who played my mother in that episode—June Kyoto Lu—was one of my best friends, and she was so helpful. I put my lines in Korean everywhere—they were written on the wall, under the camera, written on my hand, but it's hard to read lines off things. Everyone was very cool though. I tried my best. Whenever I spoke garbage, my friend June would take over and put the scene back on course, so it all worked out.

I have a lot of good memories of shooting scenes and episodes on the show. But my favourite episode is probably Lane's wedding shower. We didn't get to improvise at all on this show, because we had to be word perfect—even letter perfect. In this episode though we got to do silly things like rolling the bed through town and improvisation became a natural part of this fun scene, so it was an opportunity to do things a little differently.

I heard early on about the plans to make *A Year in the Life*, but I didn't hear anything official right away. Michael Winters (Taylor

Doose) and I were actually talking one day, and he asked if I had been cast in it. I thought by that point that I obviously wasn't going to be involved, as nobody had called me, but it turned out that nobody had contacted him yet either. That shocked me, as I assumed Taylor would have a significant part in any *Gilmore Girls* revival. Of course, we both ended up being in it, and his part was a lot larger than mine—he was in almost every episode.

It was so funny when the shooting of the revival did come to pass, because I didn't realise until the day of filming that Mr. Kim would feature in the episode. We were getting ready to shoot when Daniel Palladino came over and told me. That was fun, although I think it would have been better to leave the mystery of Mr. Kim to the fandom. Keiko and I never talked about where we thought he was—I never really talked about it with anyone. I think we all had our own ideas about where Mr. Kim was, and sometimes my theory about him would change according to my mood. It was still left pretty wide open though—he was just standing there. I think we can still have our own little realities about him.

Gilmore Girls had an impact on both my professional, and personal journey. I got a few jobs from it, which was great, because I don't really audition well. Keiko and I are still friends—I'm friends with a number of people from there, and it's nice that so many of those friendships have lingered. That sense of camaraderie outside the show has been more enduring than other television shows I have been on.

I didn't really realise the impact this show had on the fans until the fan festival was established. I would get glimpses of the cultural impact—a fan here or there. I got some fun little perks out of it—a good table at Disneyland, preferential treatment at Singapore Airlines, but these were more isolated incidents. When I went to the first fan fest, it was great because I didn't realise there were hundreds of Gilmore fans. When everyone was collected and in the same place, I realised how big the fan base is for *Gilmore Girls*. I think the *Gilmore*

Girls fans are a certain type of people—they're often family oriented, kind, and smart. You have to be smart to watch *Gilmore Girls*. It's nice because when the fans get together they always have those same basic traits and that is kind of refreshing for me.

Being on the show was a gift. Being an Asian-American actor, when I was growing up I had Miyoshi Umeki to watch on screen-but that was it. Now it's not so bad—it is still pretty bad, but 20 years ago you didn't see an Asian-American family on television —especially one that was as well-rounded and real as the Kims. Growing up, I couldn't count on one hand the amount of Asian-American characters I saw on screen that were so well rounded and invested as the Kim family. It's still kind of rare —to follow this Asian-American family through seven years—Lane dating, lying, growing up, and getting married. And it was real—there was nothing cartoony or stereotypical about it. Everything was one hundred percent real and I really appreciated that.

Shelly Cole

Madeline Lynn

I was just a fresh, young kid in Los Angeles, pounding the pavement, when I came to the show. I found an agent and I got sent the audition for *Gilmore Girls*, from one of my agents. I had a powerhouse of three agents, which was awesome. Mike sent me out to the Warner Bros lot for the scene in the bushes, in season 1 episode 2. So, I went on to the lot, and I was directed to a little trailer where my audition would take place. I went in and it was a dumpy, tiny little trailer. I don't think Warner Bros had any clue that it was going to be the show it was. It was Amy Sherman-Palladino, Jami Rudofsky and Mara

Casey casting. Mara was the one I read with, and Amy was there. It was super informal. I did the material from the scripted material that they sent me. They laughed and said "okay, thank you, bye!" On my way out, Mara came out into the parking lot and chased me down. She said Amy wanted to see something a little different. I went back in. Amy told me she wanted this character to be more whimsical and kooky. She wasn't specific, but she wanted Madeline's character to be kind of off beat and odd. I think that Teal's character Louise was specifically sexy—she was the sexy girl, the bad girl—and I don't think Amy knew what she wanted with Madeline yet. So, I did what I thought was kooky and tried to keep it funny, and they laughed really hard about it. I felt really good about it when I left. I think a lot of actors, when they walk out of a casting room, feel one of three ways:

1. "Well….that SUCKED", and you throw your script out on the way out the door
2. "You can all just go home because I booked that job"
3. "That was somewhere in between 1 and 2. I can't tell."

This job was a #2: everyone else can go home. I got the call later that day that I had the job. It was supposed to be a co-starring role. I was booked for a first episode, with the possibility of recurring. That happened for a couple of episodes and then they moved me up to guest star and it really just steamrolled. I'm super grateful, and it turned into a really cool experience. It was great to be cast in the series, and it was my first job to speak of. Nobody knew that the show would be the hit it was, or that my character would go on to keep going and going and would become a major recurring character. It was a wonderful gift to have and I'm so grateful for it. And it was really awesome to be cast in episode 2 because I was there from the very beginning of the show and became part of the original family of the show.

One time, Amy told me (well down the road), that she put a lot of herself into Madeline's character. I was surprised, but she said that Madeline was very odd, whereas Louise has kind of a mean streak, Madeline does not. She really doesn't but she is also odd—you can't quite put your finger on her. She is maybe an idiot savant, just a little 'off'. So that's how I always saw her. Amy said when I auditioned she wasn't sure what she was looking for in Madeline, but I found it, and continued to find it throughout the episodes.

Off set, the best experiences were Amy and Dan's Christmas Parties every year. They had it at their house which isn't too far from where I lived. Those parties were so great. They were catered to the nines, and they spared no expense. They had a pool table. It was always a really magical time. I can't say that enough.

On set, I loved wardrobe sessions with Brenda Maben and Valerie Campbell. Those were always really fun because they always had so many choices and so I would go in there and try on clothes. It's fun trying on clothes, and especially ones that I couldn't even afford. Every once in a while Brenda would give me something, like that pink leather jacket I wore in the Bangles episode, or my bathing suit from the spring break episode. She gave me my Chilton uniform too. So for the fan festival two years ago, I wore my shoes. It was really fun.

There were many other awesome experiences on set. The Bangles episode was really fun. The spring break episode was my favourite to film because they put us up at the Sea Sprite Motel and we basically partied the entire week. We just had a blast and hung out. It was just really fun. I always loved it when we filmed at the Greystone mansion because Liza Weil (Paris) and Teal (Lousie) and I would always take off and explore all the nooks and crannies of the Greystone mansion, beyond the 'do not pass' signs and ropes. It was really creepy. The Doheny family owned that mansion and obviously donated it. It was used for a lot of different things like an antique festival every year, and I think there was a murder at the mansion. I think that Mr. Doheny was shacking up with the pool boy. I could be wrong, but as I recall, Mrs. Doheny was rather upset about it...

It was always fun when I filmed with Ed Herrmann (Richard) or Kelly Bishop (Emily). Those episodes were always fun to film because they were both wonderful, gracious people. I loved the Bangles episode because I got to work with Melissa McCarthy and she is a really wonderful human being. Anytime I would see her she would be that person who came up to me and asked how I am, asked about my relationships, talked about recipes etc. She wanted to know about me. She was a 'Groundling' from The Groundlings Theatre which is the big improv theatre in Los Angeles where Will Ferrell, Kristen Wiig and lots of other legendary actors like Lisa Kudrow got their start.

The biggest challenge of working on the show was the working hours. The hours were really difficult. I would start out on Monday morning at 5:30 am and the cast and crew would all be arriving. According to SAG AFTRA contracts, actors had to have a 12-hour turnaround from when they got released, to when they came back, but the crew only had an 8 hour turnaround which was really unfair. So each day it would get later and later, going over by several hours. By Friday we would get there at maybe 5:30 in the afternoon, and have to film all night. The hours were really hard also because Amy required that every word was said exactly the way it was written—nothing could be left out, changed, or added. That made for very long work days because as you know, *Gilmore Girls* had a lot of dialogue for a 60 minute show (44 minutes running time). You usually have less pages than minutes per show, but for Amy's shows there are way more pages than minutes. So that's a lot more dialogue and that's one of the reasons for the long days. That was the most difficult job I've ever had. The problem for the crew is they don't have a relaxing trailer to rest in, and only an 8 hour turnaround. It's really hard—the pressure to get it right so they can go home. The crew, hands down, deserve so much props for what they did—more than anybody else. The reason it was such a hit show was because Amy was very specific about how she wanted it done.

I have a lovely memory of filming the Bangles episode. There were two guys that were cast to sit behind us, who Louise and Madeleine would hook up with and leave the concert for. The taller one, Brandon Routh, eventually went on to play *Superman*. We were at the boys' apartment when Sookie and Lorelai came to retrieve Madeline and Louise. Brandon was standing there right next to Lauren. It was really late at night, and his phone started ringing during a shot. The entire crew by this time was tired, annoyed, and they let that be known to him. The soundstage bell rang and we all had to return to 'one' (our original starting points for the scene). Lauren, without missing a beat, put her hand on his shoulder and said "Yep…..happens to the best of us". It was such a nice gesture because he was so embarrassed.

I always loved it when director Michael Katleman was on set with us. He was so fun and easy to be with. I remember one time I had booked an audition for an episode of *ER* and it was on the Warner Bros lot. I said to him that I had an audition across the lot. I was wearing my Chilton uniform and he worked around me while I raced across the lot to the *ER* casting office, who got me right into the audition room. I did the audition for the part of a girl with meningococcus. I ran back to the *Gilmore Girls* set just in time, and an hour later I got the call from my agent that I had booked the character on *ER*. I was really grateful to Michael for helping me out that day.

When they decided to green light the *Gilmore Girls* revival I got a call immediately to be in it. I was really excited, but I wasn't really surprised. I couldn't really see how they could do a revival without my character—Madeline and Louise were such an integral part of Rory's Chilton experience. We were a big part of the show from the onset. Then I got a call that it wasn't going to happen and I was so upset. Due to some complications, they couldn't make it work. I later realised that the reason they didn't cast me in *A Year in the Life* was because Teal who played Louise was unavailable, and the show didn't want to bring back only one of us, as they felt like that wouldn't fit. Teal was living in Minnesota and has no interest in acting anymore. I was excited to have that ticket to see everyone again, and I was disappointed that it didn't happen.

It was my first job and an amazing experience in a lot of ways. After I moved to Denver I had so many dreams where I was on the set of *Gilmore Girls* and I'd wake up and realise how much I miss that time in my life.

Professionally, *Gilmore Girls,* impacted my career in several ways. Firstly, I learned immediately that when you are an actor in a television series—whether it's a series regular, guest star, etc.—you say those words exactly as they are written. Memorising lines after that became very easy because nobody writes as fast paced and complicated as Amy and the only direction I ever received was "faster! faster!" By Jamie Babbitt who directed those episodes.

It also instilled in me—which I already think I had to a lesser extent—a really good work ethic. I made it my rule to never show up late...ever. I was also always respectful to the crew. For instance, the first thing I would do in the morning is go straight to hair and makeup and then get my script. At the end of each work day I would put my costume for the day, or costumes, back on their hangers and take them all back to the wardrobe because that's just one more thing they don't have to add at the end of their day. And I'm just one person, but they have to do that for every single person. A lot of actors just leave it on the floor in a ball. So that was another thing—learning how important it is to take care of the crew. Also, never walk out of your trailer if you haven't flushed the toilet. Don't leave it filthy or dirty because the teamsters have to clean it up after you, and you don't want to piss off a teamster. I've heard horror stories like people getting polaroids of their toothbrush on the last day of filming. You always take care of the teamsters and the crew.

There was another thing that I learned that was really important. Anytime I had a comprehensive scene to do, or my close up, I would always stand in for myself. They are lighting for me, not my stand in. I rarely had any scenes with Lauren Graham so my stand in often times would be Patty Malcolm if she was available, who is Lauren's stand in. Patty is a different colouring to me and has a different hair colour. She just happens to be the same height as me, with dark hair, and was available. However, I just felt it was important to stand in for myself when I could and I took that conviction into other jobs that I did where I had really intense work to do and it kept me focused and in the moment. The most important thing I learned from *Gilmore Girls* was to be respectful.

Working on *Gilmore Girls* boosted my career in terms of getting more roles. There is something to be said about a working actor. Working actors, beget more work. When I got to that place in my career where I really was about to break through the glass ceiling, my Dad got really sick, and ended up in a veterans hospital in Texas. I had gotten a huge opportunity to take on the role that Pauley Perrette ended up booking in *NCIS*. This was the role of Abby Sciuto—the scientist who performs autopsies on the show. On the day that I was supposed to test for that role I had a panic attack. I was having a lot of them back then. I ended up calling my agent and saying that I couldn't do it. "I just can't." Donald Bellisario, the creator of the show, called my agent and was livid. He asked, "What do you mean, she can't do it?" My agent didn't know what else to tell him. It's a difficult memory to wrestle with in some ways, because that show is still on the air. That would have been such a secure acting job if I had booked it, but I didn't even show up.

Later on, I was riding to Coachella with Michael Weatherly who plays Anthony DiNozzo on the show. I had guest starred on an episode on *NCIS* and we were sharing a car after a long night of filming. I was talking to Michael about my lost opportunity at the permanent role on this show and he said, "maybe things work out the way they should." When I questioned him, he said that Pauley Perrette who did book the role was in a bad place in her life before that job, and she really needed it. He even said that the role saved her life. After hearing that, I was pretty content with what had happened, and felt that perhaps things did work out the way they should, like Michael said.

At this time, I was having panic attacks left and right—anytime I had an audition. My agent called me, when I was on set one day. I told him, "I have to take a break." He asked if I was sure, and I said "yes". He was concerned about the timing of this break. He said, "You are really about to break through". I said, "I think that's probably true, but I just can't do this right now." I was having panic attacks, my hair was falling out, I was rail thin. I wasn't happy. I was afraid all the time, and I know that it was because my one and only family member was dying, in another state. During this time in my life, I was jumping back and forth on aeroplanes to be with him. He was my only family member—we only had each other. Later, after he died, my agent pointed out that if I had taken the job, I wouldn't have been able to spend that time with my Dad. Looking back, I realise that things worked out for me too.

After that, I took about a year off from what I call 'hard' auditioning. I started booking jobs slowly and I thought, I don't want to do this anymore. It's too hard. I plugged at it for a few more years and then got to the point that I felt I was over it. I packed up and moved to Denver, to follow a guy here. That didn't work out, but I came here with the thought that I would love to transition into teaching acting to kids because I enjoy working with kids and I think I have a very nurturing spirit. I transitioned into coaching acting with kids and it certainly does not pay the same, but I love it and I would never want to go back to that life. It's very hard. When I think about aspects of the job like doing interviews on the red carpet, I remember how much I hated that. It was not my jam at all. So coaching is where my life is now, and I'm really glad for it. Every now and then someone will recognise me from *Gilmore Girls* or one of my other roles and ask what I'm doing in Denver. I tell them it's a long story.

Michael—my boyfriend—and I, were at a little beer tasting bar at the beginning of our courtship about four or five years ago. It was a round bar and we were sitting playing Trivial Pursuit and sipping our beer. We went to leave and pay, and the bar woman said our tab had been taken care of. She brought over a receipt with a little signature at the bottom that said "We loved you on *Gilmore Girls*. Thank you for your service." I tried to find the people who did it to thank them, but the lady at the bar said they wanted to be kept anonymous. I thought that was so generous and kind. They had no desire for any fanfare or gratitude.

On a practical level, *Gilmore Girls* also impacted my personal life in more ways than one. Firstly, the health insurance I enjoyed for years was fantastic. Secondly, it was my first job and so it really helped open the door to other opportunities. Thirdly, I have a pension through the Screen Actors Guild (SAG AFTRA) and I still receive royalty checks. I also came from a pretty rough young life and acting truly was a saviour to me when I discovered it. *Gilmore Girls* was a true gift because it helped me find confidence in myself and a sense of value and community. I didn't have much community in my young life so that was very much a foreign idea to me. I had such kick ass friends, some of which I will always be very close with. It gave me that sense of confidence and belonging which is priceless for someone who didn't grow up with it. I found that the more I put into my relationships on that show, the more I got out of it. The more respect I got the more I received in return. Liza Weil (Paris) and I were very close with each other for a long time. I was at her wedding to Paul and then I moved, and things eventually fell away with some people. The fan festival has been such a wonderful community that Marcus and Jennie Whitaker created. I didn't become involved in the fan fest until a couple of years ago, but I'm really glad that I get to be involved in it now. It's been 20 years since I was cast in *Gilmore Girls* and to have that experience still of my original life in Los Angeles and the beginning of my career is really cool. Valerie Campbell from the wardrobe department is a really wonderful person, as is Liz Torres (Miss Patty). I've gotten to know Nick Holmes (Robert Grimaldi) really well. I've been really under the weather the last week and a half and Nick and his wife Virginia kept checking in, which made me feel so special and loved. George is a really wonderful guy and I got to meet Olivia Hack (Tanna Shrick) for the first time at the festival. The relationships that I have with the people who have made themselves available for the fan festival have continued to grow, and that's been really great.

Gilmore Girls had this amazing following because at the time there weren't too many female driven shows. It ran on the CW network where teenagers and people in their 20s and 30s were watching, and it had several elements that would appeal to these age groups. First—being female driven. Second—I think that the pop culture references and the music were so well placed and smart that it appealed to a wide audience. I think it's something that people have spent time watching together. Beyond just being a funny witty poignant show, there is also a community to it, which is universally something that we all need. So many mothers and daughters have told me that they share it with each other. Obviously the great casting contributed, and the wonderful star appeal of the main actors, surrounded by so many great supporting characters. I believe it was just the right time for Alexis and Lauren to break through. I think Milo (Jess) was amazing casting, as was Jared (Dean). I think that Sally Struthers (Babbette), Liz Torres, and Ed and Kelly brought something unique—it was just amazing casting. *Gilmore Girls* was an amazing bringing together of very interesting kooky characters. And, let's not forget the setting of the town—who doesn't want to visit a perfect New England town with a gazebo? The whole show was just a bunch of little perfect elements of magic.

Dakin Matthews

Hanlin Charleston

I came from the San Francisco Bay Area—from Oakland actually, but I was working in Los Angeles, and had been since about 1984, when I was cast in *Gilmore Girls.* My agent called with an audition for me, for a new series which I knew nothing about. The audition was for the role of Lorelai's father, Richard Gilmore. I went to the audition and thought I did rather well. I didn't get it, but my friend Edward Hermann did. They called me back quite quickly and said they would like me to come in for something else. This time, I didn't even audition. I was offered the role of Hanlin Charleston, the headmaster of Chilton—Rory's high school.

I knew from the start that my role would be recurring, and I was happy about that. I had done a number of series' by that point, and the world of television had changed a lot in my time. The amount of dialogue crammed into the large amount of script pages for *Gilmore Girls* was initially shocking. Different showrunners and different writers have different attitudes to their scripts. Most of them want you to stick to their scripts but are not terribly hawkish about it. Amy Sherman-Palladino wanted the actors to follow all of the words she wrote and be word perfect. She also wanted us to talk as fast as we possibly could. I was warned early on that if I took a pause anywhere in my speech, they would cut away from me, and fill that pause with a reaction shot, closing the gap up. With that in mind, I knew I may as well keep talking during my lines.

I first appeared on episode 2, so it was too early for me to know anything about the show. However, in those days, they would send out the whole script when you got a part, so I read the whole script and was very impressed. It was a charming script, with a wonderful writer. It was very literate. In this town, I feel very grateful when I get a really literate script, and this one had more depth and style than usual. I myself am an ex-English professor, and I have a theatre background so I really appreciate good writing when I see it. Amy writes more like a playwright than a television writer, and it was clear right away that this was a quality project.

Everyone on the set was charming but overwhelmed with their work. The number of pages that one shoots in Hollywood in a day is a measure of how hard the work is. On *Gilmore Girls,* a lot of pages were shot per day, and the pages were crammed with a lot of language.

I'd estimate that the scripts on *Gilmore Girls* were 10-15% longer than the average television script. Also, on most shows there are many writers, and there's not always a clear voice across each episode or season. On *Gilmore Girls*, Amy was writing, and rewriting everything, so there was a singular voice. Being a mostly stage actor, I am used to the singular voice and style of one playwright. Some series have a dominant visual style, or decor style but the thing about *Gilmore Girls* was that it had a dominant linguistic style.

One of my favourite moments on the show was the episode where Anna Fairchild goes to stay with Rory at Yale. I was very happy to get an episode after Rory graduated. Once she left the school, I knew my time on the show was over unless my character somehow attached itself to the Gilmore household. I kept hoping Hanlin would be invited over to Richard's for dinner, since we know that they were friends, but it didn't happen. Coming back for that episode was very pleasant.

There were no unpleasant moments during my time on *Gilmore Girls*. I'm a fast learner, with a very good memory, so I had no difficulty getting the lines correct. I always enjoyed it. There wasn't a lot of downtime on the set, which I always thought was great. On most sets you can spend an hour working, and seven hours in your chair reading, or doing crosswords. Amy ran a pretty tight ship, which I always appreciated.

The only difficulty I ever had on *Gilmore Girls* was around my contractual obligations. My role was recurring but there was no promise that there was ever going to be another episode. At that time, I had about three recurring roles on television shows, including my role as Reverend Sikes on *Desperate Housewives*. I was working on stage pretty regularly, so I had to have clauses in my stage contracts that I could have time off if my recurring television roles came up again. In the event that my recurring roles called me in, my understudy would cover for my stage roles while I went and shot the episodes. I felt fortunate to be recurring because it left me free to do other things. I could be in the theatre, or on multiple shows. For one of my stage shows, I had shaved my beard and moustache, when I got called back to *Gilmore Girls*. When I told the production team I was clean shaven, they were insulted, and felt that I had not lived up to my contractual obligations. I was told that I would need to pay someone to get a matching goatee and moustache made or they would write me out. Amy was very strict about that continuity.

I tend to play authority figures, and I love working on regional accents. Casting directors tend to cast me as old Southerners—senators, and sheriff's, or they cast me as upscale lawyers, doctors, and judges. I also get cast as priests, and ministers. The accent I used for Hanlin ws pretty unique—I've never used it on anything else. It was kind of an upscale mid-Atlantic accent, from a time when people in America sounded more British. It had a higher tone, from when people spoke in a very careful, Boston accent. I was trying to represent that stereotype of an extremely educated upper-class New Englander. Ed Herrmann was also a great dialectician. He did a great American Irish accent in a film. I have always been a big fan of Ed, and I miss him a lot. He was very bright, and very well read. One of the great features of the show was the multi-generational aspect, because the older characters, like Richard Gilmore, got really good on-screen time, and good stories. Amy wrote well for every character. She was just as concerned about all of the generations.

A Year in the Life was a wonderful opportunity to get back together with everyone. There were rumours going around in 2015 about a revival, and then it was confirmed. Not long after, my good friend Michael Winters (Taylor Doose) got the call to come back. I was in the middle of doing *Waitress* on Broadway with Sara Bareilles when I got the call for the reboot. *Waitress* was loved by young women, some of whom would wait in the line outside for my autograph, because they wanted to meet Headmaster Charleston. I started carrying pictures of myself with Liza Weil and Alexis Bledel and if anyone mentioned *Gilmore Girls* in the autograph line, I would sign the picture of me with two cast members from *Gilmore Girls*. One girl who I did this for, was so excited she thought she was going to throw up.

I got a few days off from *Waitress* and flew back to Burbank to shoot my episode of the revival. I loved being back and filming that episode. The alumni reunion episode was wonderful because in a way it was a real reunion, and we were all feeling nostalgic. Some of the people who came back had become really good friends because of the show, and it was wonderful to see them again. Michael Winters and I have been friends since we started in theatre years ago, and Emily Bergl (Francie Jarvis) has been a good friend for a long time, before *Gilmore Girls*. It was also nice to revisit my character. Through most of the series, Hanlin was a hard-ass, and not particularly sympathetic. He was almost always seen when the girls were in trouble, so we always saw his hard side. The character was a bit more sympathetic and comic in *A Year in the Life*.

The mother-daughter relationships on *Gilmore Girls* were unique and worked very well. Having two relationships—one so strong, and the other so troubled—was a fantastic dichotomy. It was appealing to those who have wonderful relationships with their mothers, and those who have troubled ones. One relationship was perhaps too close, while the other was too distant, and estranged. Having the two possible extremes meant the show captured a wide audience. Everybody has a mother, and that relationship sits somewhere on that spectrum. There was a universal truth to the writing which was enjoyable to explore. That's the heart of it. It's a show that mothers and daughters watch together.

Ted Rooney

Morey Dell

    My journey on *Gilmore Girls* started like any other, but I ended up being very close to being recast.

    The audition was just one of many auditions that week. As an actor, your real full-time job is auditioning. When I went in for the part of Morey, they didn't have any real lines for me. I walked in the casting room, and the casting directors Mara and Jamie were there along with Amy Sherman-Palladino and Dan Palladino. As soon as I walked in, they all laughed, which I hoped was a good sign. I got the part almost immediately after that. I later realised that what they were laughing at was the thought of my long, skinny body next to Sally Struthers who was so much shorter than me.

At the audition, they had me sit at the piano and act like I was playing it, and say something like, "Hey honey? Come listen!". That was my audition. After I left the lot, I didn't think twice about the audition again. I had a trip booked for the next couple of weeks to go to Mexico with a buddy. So, I got on a plane and went and had a great time. For a lot of the trip, my pager was out of range, so when I could, I checked my messages. To my surprise, there were four from my agent, over several days, sounding increasingly desperate. The last message was from the same day as I was checking them, and he said "they are about to recast you if you don't call today". I quickly called him, and he recommended that I get on a plane right away as they were setting up to shoot my first episode. So I headed to the airport, shot my episode, and then flew back to Mexico to meet up with my friend and finish our trip. I was that close to not getting on the show because of my lack of industrious attitude.

I had no initial impression of the show. When I auditioned, I didn't even know what it was about. I didn't know that I would be cast opposite Sally, and that was interesting because she was the 'movie star' from my high school. My dad was one of Sally's teachers. The whole time I was growing up, we had an *All In The Family* photo on the desk, signed by her, to her 'favourite teacher'. She was a rock star to us—to everyone in Portland, and especially those at Grant High School. I was excited to actually get to meet her. As far as I knew it was a one-episode job. I showed up on the set and Sally was there. I sat next to her on one of those actor folding chairs. She commented on how hot it was, and I said "yeah…it's not like the summers in Portland, Oregon, huh?" She looked at me, gasped, and said, "You're Ed Rooney's son!" She had heard my name already but hadn't connected it to my dad until I said that. She was, of course, 15 years ahead of me, so she didn't know me from high school. Later on down the track, my dad came to the set to watch one of the episodes get filmed, and to hang out with Sally. That was really exciting for him.

When I auditioned, I was told the role was possibly recurring. They tend to say that to leave the possibility open, but they don't want to promise anything. 'Possibly' usually turns into not at all—never again. When I got called back for another episode, I knew that I was going to be in the next few episodes. In my mind, I thought it was starting to look like I would be recurring. Technically, as soon as you are called back for a second episode, you are a recurring character, but you never know when you are going to be called back. A few episodes in, I really felt that I might be a long-term character. After I had done a few episodes, we were shooting the episode where I attended Rory's 16th birthday party at the Gilmore house. I realised at that point, that if I was attending the birthday parties of the show's leads, I was a part of the inner circle. By that point, Babette and Morey's characters had been in a lot of the major storylines—we were the next door neighbours. That was when I really felt that my character had become a part of the show.

After the birthday party episode, I shot one more episode and then heard nothing for 14 episodes. I had known this would be the case because Sally had planned a vacation before she was cast on the show. It was her intention to travel to Italy. Even though she had been cast on *Gilmore Girls,* she went on that vacation. Because it was early on in the show, and she was going away for an extended time, the two of us were officially uncast. I had tried to get her to delay her trip, but she had her reasons for needing to get away. I figured we would not be asked back on to the show again. To my delight, I was asked back at the end of season 1, but the large gap in my character's presence on the show dashed my hopes of ever becoming a series regular. As an actor you tell yourself to never, ever, get your hopes up. You never count your chickens until the cheque is in the bank. I did hope a bit there.

I didn't expect to be called back for *A Year In The Life*, because I never get my hopes up. I was really glad to be asked back for one little scene. The best part of it was that I got to bring my daughter down to Los Angeles for the filming. That was really special because the last time I was on that show she wasn't around. She was about 10 or 11 at the time of the revival, and got to come and hang out with the cast and me in LA. It was a really lovely father-daughter trip. Being back with everyone after such a long time felt the same as the original run. It was great to see everyone—they are a very sweet group of people. I always felt like I was a visitor in the family because of my sporadic appearances. It felt a little awkward, a little fun, and exciting. I hadn't developed close relationships with people from the cast because I was so rarely on, and when I was it was usually one scene. But everyone was really nice and I was really excited for my daughter to meet everyone because she had watched the show. And it was a free trip to Los Angeles where we got to hang out on the set and tour the Warner Bros. lot.

Sally and I have kept in contact over the years. We email and text. She is from Portland, so she comes back to see family once in a while and we catch up when she does. My family and I live in the same neighbourhood as Sally's, so we hang out for a bit when she is here. When we adopted our first child, Abe, she asked if she could be his 'fairy godmother'. So, that is her official role in our lives, and we send her updates.

My favourite scene is the big scene that really brought us into the fold—Cinnamon's wake. I got to do a little more acting than just wear my hat and glasses and say something flatly, which was often what I had done up until that point. Sally and I ended the episode with a nice little moment on our porch and a pan shot from above. The moment was scored by Sam Phillips—the song in that moment was written just for us, which just gave it a really nice touch. I had been a big Sam Phillips fan since high school, so I was thrilled when I got to meet her at the cast Christmas party. It's a really weird moment when you meet people in Hollywood who you have admired all your life and they are now working with you. She was married to T Bone Burnett at the time, and he suggested that I introduce Sam to Lauren Graham. So, I took Sam Phillips to meet Lauren and it was just odd for me—taking one of my most admired artists to talk to another famous person—very surreal.

I also enjoyed the Halloween episode where Sally and I are rigging a gallows. The trap door would open up and I would fall down, and wriggle around with a noose around my neck, to look like I had been hung. It was funny to me but not to anybody else. There was a fight coordinator there to make sure everything was rigged accordingly. I had wire rigged to my groin and waist so that all the weight would fall to my crotch and waist, which was not exactly comfortable, but saved me from injury. The noose was then hung loosely around my neck. When the time came to rehearse the drop, every time I dropped it it was very jarring, and I wished I had a stunt guy to do it for me. Then when I got to the actual shoot, and the cameras were rolling, the gallows dropped like it was supposed to, but it broke, and I fell to the ground. And because I'm a Rooney, I'm just wired to try and make this into a prank. So, I took the opportunity. I started crying for Sally. "Sallllllyyyyyy…….Saaaaaallllllllyyyyyy!!" I could sense the air just turn ice cold. There was fear shooting through everybody and I thought "Oh dear….I've gone too far again". I stood up immediately through the hole in the floor and…if looks could kill. It's an example of my sense of humour. I might have lost a couple of episodes because of that. That director hated my guts after that. There were a lot of people uncomfortable with shooting that scene anyway—it's pretty gory and realistic.

On *Gilmore Girls,* I was hired to look incredibly handsome and tall and to keep my sunglasses on. Sally would occasionally tell me that I have nice blue eyes and would tell me to take the sunglasses off. So I did, and someone would very quickly, and dutifully, come by and say, "Could you put your sunglasses on Ted?" Early on, it was decided that wearing sunglasses would be my signature look. In one scene I had them off and it never happened again. Sally was the instigator. She was a troublemaker. She and Liz—old school Hollywood comedians—would always be joking. If you put them together you knew everything would take twice as long because they would be telling stories and laughing. It would get to a point where people were starting to wonder how they were going to reign it in. They were old enough that they knew it was all going to be fine.

The vibe on set amongst those of us known as 'dayplayers', guest stars, and supporting actors, was really fun. We were all there to have a good time, and happy to be working. I never spent a lengthy time on set because my scenes didn't call for it, but I sensed that among the leads there was some stress about getting things done, and not taking too much time to do it. Knowing the industry like I do, I feel that this was understandable. When you have a show that spans years, and the actors are working their butts off to learn such dense lines, you understand that it doesn't go smoothly 100% of the time. I was interviewed recently by Scott Patterson. He was talking about different actors, and he brought up Lauren Graham. My advice was "just stay clear of her". She was a force to be reckoned with. She is a perfectionist. Scott was hesitant to include this in the interview. There were a couple of things that I said in that interview that were ultimately edited out. I told Scott the Halloween story too and he was like 'yeah…that's not funny'.

I also mentioned something about how in Los Angeles, every actor—if he or she has hung around long enough—has five or six disappointments. Just five or six times where you really had your hopes up, and things went awry professionally speaking. I was lucky to get in any shows. I felt so blessed and happy to be making a career in Los Angeles. Part of me thought that was never possible. I was always happy, and as giddy as a schoolboy to be on sets. You never get your hopes up, but sometimes they dangle the carrot so closely that you can't help it. And sometimes, they would even let you take a bit of the carrot. And…I would get my hopes up. How could I not, when I had been allowed to eat the carrot? You bury that stuff because you have to go on working, and it happens to everyone. It's harder when you get your hopes up though, and knowing that Scott's interview was coming up, I did a bit of research and my experience on *Gilmore Girls* all came back to me. I think that 14-episode gap was one of those disappointments for me, since I had hoped to be picked up as a series regular.

While on the show, I was taking other jobs on and off. There were conflicts sometimes with my beard. Sometimes I had my beard but I had to work around it. One time I had to shave, and it was for an Abraham Lincoln role on stage, and the production crew for the stage show just built a beard for me. I was ready and available. The year that I wasn't on *Gilmore Girls* for 14 episodes I was shooting *Joan of Arcadia* on the Warner Bros lot and I crept around the set to say hello to the Gilmore cast. Some of them knew what happened with Sally going away and they felt bad for me. They figured I was not coming back to the show, and were avoiding eye contact, and acting super awkwardly. I never got to talk to anyone about it, but those visits were my confirmation that everyone thought I was not coming back.

I had a much bigger disappointment with the television show *Community*. I was cast in the show as a regular character. The table read happens the week of shooting, so I went along to the table read and met everyone. There were hugs all around, the producers were saying things like "it's great to have you in the family" and it was just great. Then, the day before shooting my agent called and said "actually no, they are going another way". My wife and I had considered moving out to Los Angeles to an apartment because we were living in Portland by then. I had finally got the part I was waiting for, and it all fell through. That's an example of tasting the carrot, and then having it ripped away. If I'd never got it in the first place, I'd be fine. But I got it, I showed up, rehearsed, made plans around it, and then it was over. Those are the hard ones. Every actor who has been around and auditioned a lot has those stories. Famous actors have been recast right before shooting a film where they had a lead part. That's got to be devastating. In Hollywood you are never given the reason why. You are given reasons—but you can't trust them. The answer is always something like, "you're awesome but we had to go another way". And you always get told things like, "It's nothing to do with you", but it's almost impossible not to feel that it is you.

Gilmore Girls, and its fans, are unique because the average fan watches every season three times and some a lot more than that. For that reason, everybody on that show who did more than about 10 episodes gets recognised. We were at a wedding one weekend, sitting across from women in their mid 30s. One leaned over and asked, "Are you an actor?" I said I was. And she said, ".....Gilmore…Girls….?" We ended up taking photographs, and she was blushing. I was Morey, barely on the show and they turned red because anything attached to that show sets them off. Every image in that show is etched in the brains of the fans. It's so much a part of their life that it is like I'm a part of their life and so fans often relate to me as if I am someone from their past. It's a strong reaction. I was once at the airport in Chicago, waiting on a red eye, looking for a corner to sleep in. Three young ladies from New Zealand tapped me on the shoulder and they were all excited because they knew I was Morey from Gilmore. I've got plenty of those kinds of stories. I'm not a movie star like Lauren or Alexis Blededl but I still get recognised.

I do have people say, "you were my favourite character". It's hard for me to believe that, but the fans are drawn towards certain personalities because they are part of the Gilmore world. My experience is that G*ilmore Girls* has actually been so few days of my life. I usually shoot everything in one day so in reality, the show occupied less than a month of my life. Also, Sally does all the talking for us. I get a line or two and the flatter I deliver it, the better. In that sense, it doesn't really even feel like an acting experience. Most of the comedy is just in the words and delivering them in a matter of fact fashion, and that makes it funny. From my experience, it's one of the lowest challenges of my career acting wise. Nonetheless, it's cool. I love it. It was still fun and satisfying, I was never bored. I felt really lucky to be on the show.

Gilmore Girls' popularity is built around small town life. The fans feel they are a part of Stars Hollow. For some, they grew up in that world and the characters were a part of their life. The particular writing from the Palladino's also made it one-of-a-kind. Their style is very specific. The pop culture references, speaking twice as fast as normal humans can, and the tongue-in-cheek humour all made it unique. *The Marvelous Mrs Maisel* is a continuation in a way of that brilliant, tight writing. I think that show is elevated, it's on a different level compared to *Gilmore Girls*. It's a little more complex. For Gilmore, it's just that comfort of knowing the characters—it's the 'old reliable', and it's seven seasons so you can really sink your teeth into it. It's always pleasant. You can turn it on and feel like you are visiting family.

The fans of this show are unique too and give it the afterlife it has. We have even had reunion events—the fans can never get enough. They will hope for more Gilmore for the rest of their lives. I don't think about more *Gilmore Girls* reboots at all, but I could imagine it would happen again, and the fans would love it. I'll ride whatever boat comes my way.

After the show ended in 2007, we moved back to Portland. My wife and I had been married for two years by then. She was from the South, living in Los Angeles with me, and it wasn't exactly her style. Los Angeles is the least conducive city in America to community and it takes extreme effort to make any kind of feeling of community there. My wife really disliked this aspect of Los Angeles, so when the show was over, we moved back to my hometown. Initially I was still working in Los Angeles and flying to auditions, but it was breaking up our lifestyle so much. We had moved back to Portland to have community, and we weren't able to have that with such a disjointed lifestyle. So, after two years we decided to make the decision to either stay here, and really be here, or go back. We stayed and I started teaching on-camera acting. We've been here ever since. I'm also a theatre actor and so I've been in plays up here too. Michael Winters (Taylor Doose) is primarily a theatre actor, and he lives in Seattle so we did a play two years ago and Michael came to see it. He had done shows at the same theatre company and then I just saw him a few weeks ago at the theatre's anniversary. I told him about Scott Patterson's podcast and hooked him up with that. Theatre's really where I get my kicks. There's small film and television parts that come up here too, but it's not full time when you have a family to support. Teaching is definitely a passion of mine. I love it. It didn't feel like a compromise for me. It felt like moving up here put a fire up my butt to do something that I've always wanted to do, and that I always thought I'd be good at, but I couldn't know for sure until I did it. I'm so happy that I was forced to become a teacher because I wouldn't have done it if I wasn't backed into a corner. In Los Angeles it's easy to get comfortable if you are making a living. My studio partner and I just moved into a theatre and our first show is being produced this week. We are very excited about what the future holds.

We've adopted two children and that is the primary focus of my life—family. It's been a real journey figuring out how to raise two kids in this day and age with internet access and phones. Adopting has been a very storied, arduous journey, but has also been a huge blessing, and a learning experience. It's made us better people.

Carla McClosky

First Assistant Director, Director, and Unit Production Manager

I was First Assistant Director on *Gilmore Girls* from the beginning, then became a director in season 3, directing episode 11. I had worked previously on *Ally McBeal* which was such a popular show, and had been the Assistant Director on feature films such as *Jurassic Park* and *Hook*. When the team at *Gilmore Girls* called me, I had switched from film to television so that I could be more present at home. I had two daughters and felt that I didn't get to spend enough time with my family. I had worked on a few sitcoms which were a light workload because you would rehearse for a few days and then film all in one day. I broached the subject of job-sharing with the production team on *Gilmore Girls* when they offered me the work. It was not really well received. They said they didn't want anyone else doing the job, just me. My girls were a little older by that time, and it was an amazing show—very high quality, so I said yes, and took the position. Initially, I thought I had perhaps bitten off a bit much, but it worked out well in the end.

One of the funny running jokes of the series, behind the scenes, was the amount of flowers on that show. Richard and Emily's house was always filled with flowers. These weren't just small posies, they were the huge arrangements that you order for a wedding, or a funeral. On a Friday night, when we were done filming for the week, the crew would take them home. The same happened with Sookie's kitchen—we would take home the fruits and vegetables.

Lauren Graham was fantastic to work with. She was so smart, constantly memorising enormous amounts of dialogue. On feature films, it's a much slower pace. We would shoot two to three pages a day, but we could easily shoot 8-10 pages a day on *Gilmore Girls*. Lauren was also so funny. I remember one scene where she couldn't stop laughing. There are pictures somewhere of her rolling around on the floor, laughing uncontrollably.

The show was filled with many young, adept actors. Alexis Bledel had never really done anything before *Gilmore Girls*, but she was such an angelic vision. I've only felt that way about one other actor—Keri Russell, on *Felicity*. They both had that ethereal quality, and were sweet, darling women. It was amazing to watch the young male actors like Jared and Milo on the show grow too, from boys, into men.

One of the things I loved about working on the show was the interesting things that we got to do, and the learning opportunities that it provided. This is true of a lot of things in the filming industry, but the themed episodes on *Gilmore Girls* were especially interesting. For the dance off episode I went to swing dancing clubs and hired swing dancers for the shoot. For the episode where Rory has her 'coming out into society' at the debutante ball I researched those balls and how they play out. I also got to research medieval dinners, in preparation for The Bracebridge Dinner. I learned so much and got a little window into a lot of different creative niches. The episode I got to direct was the fencing episode, so the girls had to go and learn how to fence for that scene. It was amazing to see each episode and scene grow from nothing and learn new things which would bring the episodes to life.

Some of the episodes were difficult to shoot. There was a lot of shooting at night, being outside, and working with a large cast of extras. There was added stress if something didn't work, or systems broke down. Despite this, and the long hours needed to make the show great, there was a real camaraderie amongst the cast and crew. We were all very close, and we would hang out together outside of the show. That same camaraderie isn't always found on every television show. On *Gilmore Girls*, it was like family. Even when the working conditions were tough, we were all in it together. When I had a stroke during my time on the show, the cast and crew were really supportive. My hospital room was full of flowers sent from the show, and from Alexis and Lauren personally. They came and visited when I came home too. Overall, working on the show was a fantastic experience.

When they asked me to direct an episode, I thought about it for an instant because we rarely got any preparation time, as we usually got the scripts late. This would mean I would be shooting and prepping at the same time. It was my intention to direct many more episodes of *Gilmore Girls*, after directing 3.11, but I suffered a stroke. It started with a unilateral headache which the doctor suggested might be due to stress. It wasn't. During the fourth season, I was pretty incapacitated. Assistant director work keeps you on your feet for 18-19 hours a day, so I wasn't able to return to my role. During this time, my husband wanted me to quit the show altogether, but I felt it would be difficult to replace me. I continued to work from home while I was recovering, breaking down scripts, and speaking with people. In the fifth season, the show brought me back on as the production manager.

Both of my daughters were in college by that time and they were able to visit me on the set sometimes. They even worked on the show as background actors, so I still saw them. Eventually, one of my daughters took over as a dialogue coach on Fridays. They loved her and she ended up doing the rest of the show. That meant one person from my family was on the show the whole time.

By the time *A Year in the Life* came around, I was retired. It was too many hours, and I had moved on. I had written two books by that time and was in a new space. I went and visited when they shot out by my home in Malibu, and I attended the premiere. Alexis was all grown up, married, and a mother. It was lovely to see her, and everyone again. It was like going home to an old friend.

I try to attend the fan fest every year, and while none of the main cast have attended, I have become close to those that do. Sheila Lawrence was a writer on the show. I didn't see her much while I was working on *Gilmore Girls*, but she is a delight at the fan fest and we have bonded over that shared event.

I retired in 2008, so *Gilmore Girls* was near the end of my career in the film industry. I was winding down, after my heyday, doing films with Stephen Spielberg. I was one of the first female assistant directors in Hollywood and had enjoyed a wonderful career.

I had been friends with George Bell for years, who went on to become an actor and dialogue coach on *Gilmore Girls*. I brought George on to work with the lost boys on *Hook*. They needed someone to work with them and run lines with them. I tried to get him onto everything I was working on. I knew he was a good actor, and could get along with anybody, so I approached him when *Gilmore Girls* needed a dialogue coach. He accepted, and had a long run on the show, as both an actor, and dialogue coach, even coming back for the reboot.

What made *Gilmore Girls* so great was Amy Sherman Palladino's complete 'umbrella' oversight. I could go directly to her about everything. She made herself completely available. She was there to get it the way she wanted it.

I don't think I realised how popular *Gilmore Girls* was until I heard about some soldiers who were posted overseas, watching the show all the time. When we renovated our house I found all my old scripts, and I ended up giving them to fans who were thrilled. People find things, relate to them, and love them. *Gilmore Girls* is not time specific. It's as viable today as it was then and will be in 20 more years. People continue to relate to it. If you spend so much time on something, you want it to be timeless. *Gilmore Girls* ran for seven seasons, then came back for another, and people are still discovering it. *Ally McBeal,* for instance, was very popular at the time but doesn't have the same longevity. It's wonderful when young people discover a show. There are certain shows that go through generations and are important to each of them. *Gilmore Girls* is more popular now than when it was on television.

I related to the show myself in a lot of ways. I grew up in a small town in Wisconsin—Lodi—that felt a lot like Stars Hollow. My daughter was so much like Rory. She read a lot and took books with her everywhere. I told Amy and Dan a lot about the town. They used to ask me what my daughter was reading at the time to inspire Rory's reading on the show. The people of Stars Hollow are simple, but colourful, and they bring so much richness to the show. I like the way that the show reminded me of my own life—my daughter, my little town, and all the crazy people in it. Those things are important. This was a show about family, friends, and what you love. The show is a picture of what is important in life. We get caught up in angst and craziness in the world and the show helps to remind us of what we love, and what is good in the world—what grows in our life. If we focus on those things, we will all share something wonderful and be much happier.

Robert Michael Lee

Background

I didn't start on *Gilmore Girls* like an actor usually would. By profession, I am a computer consultant specialising in Macintosh computers. Before *Gilmore Girls,* I was working on the set of *Babylon 5* as a computer consultant, and I worked with the First Assistant Director Carla McClosky. Carla went onto work on *Gilmore Girls* and brought me on as a regular background actor. The funny thing is that I was vastly overqualified for background acting, and I didn't go looking for it. I did it because I enjoyed being on set, I enjoyed the entertainment industry, and I enjoyed the company of the people I was working with. I promised myself that when it got onerous and boring I would get out of it. It never did.

One day they decided to make me the regular bus boy at Luke's diner and that role turned out to be a good fit. Since we had so much talking on the show, the scenes in the diner were always five or six pages long, which was a lot of talking. They needed someone who was intelligent enough to understand the blocking, and camera angles and be able to navigate the set and understand where I should and shouldn't be crossing in the shot, while all of that dialogue took place. I was technically minded, and sharp enough for the job, so it worked out to be a great job for me.

Over seven seasons, I was usually always available, but there was one day where I wasn't, so they brought in another background actor. I heard that this didn't go well. They weren't used to needing to micromanage me in the diner, as I was efficient at what I did, and experienced in the role now. This cover person needed a lot more assistance and it caused a bit of stress that day. There would be six tables and the counter to fill the diner for a scene at Luke's. This meant there would be 20-25 people in the diner, and then you would have another 20 people walking outside the windows. That's a lot of people for the assistant directors to keep track of. They didn't want to have to micromanage the bus boy as well, so it turned out that I was valuable because I would come in, memorise the scenes and then take notes about my crosses. I would then do everything the same way over, and over again and this made them deliriously happy. So, for all seven seasons I was the bus boy, but it had just happened by way of being in the right place at the right time.

I am a very unusual background actor. Most background actors want to work everyday, because they are either chasing a paycheck, or trying to break into acting. Understandably, they want to work across as many shows as possible for exposure, and for income. However, I was a background actor/computer consultant hybrid, even once I became the bus boy in Luke's diner. My experience with computers was still a safety blanket for the assistant directors, in case anything went wrong, and I still enjoyed that work. Having me on set all the time was valuable for them, because I could fix computer issues while I was working background. There were computer disasters sometimes, and I would fix it. Even though I was working as a background actor, I always kept my equipment on me. This meant that I wasn't looking for other work on other sets or asking my agent to put me out for any other roles. I didn't really have high aspirations of being an actor at the time. I was just extremely fortunate with the friendships that I had, to get this kind of unique role on *Gilmore Girls.*

The best moments I had on the show were when I interacted with other background actors on the show. Throughout the years—particularly in the later seasons—people would get on the show as background because they were huge fans of the show, and they would be really happy about being there. I really enjoyed talking to those people and helping them enjoy their day at *Gilmore Girls.* Specifically, the ones who got to sit in the diner—that was a real treat for those people. Occasionally there would be raffle winners that had won a day on *Gilmore Girls,* and they were always so excited to be a part of it. I loved hosting them, chatting with them, and making sure their dreams really got to come true for their day in Stars Hollow.

An episode I had a lot of fun filming was the civil war reenactment episode, where Luke's uncle had died. It was an interesting experience as an Asian man. I got to dress up and pose as a reenactor which was funny, because you can't reenact the civil war with an Asian soldier—there were no Asians in the civil war who fought for America. That was ironic, but a lot of fun.

My second favourite episode was 'Pulp Friction'. The episode was full of Quentin Tarantino movie references like *Pulp Fiction, Kill*

Bill, and *Reservoir Dogs*. I was initially asked to help with computer technology for this episode but ended up acting in it. Hair and makeup came to me and asked if I could take screenshots of the Tarantino movies from their computers, so they could recreate the looks. For copyright reasons, you shouldn't be able to take screenshots of movies that are being played on DVD, and the people in hair and makeup had been blocked when they tried. But, being a computer specialist, I was able to get around those restrictions, and get the screenshots for them. In the process, I saw the different characters that they needed to dress people up as. One of the characters they needed was the teacher from *Kill Bill* so I put my hand up to be that character. They were a little hesitant at first, because it was supposed to be a college party, but I was so keen that they let me do it. Growing up, I always had a huge fondness for kung fu movies. Gordon Liu, who played two characters in *Kill Bill* (including the one I wanted to dress up as) was one of my favourite actors. Getting to take on this character essentially meant being able to dress up as Gordon Liu. I had to wear a wig, and a big bushy moustache. If you see the kung fu master in the scene dancing behind Robert and Rory talking, that is me. I am also quite visible to the left during the reenactment of the *Pulp Fiction* dance. I had a blast. It was definitely one of the highlights from my time on the show.

One of the things that was very interesting about my time on *Gilmore Girls* was the controversy about the 'Asian Caesar.' Every show has a budget of course, and so sometimes Aris (who plays Caesar) was not in an episode because of budgetary reasons. A cheap way of including him in the story, was for Luke to run out of the diner and yell to Caesar who wasn't actually there. That happened in quite a few episodes, where you might see Luke yell for Caesar to lock up or something, but Aris was not actually on set. In those episodes, the only person you could see working in the diner was me. This made it seem like I was Caesar, and Luke was directing his lines at me. This led to online discussions and an underlying internet theory about the elusive 'Asian Caesar'.

Another theory, which led to rampant speculation online, was that I am Mr. Kim. A lot of people were expecting me to come out as Mr. Kim in the revival. I was hoping to be involved in *A Year in the Life*, but knew realistically that wouldn't be the case, because none of the original assistant directors that I had worked for were involved. I was, however, working on the lot when it was filming, so I got to go and say hi, and had a chat to Amy Sherman-Palladino, Michael Winters (Taylor Doose), and many of the crew.

Now, I am working on a television show called *Good Trouble*, which is a spin off from *The Fosters*. I play the father of a homosexual daughter, and it's a nice story about how she navigates those waters. The show's name comes from a wonderful quote from John Lewis who was a civil rights activist, and congressman. My acting career developed after I became good friends with Ellen Morano, the mother of Vanessa Morano, who played April Nardini on *Gilmore Girls*. Ellen was having some issues with her computer so I went over to their place and fixed those issues. Ellen has raised two girls who are working actors in Hollywood and are very talented. She is a very savvy woman managing her daughters careers, but also raised down to earth, friendly, grounded girls. Ellen sat me down one day when I was fixing their computers and told me that I should be in commercials. I thanked her but said I didn't know anything about the acting industry other than working as background. She called her agent and within three months I had booked my first national commercial. Through *Gilmore Girls,* and this relationship with Ellen, I am now a bonafide, principal actor. Ellen considered me worth it enough to pick up the phone, get me an agent, and tell me I was good enough to be an actor. So for all intents and purposes, *Gilmore Girls* is the reason why I'm a fully fledged actor now.

Gilmore Girls was brilliant because of Amy's writing. She is a perfectionist, and a genius. She was wonderful at bringing out the fun in the characters, and bringing life to every individual character, to every storyline, and to the town of Stars Hollow. That's what *Gilmore Girls* was really—a celebration of everything that makes you alive. This comes out in all the cultural references—the books, the movies, the music—and the relationships. What could be more celebratory about life than the relationship between a parent and a child? The show really stood for relationships between family, and parents and their children. The camaraderie and sense of family, and the good people on that show, changed my life. *Gilmore Girls* was unique and very special.

Michael Winters

Taylor Doose

During the first season of *Gilmore Girls* I was living in Los Angeles temporarily, and going out on auditions while I was there. I used to live in Seattle and do theatre, then fly to Los Angeles for 'pilot season' when lots of shows and auditions were coming out. While I was in Los Angeles for pilot season that year, I got sent out for the part of Taylor Doose. This role would have four episodes, and the possibility of more. Of course, we quite often hear this as actors, but it doesn't happen, so I didn't get my hopes up. I got the job, but I had to tell them that I live in Seattle normally, and I would need to go back and forth for my episodes. I took the job but told production that if the role went beyond those four episodes, it might be a problem, since I didn't actually live in Los Angeles.

So, I took the job and did the four episodes. When my role did end up expanding beyond those four episodes, they flew me down for shooting, and when I was back in Seattle I would do theatre. *Gilmore Girls* would break in spring and start shooting again in August so I would come up to Seattle and do a play in the summer. As the years went on, I also went to other places to work. The pay for television was better than theatre work, so it was worth my time going back and forth. After the first couple of years, I started doing theatre in L.A. and spent most of my time in Los Angeles until Gilmore *Girls* was done, when I went back to Seattle.

I started on the seventh episode in the first season, and then was on regularly for seven years. Every single season, I would leave at the end of the regular season and tell the producers that I had work in Seattle, and that I wouldn't be available to shoot for the first episode of the next season, because I would be still working in Seattle. Every year, they would write me into the first episode. So for six years, I would have to do all my *Gilmore Girls* shooting on Monday (my day off from the theatre). I would do a show on Sunday night, and my friend would be waiting outside with the car running for me to jump into as soon as the show was over. He would take me straight to the airport where I would take the last flight to Los Angeles. I would work all day Monday on *Gilmore Girls* and be back in time for Tuesday's show. After 9/11, they stopped offering flights at that time, so I would have to leave as early as possible on a Monday, and get to set as soon as I got into L.A.

When season 3 came around, I was done with my play in Seattle, and was planning on making my way to Los Angeles by car, over a couple of days. On the day I was due to leave, I fell and broke my foot. I called the show and told them what happened. I could get around okay, but I wasn't sure what I would be able to do physically. When I got to the set, they had written into the script that Taylor had injured himself when he slipped on a banana peel, and my scene was shot with me buzzing around in an electric wheelchair.

Another season, when I came back for the first episode, I was clean shaven for another role that I had in Seattle during the break. Hair and makeup got me to come in early so they could paint my beard on. They did a really good job. I'm not sure if anyone would notice.

My role on Gilmore Girls was unique for several reasons. Firstly, just because it was recurring. The whole time I was in Los Angeles, I never had a job that spanned seven years like this one did. It allowed me to get used to the situation, to get to know the cast, crew, and writers, and to become familiar working on the same town square set. I also got to settle into my character and know Taylor—how he was likely to react, and how other characters reacted to him. My main job was to be an annoyance to everyone, and to get under everyone's skin. It got easier and more fun, as I settled into Taylor over the years.

Secondly, I got used to all of the language that was thrown at us. Dakin Matthews, who played Headmaster Charleston on the show, once told me that theatre actors like ourselves were used on the show, because the casting directors felt we were more adept at delivering large amounts of the dialogue, which this show was full of. I had speeches all the time that were very complicated, and long. These were usually part of town meeting scenes.

Those scenes were always difficult because they were not shot how it looks on screen. I would sit on stage all day long with Liz Torres, reading my lines, while they shot all the footage of the town members reacting, and talking in their seats. Then, at the end of the day, they would send everyone away, and I would deliver my lines to empty seats, while they shot the footage of the stage in Miss Patty's dance studio. My speeches would be complicated, and long, with lots of little tricky verbal things that were hard to memorise, and deliver. The Festival of Living Art was shot the same way. I was the announcer, so I would deliver all of my lines while the cameras were turned to the audience. We shot all day, and deep into the night. I had been sitting around in a tuxedo for hours and then all of a sudden they were done with the audience footage. It was my turn to do the introductions in front of the camera, and this time my dialogue was full of Italian names. The director came up to me and said, "I don't want to stress you, but in about 20 minutes, the sun is going to come up, and our night time illusion will be gone". I had 20 minutes to rattle off all of the introductions, one after the other, before the whole set became bathed in sunlight, and the shoot would be over.

I remember one Monday where everything had to be shot on one day because I had to go back to Seattle. The episode was the one where an old thunderbird had to drive through the window of Luke's Diner. That had to be shot all in one day and it was an incredibly technically difficult episode to shoot. They, of course, also had only one shot at getting the crash right. I had to be there to shoot the part before the crash, and after, and I kept messing up the lines because of the time pressure, and intensity of the episode. My parts had to be shot before the crash, while the window was still intact, so it was sort of holding up the rest of the shoot. It was also very hot that day, and we shot a lot of it outside. Everyone was uncomfortable, and the cast had to keep getting powdered down. Someone actually fainted from the heat that day and was sent home, so it was a scary and difficult day.

My favourite moment was when I was running for town selectman and my character was convinced that the win would be a sure thing, since Taylor got elected every year. In this episode, Jackson decided to run against Taylor, and won the election. There is a scene where Lorelai is in the diner late at night, and all that can be seen through the diner window is me, commiserating my loss, with the lights off. I picked up a whipped cream dispenser and just turned and shot a mouthful of whipped cream into my mouth to make myself feel better. That was a really fun scene to shoot, and it came out great in the episode.

In 2016, I heard through the grapevine that Netflix was going to be doing a reboot of the show. My part was sort of borderline in terms of necessity. I wasn't a major character, but Taylor wasn't insignificant. I hadn't heard anything from anyone though, so I thought maybe my character wasn't going to make the cut. A couple of weeks later, someone called from a local theatre and said that the people at *Gilmore Girls* were trying to find me. Amy Sherman-Palladino called and said she hadn't been able to track me down. It was quite late in the process, but they wanted me to come back, and were counting on it. There were four movies in the new series, and I was in three of them. They booked me at the Hilton Universal City for six weeks, which turned out to be a really nice vacation. I had a lot of free time and got to catch up with all of my Los Angeles friends when I wasn't shooting. Getting paid to stay at the Hilton was definitely a great *Gilmore Girls* memory.

I thought being back on the show, and on the old set would be weird, but it wasn't. It was heaven. Everyone was so happy to be working, and to see each other again. Even the main actors were happier. In the original run, they worked their tails off all the time. They carried everything on their back and it was really hard work. This new limited series was only three months of filming, so the pressure wasn't as intense. It was wonderful to see everyone again, and it was a truly joyful time.

It was a great show to work on. It was high quality work, and even when it ended, we knew we were going out with a bang. The relationships on the show are really what make it so beloved, because those connections are universal. I've watched the show with my mother, and had people stop me on the street and tell me about watching the show with theirs. The mother-daughter relationship and friendship was so different to everything else on television. Lorelai and Rory were always good friends, no matter what tension was present at the time. The timing of the original show was also important. On the WB at that time, the rest of the popular teen shows were sex dramas. *Gilmore Girls* was lighter in tone, cleaner, more comic, and ultimately, sweet. It was a great balance to what else was on at that time.

Valerie Campbell

Costumer / Costume Supervisor

    My time on *Gilmore Girls* started when my friend Brenda Maben called and asked if I would like to come and work on the show. I didn't know what *Gilmore Girls* was at the time. In truth I thought she said 'Gibson Girls' which made me think it was a period show. I started on episode 11 of the first season. I was the Key Set Costumer, and my job was to maintain the costume continuity and help the actors with anything and everything relating to their outfits.

    It was a difficult show to work on, because of the hours. It was very long hours, and short turnarounds. During the time period that Amy Sherman-Palladino was running the show, we would be shooting about 70 hours a week and my average work day would be 19 hours.

Occasionally, this would stretch to 22 hours. We worked five days a week and my start time would fluctuate based on the actors' call time. We started before the actors came in. As the week went on, we would end up coming in later though, as we would work into the late hours. The union required that we have the nine hours off, so if we worked from 6 A.M. to 11pm, then we would not be able to check back into work until 8 A.M. the next day. That nine hour break from work included travelling back home exhausted, sleeping, and travelling back to work, often in traffic. Luckily for me I lived only a few minutes from the studio, but some crew members had an hour-long commute. Now, the union requires ten hours. Gradually, it would just get later and later as the week went on. By the time Friday came along, sometimes we would be coming home from work at 8 A.M., having worked all night, so we wouldn't be able to check back in till late afternoon. This meant that at the end of the week we were shooting into the night, so daytime exterior shots would be scheduled for the beginning of the week, in the earlier parts of the day, to make sure we got them in the daylight.

    Working those long hours for ten months out of the year just became my life. I didn't go home and hang out with friends after work, I just went home and went straight to sleep. By the time I had driven home, or had something to eat, I might have had less than eight hours to sleep. I basically had no life during the week, and on the weekends I would catch up on sleep and do laundry. If I had any extra time, it would be spent getting groceries or cooking dinner. We would have April to the beginning of July off from filming, so I would use that time for projects around the house, and catching up with friends and family.

    I got married in between season1 and season 2, so for the next six years I was working this crazy lifestyle. My husband works in the industry too, so it was long hours for both of us. *Gilmore Girls* was unique because we maintained those hours for so long, and the days were longer than you would expect, but long hours are common in the industry. It was more extreme than some shows, but on every show, you never really know when you are coming home. It was also difficult to take a day off, so most people didn't. I felt it was too hard to replace myself. I had a lot of knowledge about how each character would dress, and how to set a room and make sure nothing was forgotten. For instance, I wouldn't want Richard's room to be missing his handkerchief, or his bow tie. Every character had specific things that were part of their costume. For that reason, you can't just easily give your job to someone else. When I mention *Gilmore Girls* to anyone working in this industry, they know exactly what that means. Our show had a reputation for being difficult too shoot. When I say I did the show people have a lot of respect that I made it to the end.

The hardest episodes to shoot for me were the 24-hour dance marathon episode, 'They Shoot Gilmores, Don't They?', and 'The Festival of Living Art'. The dance marathon was a challenge because there were so many people and the numbers kept falling off the outfits. They were initially pinned into place, but when they moved it tore the vintage fabric so we taped them into place but they didn't stay attached very well. Between takes I would have to repair the dresses and while we were shooting my eyes were focused on the numbers to make sure they stayed in place. The Festival of Living Art episode was very hands-on. I was responsible for manoeuvring each actor's body into position so that it exactly matched the piece of art we were recreating. It had to be perfect.

My favourite scenes to shoot were the Life and Death Brigade scenes. The energy on set was so much fun, and it was so beautiful—especially the *Out of Africa* scene at night when everyone was wearing their vintage white outfits. We rarely did stunts so it was fun to use my skills to rig the clothes to fit the harnesses for the jump in that episode. I had to sew Rory's scarf into place so we wouldn't see the harness when she jumped. I have really good memories of my time on the show. I took a lot of pictures. If you see a fun, candid, behind-the-scenes photo online, I probably took it.

When the revival was announced, I had a job lined up to work on *Grease Live* so I really had to think about whether I could take *A*

Year in the Life on. I ultimately decided that I would only come back if I was the supervisor, not just the costumer. I was offered the position of costume supervisor. I had to quit the other job, which is something I never do, but I just couldn't not do *Gilmore Girls* again.

When I went back, there was a wall of headshots in the office with a picture of everyone who had ever been on the show. Looking at it, I started welling up. Ed Herrmann's picture was on the wall. It was an interesting experience going back after having such a long break. We had already said goodbye to the characters, and to Stars Hollow. Normally, once that time in your life is over, when you have been working on a show, you don't ever get to go back. It was wild. I remember passing Lauren or Alexis and getting this recognition from them—that surrealism that we were all back. It was so weird. It was like a family reunion, or a high school reunion. It was also a very secretive set that time around. The costumers often knew more than the actors did, because the scripts were being closely guarded. It was crazy, but it was amazing.

There were physical differences in the environment when we came back which also changed the feel of it. The Gilmore house was slightly bigger and was laid out slightly differently. Lorelai's house was bigger, and looked and felt different. They had redecorated it and the structure of it was different. They had elevated the porch, as well as The Dragonfly. Those sets were elevated so they wouldn't have to be on the backlot as much, as they had limited time on the backlot. This was largely due to the nature of the episodes as representing different seasons, and the backlot requiring different set dressings. It was uncanny how they recreated those areas though, and it felt a bit surreal to be back in them.

As well as coming back for the revival, something else great came out of my time on the show. I've been making ice cream for about 20 years, and started a couple of years before *Gilmore Girls*. I would sometimes make it when I was on the show and bring it to set.

One day, I brought my ice cream maker to the set and made ice cream for a baby shower that was taking place on set for a crew member.

When I was in high school, my drama teacher left the school to go teach at another school. Her husband was a stage manager in the film industry, and he inspired me to enter this industry. When she was leaving, she said to me, this is not the end. We might be leaving here, but we can stay in touch. Her husband's words of advice for me, when I entered the film industry was to keep in touch with everyone I meet. He said that I would never know who is going to lead me to my next adventure. I always remembered their words.

I kept in touch with everyone I met. I would write every person's name down and write little notes about how I knew people. I would call them periodically, and I started having parties to keep connected, and making ice cream. Those parties became the conduit for being able to keep in touch with people. I keep people on the list forever, even if they never come to my parties. We have had people not come for 10 years and then turn up at one, or several, so I still invite everyone. For me it was more about having a reason to keep in touch, even if they were not going to be able to come to the party.

I took this philosophy into my work in the filming industry, and on *Gilmore Girls*. Those parties are really how I've kept in touch with so much of the cast and crew throughout the years. When you are working such long hours for most of the year, the people on that set become your friends, your family. We spent every day together for ten months out of every year. It's also hard to maintain friendships with anyone outside of that while you are working those hours, so those people become your life. After the show finished, the parties at my house are how I stayed in contact with everyone. When Aaron Berman was writing *The Gilmore Girls Companion,* he contacted me, and came and stayed with us. I threw one of my parties and helped him connect with the cast and crew.

In 2017, I went to the fan festival and the organiser, Jennie, suggested I write a book about my ice cream. I never thought I was a writer, and the idea of writing a book seemed like a lot of work. But, I did think it would be a good idea to make ice cream at the festival. So, we churned ice cream, and told stories, and we had a packed house. It was a great event. At the beginning of 2018, Jennie and Marcus had come to town to see one of Stan Zimmerman's plays *Pledge* and we were hanging out after the show. Once again, she said, you should really write a book. She wanted me to write a book that integrated my ice cream recipes with stories. Jennie always encourages those who attend the festival to bring their creative projects along to sell at fan fest. I went home that night and couldn't stop thinking about it. I decided that if I was going to write a book, it had to be like the one I wrote while I was working on *Gilmore Girls*.

While I was working on the show, I wrote a cookbook as a wedding present for one of our crew members who was getting married to a chef. I got the cast and crew to each give me a recipe they liked and I hand-wrote them on paper and then I bound it in leather and made it into a book. The book had different sections that represented Stars Hollow and *Gilmore Girls* related things—it had an ad in there for Miss Patty's, and Le Chat Club. Every single person except for Amy and Dan contributed a recipe. Everyone had a little recipe, or words of advice. I decided if I was going to write a book, I wanted to make it like that one. When I put together my book *The Story & Recipes of Valerie's Cat Eye sCream!* the recipes were handwritten and the titles were fun and whimsical. I tried simply writing the recipes but they didn't want to come out of me like that. It wasn't until I started drawing the ingredients in the title that I realised it would be so much easier to understand if I illustrated each step. The recipes and stories were limited to one 8"x8" page each. I found clever ways to fit complicated stories by handwriting and illustrating the words into a puzzle, so it developed into a graphic image cookbook which illustrated the ingredients and steps. As I was drawing it, I was working on the television show *Timeless* and I was drawing a picture of a phantom mask when an actor walked behind me and asked about it. It was difficult to explain why this was part of a cookbook, but it turned out he was a big fan of *Gilmore Girls*. Cast and crew members would often come up to me while I was working on it, and I realised that I had something interesting, because it was appealing to people when I told them what I was putting together. People like ice cream, and they like the style of doodle art in my book. It's been a fun adventure that would never have happened without the inspiration from Jennie and Marcus, and without *Gilmore Girls*.

Gilmore Girls definitely has more fans now than it did when it was airing. Our fan base grew every year it was on the air, and it has kept growing ever since. Mothers shared the show with their daughters, then daughters shared it with their husbands, and with their own children. It's a show that gets handed down generations, and has a little something for everyone. What makes it even more special is every time you rewatch the show there are more depths and layers that are revealed. The first time you watch the show the dialogue is so fast and the references are so obscure but when you look at each reference there are subtle messages in the humour that you might not have caught the first, third, or tenth time watching it. Many fans dissect each moment for something that they might not have caught. Groups of friends have been connected through the show in a way that no one could have predicted when it went off the air. Now, with social media, and ways to connect with other fans and discuss these things, the show keeps growing. Podcasts have been dedicated to watching it for the first time or reliving each and every moment from a different perspective. In 2021 I started a TikTok account called @valeriescateyescream. I go live often and have created a little community of *Gilmore Girls* fans where I share my experiences, life, and the positive aspects of the show.

The last few years of the original run of the show were so bittersweet. I remember the moment when Amy and Dan told us they would not be following us to the seventh season. I felt gutted as we didn't know how they would be able to tell the stories without Amy's ever-present voice. The last season was so different. It was great we didn't have long hours, but the show suffered from their absence. When the seventh season ended we still did not know if we would be picked up. When I got the phone call there was just such an emptiness. It was like someone had died. The family that was created on that show was suddenly dissolved. Of course, we could keep in touch with people if we wanted to, but it was never going to be the same. Over the years I have reconnected with many of the people from the show, and we would have reunions and parties at my house. When we see each other, it is like no time has passed at all. I don't know if I will ever work on a show like that again, but I am grateful for my time there. I will never forget working on this show.

Joe Fria

Joe Mastoni

    Before I was on *Gilmore Girls* I was doing a show on stage in Los Angeles with a company called Zoo District. The play was based on a banned Russian book called *The Master and Margarita*. The stage show went on to become very popular and industry people started coming to watch it. The casting directors for *Gilmore Girls*—Jami Rudofsky and Mara Casey were two of those people. They were friends of the theatre community, and everyone in the theatre seemed to know who they were. They came up to me right after the show to talk, and were just so complimentary and lovely. After that, I got called in to audition for *Gilmore Girls*. I got the part of the waiter in season 1 episode 12, when Jackson and Sookie double date with Lorelai and Rune. That was my first part in a big television show, and it was a great credit. It definitely opened a few more doors for me. I kept in touch with Jami and Mara, after that episode. I did a short film that Mara was a huge fan of and she was trying to help me as much as she could. I could pop into their office to ask ideas and chat to them about anything. It was a relationship that continued outside of *Gilmore Girls*.

It was a nice surprise when I got called back in a year and a half later for a bigger role in *Gilmore Girls,* and I took it very gladly. I didn't have a first call audition for the role of Joe Mastoni, but instead went straight to the callback. When I got there, there were a lot of other people waiting to audition. My initial reaction when I saw that, was that I was there to be what is known as a 'room filler'. Sometimes in television, creatives already know who they will want, but they have to audition a certain number of people according to union rules. I thought maybe that's what I was there for—to make up numbers. It turned out, they were continually keeping me fresh in the eyes of that team of people. Mara and Jami wanted to cast me on the show, in something. They were very loyal to actors they liked.

I walked into the audition room where Amy, the producers, and Carla McClosky (the director of the episode) were waiting. While we were all waiting to go into the audition room, Mara came in, and asked everybody if we succeeded in booking the role, would we be able to go straight to set to do chef training. Whoever got the job would need to learn to chop vegetables like a professional for one of the scenes. I got the part, and was whisked away in a golf cart right away to learn how to chop vegetables like a chef.

We ended up shooting the episode about a week later and it was awesome. It was an incredible experience. I had heard about problems on the set, but to me it was a loving, protective environment. When the hours got long, someone like Lauren Graham would be very protective about people working all day. The ladies took the show as their responsibility and I loved every minute of that. Melissa McCarthy was amazing. At the time I was writing a short film that I wanted to shoot, direct and produce. She offered to help out. She didn't know me at all, but offered her and her husband's assistance, giving me her email so I could get in touch. I thought that was so generous of her. I was very nervous during the shoot, as usual, but all I remember was goodness.

In the episode my business partner and I are at a conference when I bump into Sookie, who Joe used to work with, and who he has had a crush on for a long time. Sookie is with her business partner Lorelai, who meets my business partner and sparks fly between them. What is interesting about this episode is that Billy Burke who played my business partner Alex was not the guy who was originally cast in that role. The actor originally cast in that role was not very pleasant. I won't go into too much detail, but he was not fun to work with, and he complained a lot about being there. He said he didn't want to do television, and felt that this part was beneath him. I was really taken aback because this was my first big guest star part and I couldn't believe this guy was so unhappy about being on *Gilmore Girls*. Alex's role ended up being a three episode story arc about his relationship with Lorelai. It was a good part.

We shot the scene where we come out of the conference room and bump into the two women. A few weeks later I got a call from my agent saying that I had to go back and reshoot my scenes on *Gilmore*

Girls because the show had recast the role of my business partner, Alex. We did all of the shots again where Alex was present, but used some of the material from the first shoot between just my character and Sookie. This recast was an inconvenience to the production team, I'm sure, but it was great for me because I got to come back and work with everyone again. I was told by someone on set that the actor I had worked with before was 'bad energy' and since Alex's character had a continued storyline, they had decided that they didn't want someone like that on set, and ultimately recast him. I also found out at that time that my character was supposed to be recurring, but the recast had messed things up, and caused a lot of rewriting. It was cool to be back, but disappointing to hear that my character was going to continue in some capacity and then didn't. I remember going to Trader Joe's and buying two cases of 'two buck chuck' and handing out these cheap bottles of wine to everybody as a thank you present.

It was funny coming back to the show as a different character. Since we know Joe Mastoni is a chef, it's unlikely that he would have been waiting tables in episode 1.12. The show runners knew that some characters don't make enough of an imprint to be remembered in later episodes, so they didn't hesitate to recast actors they had used in the past. At that point in history, you couldn't go back and watch old episodes of the show so there was safety in that because nobody could really check. The really nice part is that I still get reactions from people—messages, and letters from people who really liked Joe from the Deerhill Lodge.

Gilmore Girls affected my career in that it taught me not to rely on anyone else. You have to be a self starter in a lot of ways even if you are given a step up. You have to be proactive and recreate your own momentum. I'm in the boat now of creating it on my own. I have learned my lessons, but I live a creative life—I direct, and act and I can't ask for much more than that. Nowadays, I also voice audiobooks, which is just a subset of my acting work. My main audiobook gig has been playing Slappy in the *Goosebumps* books. I was very influenced by Mark Hamill's version of the Joker, so I think that guided my audition, and I got the job. It's been an ongoing gig and I like doing it. Most of my time is taken up being a director of voice over and working for Netflix.

A few *Gilmore Girls* people have wandered into my life over the years. Devon Michaels, and Nick Holmes are good friends of mine. So many people drifted in and out of that show. As life went on, these people who had been a part of the show came into my life and we formed a brotherhood of sorts. I think having been on *Gilmore Girls* was kind of a rite of passage for some young actors.

Gilmore Girls is special because of Amy. The writing is incredible and the narrative arc is beautiful. Keeping it alive with all of these wonderful actors was a Herculean task. The show is so universal because of its mother-daughter relationship and the sensibilities that surround those relationships. It's timeless, specific and so free and real. Even though it was stylised it was way ahead of its time. It had this connectability but also a subversiveness that television shows then didn't have. It was subversive in terms of the amount of dialogue. The 90 page scripts were for an hour long show, filled with pop culture references. The subversiveness of throwing that much information at an audience was groundbreaking. On top of that, the show had a real watchability. It was wholesome, and magical. There aren't many shows where you can watch episodes over and over again, fall asleep to them, or pick them apart and notice things. It's the kind of show you can drape around yourself like a warm blanket and lose yourself in it. Nobody will ever get sick of it. There was a genius attached to the vision of the show, and I don't think anything will ever come close to that. That trailblazing format coupled with this beautiful mother daughter storyline makes the show always relevant.

Albert Coleman

Editor and Assistant Editor

    I was an Editor, and Assistant Editor on *Gilmore Girls* for four seasons. I had mainly been working on feature films such as

Poltergeist and *Risky Business*, so this was my first time working on a television show.

I got a call from a friend of mine who was an editor. He wanted me to come on to edit season 1, episode 7. The show hadn't even aired yet, so I didn't know anything about it. I was looking for work, so I took the job. In television, the first seasons are always very difficult. The production team are trying to solidify the tone of the show, and work with what the studio and network wants. There are different competing interests, and different ideas of what the show should be. Without that track record of success yet, it can be a hard balance to strike. Season 2 and beyond, was easier.

When I went to work on *Gilmore Girls*, my two daughters were eight and six. My wife brought them over to have lunch and took them to the set, so they got to see Stars Hollow before the show had even aired. I told my daughters not to take autograph books with them because it's a working set, and they would need to be really quiet. We were standing around on set, when Lauren Graham came up to them and asked if they wanted autographs. She said it was no problem and grabbed paper cereal bowls to sign for them. My daughters still have those bowls.

After that, my daughters came to visit me at Warner Bros several more times. The cast were always terrific, and kind to them. Once the show aired, my daughters really wanted to come and visit because their friends were watching it, and talking about it. My girls are in their late 20s now, and they still talk about these visits.

When I started in season 1, I was an assistant editor, but I became editor in season 2. Television work was difficult because you would shoot 22 episodes, and then be on hiatus for a few months. This meant I would go and look for work during the break. After season 2, I got a job that prevented me from coming back to *Gilmore Girls* in season 3. By season 4 I was available again, so I came back, but then wasn't available during seasons 5 and 6. I came back for the final season. So, there was a lot of coming back and forth for me, while I took other jobs. I got to work on other cool shows though like *House*, as well as feature films.

Gilmore Girls was technically challenging to work on. I had to edit the episodes so that the rhythm and speed was maintained, and the dialogue overlapped but the actors were not talking over each other. I felt for the actors, because they had long pages of dialogue and it had to be fast, and perfect. One of my favourite episodes to edit was 'Teach Me Tonight', where Jess drives Rory's car and they get into an accident. It was a tough episode for the actors because it was so emotional, and it was important to get the tone right. It came out great. Another favourite was the episode which included a film by Kirk. I remember Liza Weil and Melissa McCarthy both wanted to direct an episode so Amy told them that they would need to spend the day in editorial. They did it twice, hanging out all day long in our trailer, and watching the process of editing the show.

The editorial rooms were in trailers on the other side of the hedges at Lorelai's house. These trailers housed the editorial staff, assistant directors, props people, post-production, and transportation. I enjoyed that actually. In the digital age, being an editor can be an isolating job, because things can be done remotely. That trailer was always full of activity, and full of people. It was a lot of fun working in a large team, and I loved being able to go for a walk through Stars Hollow if things were a bit slow in editorial that day. I could go to the commissary to grab a coffee, stop to watch some of the shooting, and say hello to the cast and crew.

After season 7, there was a season wrap party, but we didn't know it was the end. We all had a great time, and then said "See you soon!" I heard later online that the show had been cancelled. Nobody even got a phone call. Nobody got to say goodbye.

When the reboot was announced, I was working on a television show called *Grim* at Universal/NBC. I was working with one of the *Gilmore Girls* producers, Helen Pai, on Grimm, and she left to do *A Year in the Life*. I only saw one episode of the reboot, but I didn't feel it had the momentum of the original series. The 90 minute episodes lacked the snappines that characterised the original 45 minute ones.

In 2009 I was working in Mexico City, on a show for 20th Century Fox. Every morning when I was getting ready to go, *Gilmore Girls* would play in the hotel, so I watched it while I was working on the show in Mexico. When you work on something you are clueless about whether it's a hit. All you are focused on is deadlines, schedules, and doing your job. Editorial can be an isolating job, because you don't really notice the success of the show or film because you are working in a room with the door closed, and your head down. You really don't know what an impact the show is having on its audience. In addition, a lot of the shows that are made don't go beyond one season. There are a lot of one-season-wonders out there that got cancelled, so when you are working on a first season you never really know if you are working on a hit, or a flop. Time tells, of course, but at the time, you are just doing your job. Seeing those re-runs in a foreign country really made me realise the effect that *Gilmore Girls* had worldwide. This show never gets old. There is even a comic-convention style festival for *Gilmore Girls* now, and there are books being written about it. I'm not completely surprised, looking back, and having watched the show. It was well written, well acted, and I had a lot of fun working on it.

David Sutcliffe

Christopher Hayden

    I got an audition for *Gilmore Girls*, and immediately liked the dialogue I had been given. It was well written, and I thought the pilot episode was excellent. There was already a buzz surrounding this show, even that early on. When you are auditioning in the industry, you have your ear to the ground constantly, and this was one show that stood out from the crowd. The Dad character was compelling to me. It was a recurring role, and I had come off the back of two television shows that were cancelled, so I was available for my next project.

I felt good about the audition. Amy Sherman-Palladino and the casting directors were there. I asked if they wanted it fast and dynamic, or more mellow, and they of course said they wanted it fast. I read the scenes, and felt like I had done a great job. As I left, I heard an eruption of laughter. I wondered what that was about, as it was a little odd. I was later told that they were laughing because they knew they had found Christopher. They had been waiting for that right person to walk into the room and I was that person.

A couple of weeks later there was a read through, right before Christmas. I had met Lauren Graham at an audition for a pilot called *Us* for NBC the year before and we had tested together. She had already been cast and I was testing to play opposite her. That audition for me was horrible— terrible, a disaster. There was no chemistry. I called my agent and told him that there had been no chemistry between me and the woman at the audition. At my first *Gilmore Girls* read through, Lauren and I started reading together and there was instantly a good vibe, a good back and forth. We were looking at each other, smiling, and it was natural and easy. I hadn't even realised that Lauren was the same woman from that other audition.

We shot that first episode "Christopher Returns" and it went really well. It was a lot of fun and the acting was good. Lauren had been around the industry a little bit before *Gilmore Girls,* cutting her teeth on other shows. When you are pounding the pavement and you get on a show that has staying power you want to make it work because this could be it, that could be your moment. You felt that strong intention on the set—that everyone was committed, and wanted the show to succeed. Everyone on set worked hard, worked long hours, and worked with long scripts. Some of the scenes were difficult, either technically, or emotionally. It wasn't always easy, but it was a challenge and it was fun to work on something that you are trying to make great everyday. Despite that hard work ethic and strong desire for the show to work, the show comes off light, whimsical, and fun. Over time you realise that when you have a fan base that's paying real attention to the show, everything you are doing is going to be received, and is going to pay off.

This first episode contained one of my favourite scenes of mine on the show—the scene in the kitchen between Lauren and I at the end of Christopher Returns, where she is in her pyjamas and I ask her to marry me. That was a very challenging scene. It took a lot of time to shoot, but it was also really fun. We were both in the zone and it was very alive and magnetic. That scene has to be great and that was my first episode so it was a great feeling to know that it had gone well. Once I had that in the can I felt solid and secure. I felt confident and positive moving forward.

I also liked the cotillion episode, and its little moments with Rory, being her dad and passing her on. I loved my scene because I didn't have a lot of scenes with Alexis, and she was lovely. My least favourite scene is the one where I told Lorelai that Sherry is pregnant. I'm not that happy with my performance in that scene. There was some conflict about how Amy wanted me to play it, and how I wanted to play it. The filming environment was always supportive and friendly and I love Amy and trust her. I think Amy just envisioned it one way in her head, and it was jarring when I wasn't playing it out like she imagined. I felt like I could have done a better job of it. I remember shooting that scene, and it was intense. Lauren is a very intense actress. She is amazing to watch. She is a genius and when geniuses are in their zone they are working and I like that because I'm the same way and we could meet each other there. We aren't scared to go there with each other. That scene had a lot of heat, and emotion.

I remember working on *Will & Grace* and they all realized what they had—they knew they had captured lightning in a bottle. I remember one day, the producers and main cast members were all screaming at each other. They were having this passionate argument, and it was kind of beautiful. They were fighting to make the show great. Conflict is how you get to the other side. The fighting, the bickering, the arguing, and having a space where that is okay and respectful is good. It's creative fighting. The truth is, that's what television shows are—every scene is a conflict. If there is no conflict, there is nothing to watch. That's the essence of drama. That's what I liked about *Gilmore Girls*—people weren't afraid of the conflict.

The hardest scenes to shoot were always 'walk and talks'. These are tracking shots with no cuts. That's hard because when it's rapid fire dialogue that is five or six pages long, it only takes one screw up and everyone has to start all over. That pressure is really intense. There is a lot of pressure and excitement because it's like live theatre. In other shots, the editors are turning the scene into something that isn't exactly what it was, cutting, and using different camera angles. It's not perfectly organic, whereas a tracking shot without any edits has a quality to it. It's fresh, but it has to be right. I did pretty well at these shots. I had a sharp mind for dialogue at that age. Also, when the writing is so good it makes it easy. Good writing is easy to memorise.

The intention was for the role to be recurring and it was the father so I knew if the show went on they were going to use that character. After I saw 'Christopher Returns' and saw that it all worked I knew I was coming back. I knew that, I could just feel it. The work itself was kind of year to year. They would sign me for a few episodes which was, at times, difficult. I got a lead on my own show so there was a year where I was only in one episode, due to my commitment on the other show. Overall though, I was happy with it. It was fun to be recurring and come in every once in a while. I had a sort of steady gig but with options to do other things.

At the end of season 6 on *Gilmore Girls* the story was being set up for Christopher to become a bigger part. I remember thinking that if the show was renewed for season 7 I would be working a lot. I didn't know much about Amy Sherman-Palladino leaving the show but was worried and skeptical about how the show would mimic her voice, and distinct flavour in her absence. As it turns out, season 7 feels different than the rest. There was a subtle quality that you could feel was not there. The show had a different vibe. Amy has a very strong personality and her presence is powerful so her not being there was different, and I'm sure that was reflected in some way.

Before the last season started shooting, they came to me and offered me the whole season—all 22 episodes. I didn't want to commit to that. I thought it was too much and I didn't want to be tied down. I look back now and think I should have made the commitment, but that's where my headspace was during that time. Lauren called me and wanted me to come back. We had a great time, and we enjoyed working together. We were friends and she wanted to make it work. There was a lot of stuff going on in my life and I was starting to think about getting out of the acting industry and doing other things. I agreed to 13 episodes. I knew that I had some leverage in that situation, because they had set up the relationship between Christopher and Lorelai already, and they had to play that out. So I went back for the episodes, and had a great time. It was a lot of fun working on the show that year, but you could feel people were tired. I think I always knew that season 7 would be the last. I knew it wasn't going beyond that without Amy. However, I also felt like that was the end of the line for me too. I just got the vibe that it was enough. They had told the stories. People felt like they had done enough. It was a strange thing because I was 30 or 31 when it started and 37 or 38 when it ended, so that show carried me throughout my 30s.

Overall, it was a great working environment. It did feel like stepping into a vortex, or into another reality. It had an energy to it. There was a quality to that set. That's part of what made the show work, you feel that on screen. It exists within its own world, and it almost pulls you in. When I feel like I am somewhere else, I can't help but act within the framework of this world I am in, so it helps. I was also working in Los Angeles in a studio with the top professionals in the world. Everyone is at a very high level and it was exciting to work with people like that and to work on a show that is successful. There was a lot of that banter, wit, and closeness. It was a family. We were all grateful for the experience. Actors often set the tone on a set and that primarily came from Lauren, she was the leader. Alexis Bledel (Rory) was quieter and young but Lauren took the mantle of the leadership. She likes to have fun and so there was kind of a light quality to everything. Characters like Miss Patty, Kirk, and Babette also brought a fun energy. It was hard work, but I had a great time. I also make a point of having fun. If I'm not having fun at work, my performance isn't going to be good. At the end of the day, you are a player, so if you aren't playing with it, it's too serious, or you are holding it too tight. The audience wants to see the actors having fun even if it's a dark movie—scary or tragic—you want to feel the actors in the joy of the expression, giving access to the story.

After the wrap, I ended up going back to Toronto where I am from and doing a show for Canadian television. I knew *Gilmore Girls* was playing in reruns and I noticed I was getting recognised more and more. There were rumours going around about the revival, and it made sense to me that Amy would want to come back with her stamp, and storyline, and finish the show. When *A Year in the Life* was announced, everyone was still young, and it was welcome news to everyone, I think. I got a call about one scene, and when I went back it was like no time had passed. It felt like a family reunion. We really celebrated, and it was beautiful. In some ways that was the climax of the popularity of the show. I remember going to the premiere, getting out of the limo, and fans were screaming.

When the Netflix revival came out it was crazy. I couldn't go anywhere. It freaked me out a little bit. It was very surprising. I realised then the show had become a classic. That was when I realised the true impact of the show on fans. I think all of the cast and crew that came back is glad that they did it. It wasn't a payday for anybody, it was about finishing something and honouring and appreciating what was created—what Amy created—and what we were all a part of. During the original seasons, I don't think that anyone knew when we were making it what it would become. In the revival we knew it was a television classic, almost into the *Star Trek* realm of popularity—iconic. It's really something.

I have kind of left Hollywood behind me now. I live in Austin, Texas and I have a whole different life. I keep in touch a little bit with Yanic Truesdale (Michel), and Lauren and I are still friends. Austin is a growing city with a lot of energy and it's becoming the centre for transformation type work. I'm a psychotherapist: a core energetics practitioner. I started doing that work in my mid 30s, training in my late 30s, and graduated from a four year training programme in my early 40s. I started going to workshops on the weekends and it took over. I became more interested in this work than acting. It felt more fulfilling. I started getting good feedback from people, and gradually transitioned from acting work to this.

I have a private practice now, helping people with their mental health, helping them to understand themselves. I work with them on the conclusions they drew from their childhood and how these—and their belief systems—are causing them to see the world in a way that is not entirely useful for them, or causing them suffering and pain. I help people come to terms with their childhood, and knowing that everybody has trauma, we intuitively know it's good to feel. It's about creating a space for people to go deep into their feelings and liberate themselves from those feelings to really understand what happened to them. We hold those feelings in our bodies and it's hard to get through those. I was always interested in therapy and managing emotions. I jumped around looking for different kinds of therapy and I started seeing a therapist when I was going back to Toronto for summers. Something about the technique used in that therapy drew me in and I heard about this workshop in California that was group therapy. It was about 20 people in a room together for a week, so I signed up. The things that I experienced and saw were transformative and compelling.

From that moment, all of my energy was immediately channelled towards that and acting became less important to me. That was a difficult struggle for me because I was at the height of my success and right at that moment I had all the opportunities available to me but was interested in this therapy.

My dad left when I was six years old and it was only later in life that I realised I had not dealt with it and it was causing all kinds of problems in my life. It's become important for me to become a sovereign, free person in the world. I think this work is needed now more than ever. At times, people are drawn to me because of *Gilmore Girls* and will try to access me as a psychotherapist to connect with me because of the show. They quickly realise that I'm serious about the work that I'm doing, and the therapy is quite intense. There are also people that have found me because of my acting work, but have become clients and had really powerful experiences, so there has been some crossover between my acting work and this work.

I feel really grateful to the fans of the show. I was not a popular character, and people hated me. It was a provocative character—the father. He was selfish, and unreliable. There are a lot of people with Dad issues who really struggled with my character's flaws. But when I retired from acting, I got so many messages and comments from the fans about how grateful they were for the work I did on the show. I am so appreciative of those fans who reached out to me. If someone reaches out to me on the street I do my best to accommodate and be respectful. I get it. I'm a fan of stuff too. I know how meaningful that is for me, and people just want to feel connected. People come up to me and they are meeting me with love, and openness. It's a real gift.

Gilmore Girls is an excellent show. I remember we shot right beside *West Wing* on the Warner Bros lot. Our studio was right beside them and on Friday nights we were the only two shows left working. It would be one or two in the morning, and we would be still trying to get the week's work done. *West Wing* had a similarly styled show—long scripts, and fast talking. It was the show of the time. It won all the Emmy awards, and everyone was talking about it. I remember watching it and thinking it's great, but ours is just as good. In terms of delivery, it was as good as *West Wing*, and maybe better. I think time has shown that assessment to be correct because people are watching *West Wing*, but not the way they are watching *Gilmore Girls*. It's a legitimately great show. I think it just captures something that people are longing for—perhaps family, perhaps love, or perhaps a simpler time. It's funny, and addictive. But, it's also dark. It's not fluffy. There are some hard scenes. There is a shadow element to the show. Amy and Lauren are complex people—they are good and bad, light and dark, and they let all of that be seen in the show, and people connect with that. It's not fantasy, it's not wonderful all the time. There's not a fear of going into some of the shadow places with people and I think audiences appreciate that. And, it's smart. They didn't dumb it down, or 'Disney-fy' it. The show has an edge. It's got a combo of all those things and it's got all the references and millions of inside jokes and that helps to create cult followings.

    I don't have anything bad to say about anything or anybody on *Gilmore Girls*. That's sincere. I feel incredibly grateful for that experience. If you had told me when I was a young actor—starting out, just trying to get a beer commercial—that I would be a part of one of the most beloved television series' of all time, I wouldn't have believed you. It's incredible to be a part of something that is so dear to so many people, and part of something that has lasted, and that is good. I liked the character, and what he brought to the series. It's lightning in a bottle. A group of people came together at that moment and it was magical and rare. That show was a little miracle.

Grant-Lee Phillips

The Town Troubadour

    I got a message from the production team at *Gilmore Girls* in early 2001. I was working on a record at the time, and I got this note about playing a role on the show—the part of the town troubadour. I did some investigation into it and it seemed great. I was still setting out on my solo career after being in a band so I was really eager to take on anything and everything, and this seemed like something that I would really find to be a lot of fun. Before I knew it, I was on set. I had no idea that it would snowball into a regular gig with so many seasons and so many episodes. I also couldn't have known that it would become such a special show to so many people.

    I was quite blind to the show when I got the call, so I had to do my research. Even the notion of a new network—from the WB to the CW—was sort of new. It was a good time to dive in head first though, and I was aware that the show had an interesting rhythm to it. It moved quickly and it was smart. It was a show you had to really pay attention to. There was an eccentric side to it that captivated me quite a bit. When I was growing up there were a lot of shows like *Green Acres* that had a zany kind of humour to them. *Gilmore Girls* reminded me of shows like this where the main characters were surrounded by a cast of oddballs. I really loved that. That was about as much as I knew going into it.

It was my first time on an episodic comedy like that. I had a fair amount of theatre experience growing up. Those acting and comedy muscles had gone dormant but were ready to be reactivated. I can recall quite vividly that first day on the set. It involved showing up at about 5 A.M. on a brisk winter day and the streets on the set had been hosed down to make them shine. The streets of Stars Hollow were radiant, the streetlamps were glistening, and the cars were reflected in the road. It was always picturesque. That set always felt like autumn, at the turn of winter. It was beautiful, but very cold. That first episode I remember trying to keep my fingers warm, while playing the guitar. That was my introduction to *Gilmore Girls*.

It wasn't long after that first episode when they wrote the episode called 'Love, Daisies and Troubadours' which was such an incredible leap for me. The episode involved another troubadour who was played by my friend, Dave (Gruber) Allen. A lot of folks remember Dave from the show *Freaks and Geeks*. He's also a great comic, and musician. The episode involved a meeting of the whole town. I remember that particular day because it was incredibly long. My call time was 5 A. M., and I was in makeup till 5.30. Then there was a lot of sitting around until it was time to shoot. When it was time for me to shoot, I began delivering my lines with as much gusto as I could, right out of the gate. I had decided I was going to do this—nail it, and give it my all. Not being so experienced in television, and having been raised in the theatre, I didn't realise we would do it over and over from so many angles. My actual camera time wouldn't take place until 2.30 am when I would deliver my monologue. The wonderful Sally Struthers (Babette Dell) commented that I must have incredible staying power, because she could see that I was giving it my everything and it was obvious that I was not saving anything for my scene later. At the end of the day, it was a skeleton crew, and I was delivering my lines to a folding chair because everyone had gone home. The rest is history.

It's easy to underestimate the physical grind of this sort of work. One particular episode involved a Festival of Living Art, where classic paintings and sculptures were brought to life. This was done by actors in full regalia, doing the poses to match famous works of art. The effect was amazing. The show did a spectacular job. It was like looking at the real thing. My part in this episode involved bringing the Leonardo Da Vinci mural painting *The Last Supper* to life. My character was cast as Judas, playing against Kirk who was cast as Jesus, so our characters were at odds in this particular script. It was a fun episode, but it was technically difficult. The makeup was so thick it felt like clay on my face, but this was necessary to make us resemble a fresco. The clothing also wouldn't move—as though it were heavily starched and sculpted. We had to wear this all day and night, and it got cold. One of the writers was also playing a subject from a famous work of art and had to wear a toga in the freezing weather.

When *A Year in the Life* was being put together, I got an email about coming back for it, and quickly got in touch with Helen Pai, who worked closely with Amy Sherman-Palladino. When I went back to do the revival it was so great to see everyone. We all seemed to fall back into place, and had an appreciation for what the show had been. It felt very natural being back on the set. It was almost like someone had called 'cut' and we had just fallen asleep for a few years. It was really strange that way.

Because I've been doing music, and putting out albums for so long, I have a few different strings of listeners. There are folks who have been listening to my music since the 90s, and then a whole other crowd who discovered my music through *Gilmore Girls*. Because of this, my listeners also span across different age groups. The best part is when the two groups intersect, and I have seen that happen. Usually it's Moms who have seen me open for the Smashing Pumpkins or something when they were younger, and now their daughters are fans because of *Gilmore Girls*. It's a real gift to have another set of listeners who came to my music through the show.

I'm someone who really enjoys stretching out and getting the freedom to explore film, acting, and art. I'm also a visual artist, I paint. There was a time in my life where I went to film school for a period because I had that interest. So the fact that *Gilmore Girls* gave me a chance to flex those muscles was wonderful. It isn't so often that someone comes along and says I want you to play this character who is much like yourself—playing your own songs, wearing what you want to wear.

To be a songwriter is to be a storyteller and as a performer of my songs, I have to inhabit them and bring them to life. I have to be able to dig down and draw feelings to the surface to create those songs. Actors have a similar process. It's not enough to just recite the lines, or just sing the words. For me, there was a realisation during *Gilmore Girls* that all of these art forms are kind of made up of the same stuff, and that I could be satisfied doing any of it really. That was a healthy recognition for me—that I didn't have to be painted into a corner artistically. I could sample different forms, and explore anything I wanted to. I was here for an adventure, and *Gilmore Girls* gave me that opportunity to explore another path. That was eye opening.

Gilmore Girls is a show that puts a great deal of trust in the viewer. It takes that leap of faith that the character is going to take you places, and that you will follow. The show also tosses out references and ideas—they come very quickly—but it never condescends to the viewer. *Gilmore Girls* is very witty, very quick, and most importantly it's very soulful. There are really inherent human dynamics at play and I think all of us relate to the generational aspect of the show, and the relationships between Emily and Lorelai, and Lorelai and Rory. It's fascinating stuff. The more you start pulling it apart, the more substance there is. It's unique in that way. That was a unique leap at the time because the show would have no problem taking its viewers way out on a limb. My character is a case in point. The troubadour could be surreal and goofy, but also had a lot of heart. That mix of comedy and true drama was a real leap.

It's just incredibly great to have been a small part of something that holds such a special place in the lives of everyone that has embraced it—all of the fans, and all of the new generation of fans that will discover it. I had the opportunity to visit one of the fan festivals before the pandemic and it was just absolutely wonderful to meet people face to face and hear the stories of what the show meant to them. Especially the way it created a bond between mothers and daughters, and families in general. I have nothing but gratitude for the opportunity to be a part of it.

Stephen Clancy

Director and Steadicam Operator

I was on *Gilmore Girls* for all seven seasons as a steadicam operator. I walked through every corner of Stars Hollow with a camera, while the actors walked, and talked. Sometimes it would take 20 takes to get the dialogue word perfect, while I walked backwards filming them. Some people were contentious about getting every single word right, but really, that was part of the show's goodness. I came in on the seventh episode of season 1, and remained on the show until it wrapped. I even directed five episodes, which was good for me. It was a great experience, all in all. We spent a lot of late nights on the show, but the cast were great, and we all got along pretty well for the most part. Working on the show was good for my career and I am still a working camera man. It was my longest job, and in some ways, *Gilmore Girls* put me on the map.

When I came onto the show, I was working as a camera operator and the production team on *Gilmore Girls* were having a very hard time keeping camera people. The position of steadicam operator is a specifically hard job because my job is to capture tracking shots, or 'walk and talks'. These scenes are usually shot from in front of the actors, as they come toward the camera. This sometimes meant I would spend the day walking 40 times across Stars Hollow, backwards, in the snow. When I arrived it was episode 7, of season 1, and I was already the seventh person in the job. I came in to fill in for someone that day, and told production I would be available to come back if they needed me to fill in for any other shoots. Four days later I got a call that they had fired the guy who was doing my job, and asked if I could come down. Everyone thought I wasn't going to make it either, but I stuck it out.

One of the best things I remember about *Gilmore Girls* was all the snow. I've never seen so much snow on a backlot before, or since. The whole backlot was often covered in a foot of snow. My first day on *Gilmore Girls* was actually a night and the whole backlot was a foot deep in snow, with more snow coming down. They had to have snow because Stars Hollow was set in Connecticut, which has harsh winters. As the seasons went on, the amount of snow used dwindled a bit, probably for budgetary, and practical reasons. It can be hard to have a large crew working on a show wearing winter down jackets for the snow, while actually working in the heat of Los Angeles.

I enjoyed my job as a steadicam operator, and my time on *Gilmore Girls*. I got along very well with Amy and Dan, and the members of the cast as well. It was a hard job and we spent long hours there, but there were a lot of good times. When we were making it, and as the years went on, I didn't realise that the show was as popular as I now know it is. When I tell people that I worked on Gilmore *Girls*, everyone knows what it is. When I was working on it, it was a small show on the WB, but it became bigger and bigger as it went on. If anything it's gotten bigger since it left the air.

My favourite practical joke that I have ever played in the film business, happened on the set of *Gilmore Girls*. We were filming at Luke's apartment (which was supposed to be above the diner). They had built it on the set, right across from Luke's Diner in what is called "the firehouse". It's really just an exterior facade. In the scene we were filming, Luke and Lorelai were in bed having a conversation. Up in the rafters above the soundstage, we could see a bunch of raccoons. There were quite a few of them, and they were all sitting on the railing, looking down at what was taking place below. I saw an opportunity. I went to the props people and asked if they had anything that might look like a raccoon. They had a teddy bear that looked nothing like a raccoon, but I took it, because I thought it might work. I set up this prank where the prop guy would go up to the second story and throw the stuffed animal down to land on the bed where Scott Patterson and Lauren Graham were talking for their scene. The idea was that they would think one of the raccoons had jumped down and was in the bed with them. It worked beautifully. When the teddy bear came down, they both freaked out–even Scott. In hindsight, I probably could have gotten into trouble for that, but it was so funny.

One of the coolest things about working on the show was all of the festivals that took place in Stars Hollow. When I go back to that set to work on other things I go and sit in different places, and remember the things that took place there. The Swami Dog was a favourite, as was the Hay Bale Maze, because I directed that episode. That Hay Bale Maze was probably a once-in-a-lifetime event for that set because there were a lot of permits and things that had to be dealt with. Every bale had to have fire retardant spray applied. Kirk walked on stilts in that episode, and I always remember what a great, funny guy Sean Gunn was. He always had a good humour about him, and a unique quirkiness.

Amy Sherman-Palladino was a very good writer and the show itself was mostly about the words. The words were a very important part of the show, and there was a fair amount of pressure on the cast members to say their words properly. Both Alexis Bledel (Rory), and Lauren would come into work not knowing the words, as they often weren't given their scripts till the last minute. They would do the rehearsals and be delivering their lines one hour later, when we filmed the scene. After only that hour of rehearsal, they could power out their lines perfectly, which was amazing really. I work around actors all the time who could not do that. On other shows I have worked on, five pages to get through would be a lot of work, but on *Gilmore Girls* that would be nothing. It was a very well oiled machine, and five pages would just be fired through. It was a very wordy show which was part of the goodness, and allure.

Amy had a way that she wanted everything done and that's the way we did everything. Sometimes it was difficult. For example, every single time we filmed in the Gilmore mansion there had to be new flowers. They would never have the same flowers two days in a row. I remember an episode where Amy walked into Sookie's kitchen and couldn't believe that the props people had filled the room with fake vegetables. Amy wanted real food, because Sookie was supposed to be a gourmet chef. Consequently, I took home a lot of fresh flowers, and fresh vegetables.

At that time, Amy was fairly new to television. This was the first television show she had created. She wanted it her way and that was a challenge. She would have to approve every single prop—every bag, every book. It's a real testament to her devotion to the show. She cared about every little thing that was in the show, but that level of perfection was often a challenge for every department. I remember being called into the office one time to speak with Amy, because my camera had rocked sideways during a shot. My camera did this very easily. She brought me in and had a ruler and was showing me how off level the shot was, measuring it on the screen. I couldn't even see the angle but she could. She wanted everything to be perfect.

In addition to the camera work, the dialogue words had to be said exactly as she wrote them. George Bell was brought in as a dialogue coach to help the cast maintain the show's reputation for being 'word perfect'. If it wasn't word for word we were not able to move on with the scene. There were occasions where that was detrimental because Lauren or Alexis would get frustrated. It was George's job to make sure the cast had their lines down before they started shooting. None of this is faulting Amy, but it is a real reflection of her devotion.

I was a little surprised when I wasn't asked to come back for the revival. They didn't ask anybody really, in terms of crew. After Amy was let go at the end of season 6, a lot of people stayed and there might have been some animosity there. I have seen Amy since then and she was super nice. They could have just wanted a whole new bunch of people. They just went a different direction and did not bring anyone back.

We went through quite a few cinematographers throughout the show, so we developed a rule book for how to film *Gilmore Girls*. There were quite a lot of rules and regulations. For instance, Amy did not allow tight shots, and If someone was entering they needed to enter in from behind. When new cinematographers came in with new ideas, we would have to tell them that this would not be what she wants.

Gilmore Girls was my first real job in a studio network as a steadicam operator, and I credit it with putting me on the map professionally. I have not stopped working since the show wrapped. I've done more than 300 episodes of television now and *Gilmore Girls* was undoubtedly my springboard. Working on the show definitely helped my career a lot. I learned a lot from the cinematographers, some of whom I have worked with since then. Amy let me direct, having never done it before, which was a great opportunity for me. It was a very good experience.

I still have a lot of friends from the show. Valerie Campbell is one of them. She is still very involved in the *Gilmore Girls* world. When I am on the Warner Bros lot I can ride my bicycle around and wave to people who still work there. If you work with people for seven seasons, and you've been in the trenches together making it through tough times. you end up being friends for life. We had barbecues, we went out for a drink after, and sometimes had karaoke on set. I still remember Valerie Campbell singing *Crazy* by Patsy Cline on one of our karaoke nights. The film business is a very social business in that you kind of get your work from your relationships. In this industry it's not what you know, but who you know.

I think when *Gilmore Girls* was originally released, it was a good show, but perhaps not publicised widely enough. It was very targeted towards a certain demographic, which television shows sometimes aren't. They could stay on the air with less than two million people watching because they were the right two million people. Then I think people realised that this is a good show—the writing was very good, and so was the acting. Over the years it has blown up. The revival helped it, but there was also a reason for the revival. Its popularity remained strong, and the demand for more episodes never seemed to die.

In 2020 I worked at the Warner Bros lot on another television show and it was fun to be on the back lot where I have so many memories. Everytime I go to the set, I remember things. I feel like I was 'Gilmored'...but in a good way.

Jon Wellner

Mikey

I grew up in Chicago and always knew that I wanted to be an actor and comedian. If you want to be those things, you have to live in Hollywood so I moved out to Los Angeles in my mid 20s. When I got out here, I got an agent, and my first gig was my role on *Gilmore Girls*. I had three words, in the finale of season 1, when Rory goes to the grocery store—something like, "huh?", "what?", and "no...." It was really exciting though, as such a new actor getting to go to the Warner Bros. set, and I really felt the pressure not to make a fool of myself.

One thing they don't teach you in acting school is hitting your marks. I had to be in the exact spot set out for me when I said my lines, and I just couldn't seem to get it right. After multiple tries, the crew came and laid down some sandbags so that I would feel where I was supposed to stand. It was super embarrassing.

It was an interesting time to be cast on the show, because it was the first season, and on air, but it wasn't very far in since episodes are shot in advance. Nobody really knew what a huge success the show was going to be, so over time, that part has become more meaningful for me. I had hoped at the time, that since I was working at Doose's, and that seemed to be the only town grocery store, that I might be called back, but it wasn't meant to be.

I had a friend who was working on the show, so I was aware of it before I got on, but it was in its infancy in terms of being on air. I had heard a lot of talk, particularly amongst young people that were watching it, and it seemed to be well received. I also knew Sean Gunn, and I remember being so jealous of him, because we had the same manager at the time, and Sean was from Chicago too, and he had such a great part. Years later I got on the show *CSI* and became a series regular and it worked out for me. At that point, I wasn't so jealous, because I realised there was enough cake and pie for everybody.

I remember I couldn't sleep the night before my day on set, because I didn't want to miss my call time. I had to be there early even though I wasn't on first. I was initially impressed when I got onto the lot at what a well oiled machine the show was. I drove onto the set, was shown where to park, and as soon as I set foot on the set the first or second assistant director approached me immediately, and showed me to my trailer. They told me that they would be back in ten minutes to take me to makeup, and then after I had makeup done, I waited, and waited, and waited. Eventually they came and got me for a quick rehearsal and I got to meet everybody. It was my first Hollywood thing and I was freaking out. I read the scene and was holding my lines and trying not to let my hand shake from nerves while I read it. Then we started running through it with the blocking, and that's where I had to hit my mark. I was always either in front of the beam, or behind it. Then they got to the point where they were ready to shoot, and that took a while because it had to be shot from every angle. We shot the 'master' shot, then the 'close-ups', then other 'pick ups', so it was a really long day.

Everyone was really nice, and really professional. Amy Sherman-Palladino directed my episode which was really exciting and cool. Alexis was very quiet and shy, but I was too—we were both just very polite and quiet with one another. It was very professional, but the team allowed themselves to enjoy their work. I've been on other sets where it's rough and that tension is in the air—people are complaining and yelling—but I don't remember that at all on *Gilmore Girls*. It was so cool, and I really felt that day that I wanted to do that for the rest of my life. They fed me, paid me well, and treated me nicely. It was also an exciting time because it was becoming a real hit show, and I felt thrilled to be a part of it.

I started with *Gilmore Girls* as an actor and just kept doing co-star roles on a bunch of other network shows. I then was cast on *CSI* as a series regular. That took up most of my time for 12 years. During that time I started a research company with another actor on the show. The service we provide at Entertainment Research Consultants is research for television shows. This filled a real gap in the industry because the writers on T.V. shows don't necessarily have a deep knowledge of forensics, police protocol, or law, for example. We found there was an opening for a liaison. Now, when writers are putting together episodes, they will ask us things like, "what happens if someone gets hit in the skull with a wine bottle?". We then work with a medical examiner to get the information we need, we write it up into television friendly lingo, and pass it back to the writing team. We started doing that with all different shows like *Bones, The Black List, Drop Dead Diva, CSI, CSI: Miami, CSI: New York,* and a bunch of shows that got cancelled. We have also worked with writers who are writing books.

It's an interesting line of work too because we don't necessarily have the knowledge the writers need either. We just know where to find it. So, we started working only for *CSI,* but as the *CSI* writers left for other shows, they would call us and say they needed our services over at their new show. Before we opened this company, writers would just get their assistants to just 'Google' things, but on crime shows especially, sometimes there are things that only a dozen or so people in the whole country would know the answer to. Of course, when we started, the internet was still really, in its infancy, so there wasn't always enough information. It was hard for us back then too, because we would have to call the expert, and then use a tape recorder on a landline to be sure we got the information down accurately. Of course, now everyone is comfortable over email so we email the experts, and we get responses sent back to us in writing. Over time we have created a network of 300 people in all different fields. This makes it so much easier now because if a show needs a lawyer, we already work with an immigration lawyer, a criminal defence attorney, a divorce lawyer, etc. This is the same with all fields, particularly forensics. We just wrapped up working on *DopeSick*. Whilst this keeps me busy, I am still auditioning, and working as an actor, and researcher in the entertainment industry.

I know that the *Gilmore Girls* still has a huge following, akin perhaps, to Star Trek. I put this down to how incredibly well written it is, and the unique mother-daughter relationship that it pivots around. I don't think television had seen one like this before. This one was different, and smart. There's a rumour that the scripts for *Gilmore Girls* were the thickest in Hollywood because there are so many words. I think in the same way that *Hamilton* is a new language—and a whole new way of seeing a musical, *Gilmore Girls* spoke a new language.

Biff Yeager

Tom

My journey on *Gilmore Girls* started a little before my entry onto the show as Tom. The first year I read for the part of Taylor Doose that Michael Winters got. I had known one of the casting directors from *Judging Amy* so her and her partner called me in for the role of Taylor. I went along, but didn't get the role. I'm actually really glad I didn't get Michael Winters' part because nobody could have done it better than him. He's fantastic.

Then, the following year the show had me come in for this one day character—a contractor that would show Rory what to do during a work experience day on a building site. They wouldn't let me use the power saw in that scene, so I must have looked like I couldn't handle it. Alexis Bledel wasn't allowed to stand near me when I used the hand saw either. They must have liked my performance though, because they kept calling me back. Initially I went in just for the one day, but then the next year they called me back and gave my character a name, "Tom" the contractor.

I hadn't seen the show when I got the part, but after I was on it more and more I watched it and liked it. My daughter had started to watch and enjoy it too. I've seen it twice now, and will probably watch it again soon.

That first episode was a one day shoot. I think we went in and shot the scene with the saw, then went for lunch after that. After lunch was the scene inside the building framing where the piece falls from above. I was in and out in about eight or nine hours that first episode. Everyone was kind, and fun to work with. There wasn't much I didn't like about my time on *Gilmore Girls*. Anytime I worked with Lauren Graham, she amazed me with the way that she knew her lines. She had pages and pages of dialogue and she was on it all the time. That's a lot of words to get down, everyday. I had a page or two here and there, so I didn't have that same pressure.

I had previously had a little gimmick that I did when I was on *Star Trek*. I wrote to about 5000 science fiction fans and gave them my address to write to me at Paramount. The idea was that if they wrote back, it would show my character was popular and potentially increase my appeal on the show. There used to be a show called *77 Sunset Strip* and there was an actor on it, Edd Byrnes who played Kookie. He did something similar. He had people write into the show and rave about his character. He had a story about Frank Sinatra doing something similar. Allegedly, Sinatra paid women to watch him when he was just starting out, to boost his perceived popularity. People have done that throughout time, so I thought I would give it a try. It backfired a bit because a couple of people instead turned my letter over, wrote on the back of it, and sent it to my producers. I had been called back for *Star Trek* at that point, and they commented that I was getting more mail than the regular characters on the show. I didn't get called back again after they found out what I had tried to pull. I did something similar to that with *Gilmore Girls* but on a much smaller scale, sending the letters only to about 40-50 people and asking my friends to write in about my character.

I remember shooting season 4, episode 14, where Alexis was outside the side of the house and had a very emotional scene. I was watching Rory do that scene and she was making us all cry. It was really an emotional scene and she was just fantastic. It was amazing to watch. I like to watch good acting. People ask me what my favourite movie or television shows are, but I don't really have any. What I have are favourite scenes or pieces of acting.

The most difficult scene for me to film was the scene where I was drunk at the opening of the Dragonfly Inn. Amy was directing that scene and she wanted me to play drunk but didn't want me to be drunk. She wanted my speech to be a little bit slurred, but not have me come across as so impaired that I couldn't get my lines out. To this day, I'm not sure I know exactly what she wanted, and I just couldn't get it. I was really feeling bad about it. We did four or five takes and eventually she called it. I'm not sure that she really got what she wanted from me though. All you can do in those situations is the best that you can, and unfortunately on that day it wasn't quite working.

Overall, I always found it a really fun show to work on. It was a very relaxed set for the most part. Every once in a while I would hear an argument but that's not unusual. There are arguments on every set, and the ones I heard on this show weren't vitriolic. There has to be disagreements to work through things. It was a fantastic set all round—from the casting people, to the producers—and my experience was great. One thing that I remember about Amy Sherman-Palladino was how she would always help others along. I had a friend who was not connected with the show that was interested in being a producer. She asked me if I would ask Amy to let her shadow the production team during one of the episodes. To Amy, that wasn't a problem. Amy agreed and my friend spent the next week with 14 hour days and found out what it would be like to produce in the television industry.

The first time I realised the impact this show had on the fans was when the first fan festival came around. It was amazing and I really enjoyed it. That was the first time anything like that had ever happened to me during my acting career. The mother-daughter relationship between Emily, Rory, and Lorelai struck a chord with a lot of people. Women, especially of course, but a lot of men watch it too, which is obvious by the demographic that turns up at the fan festival.

My acting career continued long after *Gilmore Girls.* I spent the next 10-15 years as a day player, but I never had a role like Tom. I work now as an artist, and author. My artistic focus at the moment is fractals, but I also have a history of acrylics. I'm learning animation at the moment. I have authored two children's books—*Smokey the Cat (Finds His Purr),* and *Silly Lop*—and want to animate them and put them up online. I've been retired now from the Screen Actors Guild (SAG-AFTRA) for 12-15 years so I don't push the acting too much anymore. My agent calls me every now and then with an audition, but I try to keep my focus on my other pursuits.

I made some long lasting friends on the show, and worked with a bunch of nice people. I felt very relaxed on set from the first day I worked, to the last. I have friends and acquaintances to this day from the show such as George Bell, Valerie Campbell, Brenda Maben, Michael DeLuise, Carla McClosky, and others. It was a wonderful fun experience and one I'll remember forever.

David Berthiaume

Location Management

I worked in Hollywood doing location management for 35 years, until I retired. I worked on *Gilmore Girls* from season 3, until it finished. I had worked with the production manager for *Gilmore Girls* on two other shows, when he called me up and asked if I could come onboard and help him with the show. I was working on other shows such as *The Sopranos* but was happy to come on to *Gilmore Girls*

when I was available. My job was to find suitable locations for when filming couldn't be done on set, and organise the shoots at these locations. This included obtaining permits if necessary, and organising things like parking. *Gilmore Girls* didn't go on location a lot, but when I got the call they thought they would be going out on location more in upcoming episodes. Overall, *Gilmore Girls* production only took place off the Warner Bros lot about 15 percent of the time. They tried to stay as close to the lot as possible. They wouldn't even be out shooting on location for a whole day if they could help it.

There was an episode we did where the girls were supposed to be at Harvard University for an episode called 'The Road Trip to Harvard'. We ended up using the University of California Los Angeles campus for the shoot, but needed to recreate the famous Harvard University gates, for it to look realistic. There is a scene where Lorelai and Rory are standing right in front of it, so the size, and details needed to be correct. The Harvard gates were recreated, and installed on UCLA's campus for the shoot. The gates were huge, and a lot of money was spent on them—over $35,000.

The location manager's job is to find something that, with a bit of help, could look like the location. It was cheaper to build the Harvard gates, than to fly everyone to Harvard University and shoot there for the day. Once props like that have been used they usually go into the dumpster, unless the studio wants to store them. Props take up space—especially bulky things like those huge gates—and unless the production team can think of a way to use them again, they get rid of them. Sometimes they donate things like wood, and recycle other items in ways they can think of—otherwise it goes in the trash. One of the reasons that props are discarded is so that other shows don't use the sets. This is particularly undesirable if the props have been built very specifically. Creators have made those things for their show, and their dream. They don't want anyone else infringing on their dream.

Driving shots were almost always done just outside the studio, usually at night. During the day it's a huge job to cover anything you don't want seen—whether it's houses, street names, or the California climate. The darkness at night covered all of that, and the team only had to light what they wanted seen. If Lorelai or Rory were driving through the streets, it was usually up and down the road outside the Warner Bros Studio. For the most part, film and television is a business of 'smoke and mirrors'. It's about finding something that could look like a location, with some work.

For the episode where Christopher takes Lorelai on a drive-in movie date, they wanted a rustic barn for the love scene. I found the barn we used in a high rent district built in the 1800s. Normally a lot of shows dont give screen credit to location managers but on that episode I was credited because of how happy they were that I was able to secure that barn. I had filmed on that ranch before—commercials and several television shows. When they told me what they wanted I immediately thought of that property. I went out there and checked that there was space for cars, and that they could project onto the barn itself. I knew it would work because it was really old and I felt that it would fit their vision for the scene perfectly. It was also a remote location where Lorelai and Christopher could cuddle up in the car watching the movie in privacy.

Location managers have huge files of ideas and have to know people and have good relationships with property owners. I drive around 50,000 miles a year on average, so I see a lot. I used to take pictures of potential locations on film before digital media became available. As a result, I have boxes and boxes of locations on film in storage. Now that things are digital, it's a bit easier because I just have a hard drive full of photos.

Griffith Park was used a lot in the filming of *Gilmore Girls* because it could be used for so many different things. Driving shots worked there, as well as anything that required visible trees or foliage.

Places that had a generic look were great location choices because they could be dressed up to look like different places. Things like golf courses, or hotels could be made to look like they were on the East Coast if we hid the palm trees and changed the interiors to look more plush by using things like darker woods. Hospitals are another easy place to shoot. We shot at a hospital where we had to hire snow people to cover the hospital in snow for days, and it looked really good. There is a scene in season 7, episode 13 where Lorelai is outside the hospital in the 'snow' and it looks great on screen. That's the smoke and mirrors effect. Trying to make California locations look like New England was probably the most challenging part of this job. This was very different from my experience on shows like *Entourage,* which was set in Los Angeles.

We used a few houses on the show, but only the exteriors. This meant that sometimes the inside of a house didn't actually match the outside. This was true of Richard and Emily's house which in the pilot shows an exterior shot, but after that scenes inside the house were shot on a soundstage. The Harvard road trip episode, and scenes where Rory is attending Yale were similar. While showing the outside of UCLA, Pomona College, and the University of Southern California, Rory's classes were shot on soundstages, not in real classrooms. The most challenging places to film are places where brand names are visible, such as sporting good stores, and supermarkets. In the United States, if brand names are visible for over three seconds, that's considered advertising. If you look carefully, you will see that Lorelai's Jeep doesn't have the Jeep logos still attached to it. That's because we took the decals off, and painted the whole car, including over the unremovable Jeep markings.

The Jeep underwent quite a few other changes to make it television ready. It was originally red, but had to be repainted because the red was a problem for the cameramen. The windows were originally tinted, but the show took these out and replaced them with clear ones. The rearview mirrors were also taken off because you can't shoot with them on.

I actually came to own that Jeep, and I still have it. When the show wrapped, the car was six years old, but had almost no miles on it. For many driving scenes, the car was being towed, so it had only around 1400 miles on the clock when I bought it at the end of season 7. I put my hand up to buy it, because it was in such great condition. The producers were initially afraid that it was my intention to buy it and auction it off online to fans, but I assured them that it was just for personal use. My wife drives it now, and even though it's a 22 year old car, it still only has 25,000 miles on it.

Gilmore Girls was a great show because it wasn't political, and I think a lot of people could probably identify with it. The mix of coffee, college, and community made for a wonderful combination, no matter how old you were as a viewer. It was just a good show.

Sheila Lawrence

Writer / Co-Executive Producer / Supervising Producer

My first involvement with *Gilmore Girls* was as a viewer. I was initially struck by how unique the voice of the show was. I had also been a big fan of Sam Phillips' music so I enjoyed the scoring of the show. Back then, not as many people knew who she was.

My first encounter with the show professionally was when my agent sent me a script for *Gilmore Girls* and set up a meeting to meet with Amy Sherman-Palladino and Daniel Palladino. It was one of those great meetings where we just really clicked. I left the meeting feeling really good about how it had gone, and hadn't been in my car for more than five minutes when my agents called and told me that the Palladino's wanted to make me an offer.

As a writer on the show, I didn't actually get to visit the set very much. Writers were prisoners of the writing room. We ate our lunches in there, worked in there all day long, and consequently, got to know each other very, very well. I remember walking through the town of Stars Hollow in the backlot on the way to the gym after work. That was a really special experience as a fan of the show. It was amazing to watch the town go through the different seasons, decorated with snow in Winter, and pumpkins in Fall. Those seasons didn't really manifest like that in Southern California. It really was a gift to get to write on a show that I loved so much, and that I had been a fan of before I came to work on it.

Before *Gilmore Girls,* I had come from half-hour sitcoms like *Mad About You*. Sitcoms can be notorious for their long hours, especially for the writers. *Gilmore Girls* was an hour long show, which is harder on the crew, but a little easier on the writers. We generally left at 7 P.M. each night. Having worked such long hours on sitcoms, it took me two years on *Gilmore Girls* to trust that I could keep dinner plans. I was used to being ready at any time, for all nighters. Amy had such a strong vision for what she wanted that we never threw out a story like we commonly did on other shows. Having such a clear vision, contributed to the writers having more reasonable hours on *Gilmore Girls*.

Gilmore Girls was the pivotal credit on my resume for many years, and has only become an even stronger credit over time. That is very unusual. Normally I work on something and five years later people have forgotten about it. *Gilmore Girls* has developed this massive second life which is much bigger than it was when it aired. It has continued to be good for me professionally. I've also worked on *Bunheads* and *The Marvelous Mrs Maisel,* so my time on *Gilmore Girls* directly led to other great jobs with the Palladino's. To this day, *Gilmore Girls* has been responsible for my best credits and a primetime Emmy award.

Amy learned from her time working on *Roseanne*, that a writer should 'make the big small, and the small big'. She shared this with the *Gilmore Girls* writers room and this philosophy has guided my writing ever since. The idea is that if something huge is going to happen in an episode—something like the debutante ball in season 2, episode 6, for instance—then it's the small things that are important. For example, in that episode, there is a little conversation about Richard being phased out. This conversation is not the focus of the episode, but it gives important insight into what is going on in his character's life, and how this might affect the other characters around him. In the foreground of this large event, small details are changing the lives of the characters in significant ways. This kind of storytelling has been a staple of my approach ever since.

I made some of my closest friends in that *Gilmore Girls* writers room—about six people including Amy and Dan. The writers would go on a retreat to Las Vegas before every season started. We got to know each other very, very well. Amy and Dan were very good at getting us to open up and tell many of our embarrassing stories so that the characters could end up living them out on screen. Many of our personal stories, and details from our lives ended up on the show.

Right from the time I started watching *Gilmore Girls,* I loved the mother daughter relationship. It was such an ideal relationship, and I was so struck by their closeness. I hadn't seen a mother-daughter dynamic like that before. Of course, adding Emily into the mix was also brilliant. It added contrast, and there was so much to explore between the two very different relationships. I am a sucker for a small town, and once you add twinkle lights, Stars Hollow becomes a pretty great place to be. Rory being a smart teenage girl on television was also phenomenal to see. I can't even think of any other characters—high school girls, who are so unabashedly smart and well read, well spoken, and care about school and not what people think. It was so well represented.

The popularity of *Gilmore Girls* comes down to a number of factors. The existence of Netflix gave the show a broader audience than the WB ever could have. I also think the relationships resonate with everyone. People fall into two categories—they either related to Rory and Lorelai's relationship, or they are on the other side wishing they had that relationship. The show has a timelessness about it. Those relationships will always exist. The wonderful thing about *Gilmore Girls* is that there are no real villains on this show. Even the characters that are villainous—for instance, Paris, or Emily—are good at heart. They aren't trying to be awful to anyone. They are well meaning, in their own way. Nobody on *Gilmore Girls* is truly evil, and I think sometimes we need a show like that. I want to live in Stars Hollow right now—a town full of fun, quirky people where people are free to be who they are.

Adam Wylie

Brad Langford

I had worked with Amy Sherman-Palladino before *Gilmore Girls*, on a show called *Love and Marriage*. It was a very short show that ran after *Married with Children* (though a lot of people got the two shows confused). I filmed five episodes, but only two or three aired. It was an amazing show that nobody ever really saw, because the ratings didn't do well immediately, and so the network just cancelled it. The experience working on *Love and Marriage* was great. The same thing had happened on another of my shows *Picket Fences* which was served with a cease and desist notice before it reached its 100th episode, at which point it would be eligible for syndication and would cost the network more money.

Then Amy created *Gilmore Girls*, and she had a part that was one scene, and four lines. She thought I would be great for it, but wasn't sure if I would want to come and audition for it, since it was only four lines. A very small audition was held for just a handful of people that she wanted to see deliver the lines. So, I went to the audition, and said my four lines, which were basically: "Brad…Langford…from fifth period Shakespeare." When I auditioned, that was supposed to be the entire thing. I ended up getting the role, and was super happy, but of course, it ended up being much bigger than what I had originally auditioned for. I guess the character of Brad got a really good reaction and inspired her to make a recurring character, and for that, I am super grateful.

By the time I was cast as Brad Langford, *Gilmore Girls* was in its second season. I had never seen it, but I knew what it was, since I had followed Amy's work after *Love and Marriage*. My first day on set was like any normal day. By that time I had been acting for 13 years, and my days were often spent on sets. *Gilmore Girls* was a one camera comedy that was familiar to me, so I went in, did my thing, and hoped I was delivering what was expected. I left the set, and got a phone call shortly after from my manager. He was calling to let me know that I had been called back for a second episode.

I knew as soon as I got that call that I would be a recurring character. Once you get a second episode, your character is 'recurring' anyway, but I knew at that time that I would be back for more episodes. It's very rare to have a character come in for a two-episode arc. It's normally one, or many, so I assumed that it was going to be more than two, and I was right.

I have a lot of favourite moments during my time on the show. My all-time favourite was coming back after my stint on Broadway. A lot of people ask why Brad disappeared for almost a whole season. When Brad comes back he explains that it is because he was on Broadway, in *Into the Woods*. In reality, I was really making my Broadway debut in *Into the Woods*. That was my favourite moment because my real life had been written into the show, and it was Amy's way of making a joke. My character's line about the *New York Times* calling me "winningly naive" was based on a real review that I received. So that was a really fun episode to film, and remains special to me. My next favourite joke and scene was the one where I talk about the robot, and say that I have tried building one. I enjoy every second that I get to play on set and to perform. The nervous, naive, nerd character was something I had gotten to play a lot before, but in *Gilmore Girls* I got to do it in a more expanded way.

Another memorable moment was when I accidentally slapped Liza Weil. It was the season 3 wrap party, and I was grabbing some sort of *amuse bouche* from somebody who was walking around with them on a tray. I went to turn and accidently backhanded Liza in the face. I remember her being shocked before tapping me back on the face and saying, "Well, I guess Paris kind of deserves it after all these years." That was a moment that was just between the two of us, but so funny because of the history of the characters we played.

As an actor, I find the most challenging part to be the audition process. It really can mess with your brain because you don't know what is going on behind closed doors, and sometimes you don't know why you didn't get a part. Once you are on set you get to relax and perform—you get to do what you were hired to do. The set for *Gilmore Girls* was the most chill set I have ever worked on in my life. I remember my first episode—I was working with Chad Michael Murray and we just threw a football around for four hours. That was half a day. The set was super chill and everyone was just dead nice. There was nobody from the cast that was full of ego or had a bad attitude. It was wonderful to work on. There were a lot of Broadway veterans in the show, and everyone was serious about the craft and doing a good job. Our script supervisor had played the main cat in *Cats* on Broadway, so it really was a set full of talented, experienced actors.

In this industry, it's very difficult to keep up with everyone. Every once in a while, I run into Alexis Bledel, or Melissa McCarthy. I follow a lot of the *Gilmore Girls* cast professionally - Alexis, Lauren, Shelly (Madeline), Teal (Louise), Milo (Jess), and Amy Sherman-Palladino.

About a third of the times people recognise me, it's for my work on *Gilmore Girls*. This increased after *A Year in the Life*. I can usually pinpoint where fans are going to recognise me from depending on their age. I get a lot of tags online, and it's almost always for *Gilmore Girls*. I was in 80 episodes of *Picket Fences,* and only six episodes of *Gilmore Girls*, but that role has come to be very prominent in people's minds.

I was hoping to be brought back for the revival, but not expecting to be. I had a crazy idea in my mind that after the events of the original run, Paris and Brad would get married. When you are expecting something, the business will trip you up. Every time I plan a vacation, I get a part and I can't go. I've worked Dec 24th, Thanksgiving, and Valentines Day. I don't ever expect to come back to a show because if I did I would be setting myself up for disappointment. When I went to New York for *Into The Woods* I thought my *Gilmore Girls* life was over. I was thrilled that I got to come back, but was never expecting to.

The fan base around this show is so nice. Every year on my birthday, I get a lot of Brad Langford memes, and it's one of the only shows where I look up memes, and Brad is everywhere! That is pretty cool to see. The best thing about this show is that there is no such thing as a meaningless character.

There are festivals about *Gilmore Girls*. The *Gilmore Girls* fan community is one of the biggest fan communities I have ever seen in my life. There are Tik Toks, podcasts, and YouTube channels all dedicated to *Gilmore Girls*! There are meetings, tours of Stars Hollow at the Warner Bros Studio set and ranch. It's like the show is still on. It has a very *Friends* type cult following. It's really cool. The fans are always super nice and super knowledgeable.

Gilmore Girls' success is largely due to how relatable it is. I think a lot of people can relate to both Lorelai and Rory, and what they go through in their lives. It has a lot of heart. The show is also very clever, and it's so appealing because it's grounded in a reality that is tangible for people to experience themselves. The entire series hinges on this relatable relationship—the mother daughter aspect. It's important when you are writing a show that you have mass appeal and in order to have this it needs to be one of two things—it either needs to be so far out you want to be it, or so grounded that it could be your own life. *Gilmore Girls* is like this—they could be us. This life could be ours. That's why *Gilmore Girls* will never go out of style. Everyone will always have these issues.

Since the show, I have continued to work as an actor. Acting is my main 'gig', and always will be. I have also, however, built a career in magic, which came about accidentally. I've been doing magic on and off since I was five years old, but did not start intricate sleight of hand until I was in my 20s. When the Covid19 pandemic hit, I was out of work for a year and a half or more. I decided to take that time to delve into social media as a creative outlet and learn how to create my own content. My magician career exploded—I even filmed a guest spot on *Lucifer* as a magician. I have also won a world award as a magician, so it's been a really amazing adventure so far. I see magic as another way to perform, and a great way to keep up my improv skills. In the future I would love to win The Magic Castle Close Up Magician of the Year, but in the meantime I am more interested in my acting career flourishing. I definitely consider myself more of a performer magician, because I can control an audience and develop a scene that really captivates.

Evie Peck

Karen

I had known the casting directors for *Gilmore Girls*—Jami Rudofsky and Mara Casey—for a long time from doing theatre in Los Angeles. I had known them separately from each other and thought they were both creative, talented, smart people. When I found out that they had joined together to cast a show I felt very excited. One of the things that made them fantastic casting directors was their knowledge of Los Angeles theatre actors. They watched a lot of plays and brought in people that they thought would be good for the show.

I had also known Amy Sherman-Palladino from when I was about 18 or 19 years old. We did improv together at the LA Connection and we became friends. She was hilarious and wonderful. I really loved her. Back then we used to buy something called a dramalogue from the 7/11 and check the ads for auditions. It was the summer before college for me, and I auditioned and got placed in a class. I moved up, and got a timeslot and was placed in a Saturday night late show. Whatever show you got into, it matched you with people and Amy became my acting partner for the shows. It was a popular place at the time and I think a lot of actors have taken classes there.

Amy and I did shows together—often to sold out theatres, and had a great time. The LA Connection at the time was a really great place to showcase our skills, and was a great place for comedians and actors to network and meet others in the business. It's funny to think about those early days, working with Amy. Our improv was often hurried, and spontaneous. Sometimes it was a mad scramble in the costume room, and we would often come up with characters on the fly. It seems like a long time that we were doing this, but it was probably only for a year. It was such a formative, and significant aspect of my career, and my life when I think back about it.

There was no social media back then, so after the LA Connection we both moved on and lost touch. I hadn't seen her in about ten years when I came onto *Gilmore Girls*. I was excited to be auditioning for a show of Amy's. I already knew of the show, and had watched it. It was a fantastic show and I felt so proud of her. Being a fan of a show can sometimes be more daunting when you are heading into the audition room because you really want to be in it. There is an added pressure. I was also aware of how different the tone of this show was, and I wanted to be what they were looking for. At the audition, I had a producer session and Amy walked in. We had a really nice reunion type moment. I didn't think that I would get the part just because I knew Amy, but I did think I might get it, because I was right for it. I got a callback, and then booked the job.

As I was already a fan of the show when I got cast, it was a really surreal experience to walk onto the set on my first day. It's always interesting to see a set in person, as opposed to how it looks on television. It looked so different once I was standing there. Stars

Hollow itself was incredible to walk around in. The town square looks different when it isn't dressed for *Gilmore Girls*, but if I am at the studio for anything, I still walk around and think of it as Stars Hollow. It was definitely really cool to see it and be there.

I was nervous on that first day, because I wanted to do well. My scene was with Lauren Graham and Ed Herrmann. I was playing his new secretary, after Margie wouldn't follow him to his new company. The idea of the scene was that he didn't want a new secretary and Lorelai was pushing for him to hire me. Before rehearsal and blocking, Ed came over and asked if I wanted to run lines with him. He warned me that I would have to be quick out there. I would need to know my lines backwards and forwards, and be word perfect. He insisted that he help me run my lines. I was so appreciative and in awe of that kindness as a youngish, new person on that set. That's my main takeaway from that experience. I was acutely aware of the fact that I was just a dayplayer and there was a demand to be really on my game. On this show, the bar is set really high, the dialogue is crisp and fast paced and you don't want to hold up the shoot. You want to hold your own. Ed was lovely and spent time with me running lines and preparing me for that scene. He was so thoughtful. When you meet a star on a show—especially a seasoned, respected stage and film actor like Ed—you don't necessarily expect that level of empathy for a nervous dayplayer. I have always remembered how supportive and encouraging he was of me that day.

Something that was unexpected was how the blocking was done on the show. Lauren Graham (Lorelai) and the director Chris Long were really collaborative about blocking and they would work through it together. Lauren was very involved which, in my experience, wasn't usual. Cast members normally don't have a hand in that, but Lauren had lots of ideas and suggestions, and worked together with Chris to plan the scene.

I wasn't expecting the role to be recurring, so it was great when I got called back the following year for another episode. By that time, I had cut my hair shorter, and it had been really long in the first episode. Amy told me that there had been a lot of fan letters for me since my first episode, which was nice to hear. My scene in the season 3 episode involved calling Lorelai to make an appointment with her father. In the show, I am speaking to Lorelai on the phone, but when we filmed it, someone just read me her lines off camera, and Lauren Graham shot her end of the phone call separately. Ed Herrmann was, again, lovely. Both of my days on *Gilmore Girls* went very fast. I wished I could have stayed longer because it was a fun set. I had a great time.

After being on the show, I was recognised a couple of times. People called me up to tell me they had seen me on the show, and I got recognised in a Bed, Bath & Beyond store. Someone kept following me around the store while I was shopping, and then eventually asked if I was Karen from *Gilmore Girls*.

I have a lot of friends that were on the show such as Nick Holmes, Sean Gunn, and Scott Cohen. Scott is a lovely, wonderful friend. Because of the nature of the casting, I have ended up knowing a lot of *Gilmore Girls* people because the casting directors brought in all these great theatre actors. It's unusual for a television show to be bringing in a lot of theatre actors. Most casting is done through agents and not all actors do theatre. A lot of the time theatre actors don't also do television work, and don't have agents. *Gilmore Girls* was a really great credit to have as an actor. The show was well respected and had such talented people on it.

Gilmore Girls was great because of the writing. It had so much wit. It was snappy, and crackly. It's a show that doesn't date—it stays young. The characters were really full, and relatable, and the humour and wit is timeless. Of course, the silver bullet was the relationship between Lorelai and Rory. Both of them had conflict with their mothers, but there was love there. Those themes are always going to be relatable, and relevant. I see a lot of young, middle school kids who are discovering *Gilmore Girls* and just love it. It doesn't go out of style because Stars Hollow could be almost anywhere, at almost any time. That whole little town is such a quaint place.

Jessica 'Sugar' Kiper

Shane

My time on *Gilmore Girls* began when I got an audition for the show, and then got a callback. At callbacks, there were only two other girls there. I remember Milo Ventimiglia who played Jess walking into the office to talk to Amy Sherman-Palladino while I was there. On set one day, later on, Milo told me that he got to see everyone's pictures and thought that I looked the most interesting.

The first episode I shot was in the town centre. Milo and I had to make out in front of a huge festival of people that was taking place. The director was Fred Savage from *The Wonder Years* and I was so excited to be working with him. Fred let us just start out doing the scene and then directed us, as it went. He told Milo during the make out scene to stick his hands in my back pockets and I thought that was so cute. After *Gilmore Girls*, I worked at a really hip diner called the

101 Coffee Shop in Hollywood. A-listers would come in all the time, and I actually ended up waiting on Fred Savage and his family a lot. I was nervous about the kissing in that first scene, and knowing how good looking Milo was made me more nervous. Milo asked me how I wanted to do it, and we decided to just go for it. If he was trying to make Alexis jealous, it worked. That scene, and that role, is still my favourite role that I got to play.

When I was on set, my trailer did not have air conditioning so Milo told me to come hang out in his. He would read on the stoop and I would nap in there. One day at lunch, Milo asked me if I wanted to go for a ride. He took me to St Charles Borromeo, a Catholic Church in Burbank not far from the Warner Bros studio. We parked, and he went in to talk to the priest. I was raised very Christian, in the south so I thought that was really cool. I don't even remember if I asked him what he was doing. I have thought about that several times since. I remember thinking he's a good guy—he goes to church, he reads. Too bad I wasn't single at the time. I was married when I did the show, and it was the beginning of a very rocky marriage. I was faithful, but I really did enjoy making out with Milo. That was fun.

Hanging out with Milo so much, clearly made Alexis jealous. Milo had commented that Alexis never came to talk to him and I thought it was interesting that he noticed that kind of thing. I knew that they would start dating once I left the show, and I had told a few people that. Life really imitated art. Maybe he knew what was happening between them too. Two years later, at the 100th episode party I saw a security guard from the Warner Bros lot who said "you were right!"

The last episode was sad for me because it didn't seem that they had written in a break-up scene so I knew I wouldn't be coming back. I was really hoping when I heard about *A Year in the Life* that Shane would come back and stir up trouble. That didn't come to pass, but I believe that Shane is still living in Stars Hollow, working in the beauty store.

I went on to book roles in movies, and television shows including *Weeds,* and *Survivor*. My Dad passed away after a three year long battle with cancer, and I had moved to New York to be with my now ex-husband. *Survivor* found me on a pin up calendar for a dog charity that I had done. They had been looking for girls and their dogs for a dog show that was being put together, so they flew me down for an interview. I turned down the dog show, and was offered *Survivor* from the same casting director. I was not an outside person, I was struggling with addiction, and still grieving my father's death. I wasn't in a good space. But, I said yes. So, I did *Survivor: Gabon* and almost won that season, and then came back for *Survivor: Heroes vs Villains*. I had some turmoil after that second season of *Survivor* and ended up on *Celebrity Rehab*.

Life is definitely different now and I'm doing okay. I continue to act, have written shorts, and am co-writing and producing a documentary about social media. One of my more dominant hobbies is being a 50s retro pinup girl, and 'American Marilyn'. But, of course, my best job is being a wife (to another man), and mother to my daughter Punky Jean. She's six years old and amazing.

George Bell

Professor Bell/Stanley and Dialogue Coach

  I started as a dialogue coach on *Gilmore Girls* in the third season, sixth episode. My first full episode was the dance marathon. Before I came onto the show, there was no dialogue coach. The first assistant director Carla McCloskey brought me on after we had been long time friends, and I had worked with her on feature films such as

Hook. Carla's husband Leigh and I went to university together, and we have been friends ever since. I sang at their wedding, and am the Godfather to their granddaughter.

When the third season of *Gilmore Girls* started, Amy wasn't satisfied with how the actors were saying their lines. She wanted all of the dialogue to be word perfect, and felt that someone should be brought in to support them with accuracy, and the rapid delivery of their lines. Amy knew that what she was asking for was difficult, and that it wasn't the normal standard for actors in the television industry. She was looking for the right person that could work with the actors and who they would feel comfortable with. Carla suggested that I was the right person, since she felt I would be a good fit for the actors' personalities. I interviewed with Amy, a producer, and then with Lauren, before I was offered the job.

I was primarily an actor, having come from commercials, theatre, and other shows such as *Grey's Anatomy* and *Even Stevens* where I had a recurring role as Louis' (played by Shia Lebeouf) school principal. When I came onto *Gilmore Girls* my acting went on the backburner. One of the things I negotiated for was to get paid as an actor. Since I was being paid as a dialogue coach, I wasn't qualifying for SAG-AFTRA health insurance. Amy and Dan were really great, and started finding ways to integrate my acting work into my time on the set. I was used as an extra, and eventually I was cast in the role of Professor Bell at Yale. In the karaoke night episode where Lorelai sings *I Will Always Love You*, I played a patron at the bar. I actually sang a song, which got edited out. I played a bailiff when Scott Patterson's character Luke goes to court, and in the reboot I played the cemetery representative. These roles gave me enough acting opportunities to be vested as an actor with the union, plus I got extra pay. In the knitting episode, I said the word "twenty" and got paid four figures. That was a nice bonus.

The workload on *Gilmore Girls* was above and beyond what I would normally expect in this kind of role. Normally dialogue coaches work on half hour sitcoms, in a kind of 9-5 day. Sitcom work would also normally rotate on a three weeks on, one week off roster. My longest day on a sitcom might be as long as 10 hours. On *Gilmore Girls* it was 12-16 hours. Episodics are longer hours. *Gilmore Girls* was even longer because of the amount of dialogue. It had a reputation on the Warner Bros lot for having the longest work hours. This was challenging when I first started because I hadn't worked those kinds of hours before, and I didn't really know what I was getting into. When I started, Carla was not there, as she alternated with another show, so it was nerve wracking not having her there to 'hold my hand'.

During my time on *Gilmore Girls* I quit four times. I was tired, and it felt like too much. Everytime I gave notice, they would sweeten the deal and I'd end up staying. I remember one time I gave two weeks' notice that evening, and the next day I came on set and I went straight to my chair. I was getting things set up when Amy tapped me on the shoulder. She had heard the news of my notice, and asked if we could talk. We went outside and she said,

> *"I don't know what happened, but I want you to know that there are about six people who are essential to making this show work and you are one of those six. What will it take to keep you? More money? More time off? Just tell me, and I will do it."*

I didn't realise the impact that my presence was having on the show so I agreed to stay. She added some extra perks and gave me a substantial raise. I think she really recognised my value on the show, and that was a nice feeling.

Another time, Scott Patterson came to work and when he arrived he heard from the crew that I had quit. He got on the phone and told the producers that this couldn't happen. He saw my role there as a safety net for the actors. I was a source of support under the tremendous stress of learning all that dialogue. I felt valued, appreciated, and loved on that show. Eventually, when I really felt like I needed a day off each week, Carla's daughter Caitlin took over as my sub on a Friday. This gave me a day to do things for my family, and this arrangement worked well until the show wrapped.

I didn't realise how popular this show was until *A Year in the Life*. Carla and I went to the premiere together in Westwood Village on a Saturday. We pulled into the parking lot and there was screaming. I thought there must have been a football game going on at UCLA, but I soon realised it was fans screaming for *Gilmore Girls*. It really hit me then how loved the show is. I love meeting the fans, and have gone on to attend every fan festival. I sometimes do double duty—sitting on panels for both the crew, and the actors. The fans are so kind, gracious, and welcoming. I look forward to it every year to meet the fans, and also to reconnect with friends from the show.

Gilmore Girls is beloved because it's like comfort food. I tell people to watch it for its great escapism. It is intelligent, witty, and full of wacky, eccentric characters. Give me a rainy day and a *Gilmore Girls* episode—it doesn't get any better.

I hope that *Gilmore Girls* comes back in some form. I would love a two-hour movie special like "A Gilmore Christmas" or a Thanksgiving episode. I want to see who the baby daddy is, and have all my questions answered. I would also love to see everyone again. I love them all dearly, and they will always be a big part of my life. I feel proud to be associated with them, and with such an intelligently written, quality television show.

Aris Alvarado

Caesar

The first time I worked on *Gilmore Girls* was September 8th, 2000. It was season 1, episode 5—"Cinnamon's Wake". But, in order to have seen me you had to look very, very, very closely, and I would still probably have to tell you exactly where I am. Oh, and by the way, don't blink or you would have missed the back of my head.

I had been in Los Angeles for a little over six months when I got on the show. I was working as a background actor, and hoping to be cast on the show in a part. To tell you the truth, I think I thought that for every television show I worked on as a background actor. A couple months later I was working on *Gilmore Girls* again, still only as a background actor, and this time it was at Rory's dance. This time you can see me clear as day, right behind Dean during the fight.

Two years later, I got an audition for *Gilmore Girls*. It was one line:

"Y lo Dooses dónde están?"

I was thrilled, but I had to borrow my uncle's van, because my car had broken down a month ago and I had donated it to the Society for the Blind. I went to the audition, said my line, and everyone in the room laughed. I was driving home when my agent called to tell me I had booked the job.

My first bigger episode was season 3, episode 15, "Face-Off". This episode had my first speaking role on the show, but also my first speaking role as an actor. I got to the set and I shot my scene at the Independence Inn. After waiting a few months to watch the episode, I was devastated to see that my line had been cut. I called my agent the next day, and he apologised. He had forgotten to tell me that someone from *Gilmore Girls* had called to tell me that my line had been cut, but that they might call me in for something at a later time. I thought "yeah…whatever, that's what they say in Hollywood." I didn't think that they would call me.

Less than two months later, I got a call from my agent that *Gilmore Girls* wanted me to come in for a fitting the next day for a recurring role. I was in Las Vegas at the time, so my agent told them I wasn't available for a fitting. Luckily, they already had my measurements from the last time I was on the show. Two days later I was Caesar, in Luke's kitchen, telling Jess I had "no ham".

Gilmore Girls has a very special place in my heart because it was my first and longest job as an actor. Through meeting the fans I've learned how much this show means to them. I feel very fortunate and honoured to be part of it and I have realised that what I do as an actor can affect others. When the show asked me to return for *A Year in the Life*, it was like coming home again. Putting that apron on again was like putting on my superhero costume.

David Bertman

Editor

 Gilmore Girls was a great show to work on, and a lot of fun. The show felt like it came out of nowhere. Amy wrote a cute little pilot, and *Gilmore Girls* was born. When the show came out, there were three big networks, and a few smaller ones. *Gilmore Girls* was on a smaller, niche network. I think if it was written now, it probably would have been picked up by a larger network.

When I started on *Gilmore Girls*, I had been doing assistant editing for a long time, mostly in comedy. I had just finished editing a television series for Judd Apatow, who directed and produced films like *The 40 Year Old Virgin,* and *Bridesmaids.* His style is "happy accidents". He allows all his actors to be writers, in a way. He would sit behind the camera, and yell things, and the actors would have to improvise. This gave them the freedom to try out a joke, or a funny line, and see what worked. Then it would all get put together in the editing room. That's why the reactions in his films are so real. Amy Sherman-Palladino's style is the complete opposite of that. She is a genius in terms of scripting, but she is very strict that her scripts are adhered to. Part of my job editing was making sure that her words are exactly what goes into each episode, right down to tiny words like "the". She prioritised word precision, even if another shot was better. For example, if there was a scene where a boom mic was visible, but the words were perfect, the boom mic would stay in.

Amy had a pace, and a rhythm similar to Aaron Sorkin from *The West Wing*. His show was patterned, and lyrical. While there was a team of writers on *Gilmore Girls,* Amy rewrote every single script. She was a very hard working woman. Because of this dedication to the scripts, the pages were often very late. Normally, in television, cast and crew receive their scripts about a week ahead of the shoot, giving them a few days to prepare. Frequently on *Gilmore Girls,* Amy would be writing right up until the shoot. Amy's expectations for word perfect episodes meant that new techniques were needed to pull it off. One of the things that we did in the editing room was take air out between words—the breaths that actors take. We also tried to overlap the lines a bit, to fit more dialogue in.

Amy was integral to the editing process. Her writing is very musical, and doesn't always make sense or sound right if a chunk is taken out of it. For that reason, she wanted to be involved in the editing process. Since she was busy doing other things on set, she wouldn't get into the editing room until night time, which made our days long. We would get there at 9am, but wouldn't leave until she had come and contributed to the editing work for each episode. She had a vision for the show, and she had to touch every part of the process to make sure that her vision was carried out. She is now doing *The Marvelous Mrs Maisel*, and that show has her signature writing style. She is a unique person, and is very warm, and outgoing. I remember walking into her office and everything was pink—pink stuffed animals, pink ceiling, pink couches. She is one of a kind.

Amy had specific preferences for how *Gilmore Girls* was shot. Steadicam was used a lot because Amy loves tracking shots. It gave a great look when two people were dialoguing back and forth because the characters could be driven forward both in plot, but also physically. Many important conversations between Lorelai and Rory take place on the way to Luke's Diner, or as they walk through Stars Hollow. Our editing rooms were in a trailer behind the shrubs in Mrs Kim's backyard. It was seconds away from the sets so I frequently would walk through Stars Hollow on my lunch break, and would sometimes have lunch in the town square. One of my fondest memories of my time on the show is walking around the snowy gazebo and having lunch in a Stars Hollow winter wonderland. Amy would always want snow, since the show is supposed to be set in Connecticut. Having snow on a filming set is a huge undertaking. It takes several days for the art department to lay the cotton material around the set, and then the machines would come in and blow the snow over the top. Because Stars Hollow is such a big area, it took a lot of work.

One of the other things I vividly remember about the set was Taylor's Soda Shoppe. It was always exciting when something new was opening on the show, and we would get to see new things built. All of the shops that you see in Stars Hollow are facades apart from Luke's Diner. There is nothing behind them when you go in. Even Luke's is a facade, to an extent. Behind the diner counters was where lawnmowers were stored. When the Soda Shoppe needed to be built, it was done in such a way that space was saved, but it looked like a big store on screen. The real depth of Taylor's was only two metres. The shop was filled with real candy which was exciting. I felt literally, like a kid in a candy shop, when I got to go in there. Unfortunately, all of the candy had been sprayed down with rat poison, so it was all inedible.

When you are in the set of the Gilmore manor, it is a very formal environment. The show spent a lot of money on the set design for that house which included a constant rotation of fresh flowers, and a working fireplace. Amy wanted luxury, but realism.

I made a lot of friends on *Gilmore Girls*. Jared Padalecki who played Dean was just starting out when he came on the show, but he was a very nice guy. He and I used to play chess on the grass outside Luke's Diner between takes. Milo Ventimiglia was also a very nice young guy, and I ended up working with him again on *This is Us*. I also worked with Scott Patterson again in *Aliens in America*, and Melissa McCarthy on Judd Apatow's *This is 40*. Ed Herrmann seemed like a great person, but I was always too nervous to speak to him. He seemed very quiet, and formal.

Being on *Gilmore Girls* helped my career a lot. Everyone knew about the show and wanted to be a part of it. I edited films and television shows after including *This is Us* after which had a similar heartfelt quality to *Gilmore Girls*. Working on *Gilmore Girls* was really fun because it was always a bundle of energy, and it was amazing to watch this finely-tuned production where Amy was integral in every part of its mechanism.

Ethan Cohn

Glenn Babble

    I had just recently moved to Los Angeles when I got the part of Glenn on *Gilmore Girls*. I was trying to make acting my career and had done some commercials and small television roles. I had been living in an apartment in New York which had enormous billboards as my view. I remember a huge billboard right outside my window for

Gilmore Girls, that I would see everyday. I had never seen the show, but I knew they talked fast, and that it was popular.

I went along to what they call a general meeting with the casting directors Jamie Rudofsky, and Mara Casey. They were coming back to a new season and would meet with new actors in town to get a sense of different actors, and who might be right for parts that were coming up on the show. I had never driven in Los Angeles before and I got hit by another car on the freeway on the way to the meeting. I felt very shaken by what had just happened, and it threw my anxiety into overdrive. I didn't want to miss my chance to meet the casting directors so I went anyway, knowing I wasn't in the best frame of mind. When I got to the meeting I just went with it and didn't fight the anxiety. I figured all I could do was the best I could, given what had just happened. I guess they liked my nervous countenance because the casting directors and I really hit it off and they brought me back the following week to read for Amy Sherman-Palladino and Daniel Palladino.

I went in the next week and ran into a bunch of people in the waiting room including Katie Walder, who went on to play Janet on the show. Her and I knew each other from summer camp. I read for a small part in the first episode at Yale. I thought the audition went well, but I didn't get the part. I was disappointed, but my agent said that they had liked me so much, they were going to write a part for me. I thought that was just a line to make people feel better, but my agent assured me that she knew the people on the show, and that if they had said that, they meant it.

Before long, I got called in again to audition for an episode with a character that had two lines. Glenn would be a Yale student who lived in Rory's building. My character would be attending a party inside Rory's dorm room where Paris, Tanna, and Janet would also be.

I remember doing the fitting with Brenda Maben in the costume department, and what a warm person she was. She was so open to talking and sharing, and made me feel so welcome. I really felt like she had my back, and I quickly came to consider her a friend. People in the wardrobe department are kind of on the front line in the sense that they are the first people you meet when you get on set. They set the tone for the day.

During that first shoot, I hit it off with Alexis (Rory) and Liza (Paris) right away, and had a very relaxed experience overall. It was my first time working on a big budget television show, but I didn't feel pressured or stressed. I felt at home there. It was a really social set. People on that set would hang out with each other, talking, and sitting on the steps of the trailers. There was a real sense that people were part of a family. They had been doing the show together for years when I came in. That doesn't happen so much anymore, with the invention of the smartphone. Actors used to read magazines together and interact with people and it was fun. Now people don't connect, they just have their head down on their phones and wait to be called to work.

After I did my episode, a couple of weeks passed before I was called back to reprise my role as Glenn, who would now be a recurring character. When I initially was shooting, the whole team would break for lunch, but I didn't know what that meant. I was fresh out of New York University and I didn't have the 'child actor, been through the mill' history. Was I supposed to bring my own lunch and eat it in the trailer? Was there somewhere I was supposed to go to eat lunch? I was too embarrassed to ask, or let people know that I wasn't sure how lunch worked so I would just go to the craft service table and grab something there. One day, Liza asked if I was coming to lunch, and she took me. I had been missing the actual lunch because I was afraid to reveal my green-ness to the other cast members. In hindsight, that show was used to young actors, and I know I was free to ask people. I just lacked confidence in those early days.

The spring break episode was the best episode for me, and for my character. It was really exciting to have started on the show with two lines and now to have this really fun part with all the best actors of the show. I really felt like I was a part of the Gilmore world now, not just this guy who hadn't felt comfortable asking where the lunch was. We all hung out at the Sea Sprite Motel where we shot the episode, as we were booked to stay there for the duration of the shoot.

The most challenging scene to shoot was the ocean scene where I come out of the water yelling "hot dog". The water was freezing, and the show had brought in a hypothermia team to look after me between takes. They set up a tent which was heated with gas, but it was February in the wee hours of the morning, so it was still cold. As soon as I ran down the beach, I would be wrapped in this big blanket and taken to the hypothermia tent to warm up. Once I had thawed, it would be time to go again.

They had also brought in a lifeguard who told me that there had been multiple great white shark sightings in the area in the month prior. At the time I thought he was messing with me, but I later realised it was true. It was a pitch black, inky ocean, so I wouldn't have seen if there was a shark in the water. When I got out into the water, Jamie Babbit—the director—kept telling me to go out a little further. I remember worrying because I was the only thing in the ocean that was moving and alive. If a shark was looking for something, I would have been its only target.

At that time in my life, I was dealing with a lot of body shame too. I wasn't happy with my weight and I think this made the scene difficult for me, emotionally. With all the challenges, I was starting to feel like it was some kind of *Gilmore Girls* hazing.

Some of my favourite moments were where Alexis and I had little scenes in the Yale dorm hallway. There was something about Alexis and her warmth that made me feel at ease. She had this willingness to connect and this ability to allow me to be myself in this way that felt really good. Since then I've been on a lot of shows and usually if you are a guest star the main cast members don't particularly want to know you. They are in their own world. The episode where we made the hats in the newsroom was also a really fun day. I remember feeling really confident that day. I finally felt that I could own my role on the show. I could be there, and be at the same level as the other actors.

Being on *Gilmore Girls* helped my confidence a lot, because then I was able to walk into rooms with the knowledge that I had gotten a part, and had done it well. I was also able to use my time at *Gilmore Girls* to get a better agent, since I now had a bonafide screen credit on my resume. It helped me professionally because it broke that barrier for me of being an actor who says they are an actor, and one who is actually a working actor.

After shooting my twelfth episode on *Gilmore Girls* I went to work on a feature film with M Night Shyamalan which prevented me from returning to the show. I used to get a call about a week before Glenn was needed back on the set, and on this occasion my agent had to tell them that I was busy on another project. *Gilmore Girls* stopped calling after that, which was difficult for me because I had so much gratitude for the show. It was hard to not have any closure. There was no last episode, I just didn't come back because I wasn't able to, and that was the end of Glenn.

Gilmore Girls has had an amazing afterlife, and the impact of the show has lasted for me, too. Katie (Janet) and I are still friends, and we have the same agent. We got to play a husband and wife on a show and it was very funny. I tell people that all of Glenn's dreams are coming true, because he is now married to Janet. The show strikes a chord with people, because it has a unique tone. It's funny, full of references, and loaded with crazy characters. It is a mix of sweet and sentimental but it has an edge to it. The show is also smart, and that makes it different. It doesn't talk down to its viewers. It assumes they can keep up with all of the references and understand them. It makes people want to learn more, know more, and grow. It doesn't pander. It plays to the highest minds. It's not condescending, but it does lift people up.

There is also a nostalgia associated with the show. It started with a generation of people that watched it after school—it was part of their childhood, and they grew up with Rory. The way that they wrote younger people on the show also played into its relatability. At that time there were a lot of shows that featured tortured teenagers. In *Gilmore Girls* the teenagers are more realistic. Glenn had an anxiety attack—there was space on that show for characters to be strange, quirky, or outsiders.

It's really wonderful to see the impact *Gilmore Girls* has had on people and I just love running into fans. I'm a therapist now and sometimes people come and see me for months before realising I'm Glenn from *Gilmore Girls*. The show made an impact on so many people.

Patty Malcolm

Stand-in for Lauren Graham
Woman #1 / Mrs. Harris / Leanne / Secretary

    I moved to Los Angeles in 2001 for my acting career. I got a small role on *Days of Our Lives* but it wasn't enough work. One thing they don't really tell you is that most of your time as an actor is spent in auditions, and you only get a small percentage of the roles that you audition for. While I was on *Days of Our Lives* I met a woman who did background work. I asked her how she made enough money from her acting work, and she said she did background work to supplement her income between larger roles. I was interested, so I registered with Central Casting and signed up for background work. I didn't like it. I did a couple of background jobs but I remember feeling like this was not what I moved to Los Angeles to do. To pay the bills, I got a job working in ophthalmology as a technician, which I had done for years in Seattle while attending acting school. I was in this work when I got the call for *Gilmore Girls*.

I wasn't familiar with the show, so I Googled it, and saw Luke wearing flannel, so I wore flannel for the meeting. I was asked if I had done stand-in work before, so I said I had. The job I was meeting them about was being the stand in for the lead star on the show, Lauren Graham. While I wasn't enjoying background work, stand-in work was quite different. I would always be on the set working, so it was full-time, and I would be working with the same cast and crew, in a steady job. The only preparation it required was that my hair would need to be cut and coloured to match Lauren's. I accepted, and was told I would start on Monday.

On Monday morning I had to check in at 7am on stage 18 which was Lorelai's house. The scene we were shooting was a scene between Lauren and Alexis. They talked really fast, moved around a lot, and then were whisked off to a trailer. I took notes. Lauren came to greet me and then went to her trailer. Alexis' stand-in and I rehearsed the scene again and again for the cameras and to set the lighting. Then they called Lauren back to film it. On that first day I worked 15 hours, and on the second, 14 hours. I was still working at the ophthalmologist's office at that time, so Monday to Friday I was at *Gilmore Girls* and then I would do 12 hour days on Saturday and

Sunday in my other job. I soon quit the ophthalmology job because it was too much.

Though we got used to the long hours on *Gilmore Girls*, we were always tired, so we tried to squeeze naps in when we could. The working day included two meal breaks because of the long hours so a lot of the crew members would run for a place to sleep on the set during these breaks. While the cast had trailers, the crew didn't, so we would all try and find a place to sleep—at the inn, in Lorelai's bed, or Rory's. The sound department used to rush as soon as the first assistant director would call lunch, to try and beat me to these places. It got really hard when shooting went into the late hours and the cast were getting tired. People would get frazzled, and on edge, and sometimes it got a bit tense when that happened. Those power naps kept us going.

While there were amazing times on the show, a few memories stand out as challenging. My least favourite scene to shoot was in the Halloween episode when Babette was hanging Morey in the backyard as a prank. Ted Rooney who played Morey had to have a noose around his neck, and be dropped down onto a platform below the gallows box. I remember we were all cold and tired, and a lot of us felt uncomfortable and didnt like it. It was very closely monitored but we just didn't feel good about that scene. Other scenes that could be hard for me were any that involved heavy snow. Everyone loves those scenes but I had to stand in the snow for a long time, so they weren't my favourite scenes to shoot. Snow had to keep being added to the set, and I had to stand in the cold with sore feet to get the lighting set before Lauren would walk in and have her magical "I smell snow" scenes. Although those scenes came out beautifully on television, I always dreaded it when I saw them in the scripts.

However, I also have some amazing, positive memories that stand out. Kenny Ortega, whom I love, directed some of the episodes, and when he did, the atmosphere on set was just so jovial. In the dance marathon episode, Alexis' stand-in and I would have to rehearse the moves for our steadicam operator Steve to get the timing of everything correct before Lauren and Alexis would come in to shoot. Kenny would do funny things like come up and grab me and dip me out of nowhere. He came back to direct a lot of other episodes for us, and gave me the part of Richard's secretary in 'You Jump, I Jump, Jack'. He was a lot of fun to work with.

Two other people I always got a kick out of working with were Liz Torres (Miss Patty) and Sally Struthers (Babette). They were always so much fun when they came to set. They would bounce off of each other, and create this amazing energy.

I also loved all my moments with Kelly Bishop (Emily) and Edward Herrmann (Richard). On the set, I was kind of like Kirk, always wearing a lot of hats—I did rehearsing, reading dialogue, filling in, and background if there were not enough background actors that day. However, Ed and Kelly always treated me like an equal. They made me feel like I was on their level. There's often a kind of pecking order on sets but not to them. Some actors just wanted me to read the lines, to give them their cues. Kelly and Ed wanted me to act with them. When I was running lines with them, or working on a scene as Lorelai's stand in, Ed would always say, "give it everything you've got". I really tried to be Lorelai for them, so that they could bounce off my lines and do a good job.

My favourite scene ever was shooting with Ed in the episode where his mother 'Trix' had passed away. They shot Lauren's coverage but she couldn't stay as she had a flight to catch to New York. It was an emotional scene and it moved me so deeply to get to play that scene with him. It was beautiful, and it really filled me up as an actress. It was so rewarding and I will never forget it. It helped me grow as an actress, to see such a professional do his work so up close. Thinking about it makes me emotional because I miss him. It's one of my highlights of working in television.

The environment on *Gilmore Girls* was different to other shows I have done. We played jokes on each other, laughed, cried, and had fun. It was a really tight knit group. We would work these crazy hours and still hang out after work. We liked each other. I've never really been a part of that again. A lot of shows are friendly and you do develop relationships over the years, but it's never been the same as *Gilmore Girls*. The men of the cast and crew would have beard growing contests, we had karaoke nights, and held barbecues and pot luck dinners. That's not something that happened on any other show I have worked on. It's really so unique. On my next job, *Criminal Minds*, I was expecting that kind of camaraderie but soon learned that on Friday nights, everyone goes home. I've been in shows I enjoyed a lot but they haven't been the same as the *Gilmore Girls* experience.

Gilmore Girls gave me confidence in myself. It gave me so much experience that I never had to look for a job again. I got offered stand-in work all the time, because I had had a long running job on a hit television show standing in for the lead. I was trusted to do the work, read, and double the stars. It really impacted my career as a stand in. I never came here to be a stand-in but I am grateful for that. I don't know if I would be as confident without that experience. After 20 years working on at least a dozen films and television shows, in 2020 I gave up stand-in work to focus on my acting career.

Gilmore Girls gave me my television family and that's the only show that ever did. It showed me what a good show is like—what it's like to work on a fun, fabulous show. I was glued to the ATX television festival when it was live in 2015. I sat there feeling like, 'This is my family…these are my people'. I haven't felt like that about any of my other shows, even though I have worked as long on others. I just have such fond memories. I listened to Lauren Graham's autobiographical book *Talking as Fast as I Can: From Gilmore Girls to Gilmore Girls (and everything in between)* and cried through most of it. It really hit me hard because I was there for a lot of it and I remember a lot of the things she talked about. She talked about her dad and we all loved her dad. He worked at a candy company, and used to bring us bags of candy when he came to the set. We also met her mom and her sister. We all cared about each other, and it's just a rare thing. We had parties on set—baby showers, and wedding showers, and we sadly lost a few people along the way. If someone was going through something we celebrated together, or grieved together. It's hard to believe that it all ended in 2007. It was so long ago and I still feel so warm about it.

Peter Klausner

William

I came onto *Gilmore Girls* in season 4, playing a Yale college student. I thought that I was going to have a professional acting career, so when I graduated from college in 2003 I had a manager but not an agent. I travelled a little that summer, as people do right after college, and when I came back the plan was to get my acting career going. *Gilmore Girls* was my first professional audition. At the time, I had never seen the show, I had only vaguely heard of it. I wasn't watching a lot of network television then, so I looked it up and what caught my eye was Edward Herrmann. I really liked him and thought the show must be pretty cool if he was in it. I asked around, but not too many of my friends had watched it regularly. However, from what they had seen, they knew the dialogue was fast, and clever. I Googled it and read that in the next season, Rory's character was headed to college, so I got the sense that I would probably be a fellow student. I also got the feeling that the show was moving away from Rory having boyfriends in Stars Hollow, and that she would be starting a new chapter in her life, romantically. The producers had this plan to bring in a lot of guys, and parade them in front of Rory, and see what stuck, and I think I was ultimately part of that parade.

They brought in every young male actor of a certain age, and certain type to audition for this. I'm not sure why, but they basically scheduled everyone at the same time for the audition at the Warner Bros lot. When I got there, the lobby became one big waiting room for 25-30 actors, all the same age, all the same look, all there at the same time. If you were like me and hadn't shed all your insecurities from youth, it was a really intense environment to be in. Everyone was looking at each other, sizing each other up. No one was friendly—it was really intimidating. I had just never been in that environment before. It was really hard to focus on anything but this meat market I was thrown into. One guy was giving everyone the nastiest look.

They gave us sides—the script you read off for the audition. They didn't have any scripts written yet for my part, so the sides were from a scene featured in an earlier episode, and season. I went into the audition and there were three women in the room, all of whom were so nice, and so lovely. They immediately put me at ease. I could tell right away that I was right for whatever they were looking for. They gave me a lot of positive reinforcement. They made contact with my manager to bring me back for another audition and found out I didn't have an agent, so they referred me to agents to interview with. From those referrals, I got to meet a few agents and choose one. They all wanted me, because a casting office had referred me, so they all wanted to jump in there and represent me before I got paid. So, *Gilmore Girls* helped set me up with a good agency.

Like most parts, I got the job after a series of auditions. At the second round of callbacks it seemed like they had brought back all the same people. Once again, there were the same 25-30 guys including the one giving everyone nasty looks. I had initially been pleased to be called back, but once I saw them all again, it seemed like everyone had been brought back. Maybe it wasn't so meaningful after all. When it was my turn, I went into the audition room again, and the casting directors were full of great things to say about me. I hadn't gotten positive feedback like that before. There were another two more rounds after that. By the fourth audition, Amy Sherman-Palladino was in the room. I didn't really know who she was back then, but I could immediately tell that she was important, and the key decision maker. It was only at that last audition that I had the sides for the scene that I would actually be doing in the show—the scene in the laundry room. In the script, there is a line in there about listening to the Smith's, so I listened to the Smiths album to get a sense of the style of music, and what it might mean to my character.

I remember getting the call from my manager saying that I had booked it, and that she had a date and time for me to show up. It was a huge thrill because it was my first audition. When you set out to be an actor you have no idea if it's going to work out. For everybody who gets work in the business there are thousands that fail, and there's no reason to think that you won't be one of those people. It was ultimately my Mom's dream for me to be an actor, so I called her to tell her I would be on a major network show. She was thrilled, and being able to call her up and tell her that was amazing. She passed away in an accident a few years later. That phone call with her is one of those really cool moments that will stick with me, that I will always associate with *Gilmore Girls*.

A week before filming I went in for a costume fitting and that was fun. I am quite fashionably inept and a bit in between sizes so I have trouble finding clothes off the rack that fit me well. Having access to all these clothes, I felt like a cool guy. They gave me a collared shirt with a t-shirt over it and a rhinestone belt. The jeans that I turned up in fit me so well that they told me to wear them when shooting. I also got to wear my own shoes. When the show was finally on television I thought it was so cool to see my own jeans and Chuck Taylors on the show.

The day of that first shoot I was nervous as hell. I hadn't done anything like that, and then a set production assistant was walking me from hair and makeup to my trailer. As we were walking towards it, we passed Alexis Bledel so the production assistant introduced us. We shook hands, and she was friendly. It was a surreal experience for me, but probably a completely different experience for her. She was the star of a very successful show, but she was just meeting the latest actor to walk onto the show.

They brought me on set and it was a bit jarring. I wasn't exactly star struck but I had never done this before. It felt like I was in a movie about someone getting fresh off the greyhound and walking straight into Hollywood. When I got onto the set I walked past all these facades, and then past a fake dorm room, and was taken into the laundry room where I would shoot my scene. There was all sorts of excitement. People were walking around, carrying things, there were lights, and cameras, and all sorts of weird noises I had never heard before. When they were about to start shooting this loud bell like a fire alarm went off and it gave me a fright.

When I read for the part initially, they didn't have a name for the character. He was just 'guy in the laundry room'. They eventually called the character William because they said I looked like a dirty Prince William. My portrayal of William in that episode only took an hour or so. We blocked it a couple of times, rehearsed it, and then when Alexis got on set we rehearsed it again. They marked my place on the floor with neon tape so I knew where to stand, and we filmed it a couple of times. The director was a woman called Neema Barnette and she was really nice, supportive, and positive toward me. She said something like let me see that 'Peter smile' of yours. Amy Sherman-Palladino was on set, sitting in a folding canvas director's chair. She was on her laptop, writing scripts. I remember thinking how amazing it was to see her in action—on set, writing, and working hard to make the show great. That first filming day came, and went, and my mom wanted to hear all about it. I was 21 at the time. I called her up as soon as I left the soundstage and she was really thrilled. I had shot my first episode.

I remember when I left that day that there was some indication that I would be back for another episode. Eventually, I got confirmation that I would be coming back to my role in another episode, and that my part would be more involved. I was in four scenes, and would speak in two of them. For that episode I got invited to the table read and I thought that was pretty cool because I hadn't met much of the cast other than Alexis, so I thought it would be great to meet everyone else. Unfortunately, I was cast for a guest spot on another show and needed to do the final audition for that on the same night as the table read, so I had to leave as soon as my part was done. I didn't get to hang out with anyone, but I did get to sit next to Lauren Graham.

We filmed all four scenes on the same day. Back then when I drank a soda from the soda fountain, I would have a bit of each drink in my cup and I thought this character might be the kind of guy that does that kind of thing. So, I did it in the scene. One of the scene directors came up to me at the end of filming and told me they could see me doing that, and asked if it was on purpose. I told them it was one of my character's 'things'. When we went to shoot the scene in the classroom there were snacks on the table for the students and they said if we wanted we could fill up a coffee, and put a snack in front of ourselves. There were bagels, so as a nod to my Jewishness, I put a bagel in front of me. I even took a bite out of it to show that my character was in the process of eating it. I remember filming that scene a couple of times in the classroom, not really being able to digest what anybody was talking about in that scene.

I remember waiting between camera sets in the hallway outside the classroom with Alexis and Liza Weil (Paris). I remember trying to butt into their conversation but not making much headway. The gist of their conversation was that they were exhausted from the demands of the show. However, they didn't want to talk to me about it. This was their permanent work, and I was just the dayplayer.

The last scene we filmed is the one in the cafeteria where I talked to Rory, and told her the story about the girl who was stalking me. I was nervous, and excited the whole time. It was a different director, but he was very supportive. The guy who was my stand-in, was also really positive and so nice, and we chatted while I was waiting to go on. After it aired, my mom was annoyed with me, because while I was talking to Rory in that scene, I was holding my fork. Mom said it was rude and uncouth of me to wave my fork around at her like that.

In the meantime, I had booked an episode of the show *Judging Amy* and it aired the week that we were filming my second episode on *Gilmore Girls*. This meant that I was actually in the promos for the *Judging Amy* episode while I was shooting *Gilmore Girls*. Some people in my life didn't even know I was working as an actor, and suddenly I was in commercials, and shooting episodes for another series.

When we were filming that second episode, there was some expectation on my part that I would be coming back. However, when the episode aired, I knew they were going in another direction. We had filmed that last scene in a number of ways, but the one that was chosen and made the final cut was the more antagonistic one. I didn't think that's the one that would have been chosen if that character was going to go on and become Rory's boyfriend. Years later, there was an article on Buzzfeed that ranked all of Rory's boyfriends over the course of the show. Someone sent it to me and I was dead last on it. It said something like. "Can you believe this guy turned Rory down?" In my mind, if you aren't going to be at the top of the list, it is better to be at the bottom of the list, than in the middle. I at least got the distinction of being the least favourite of Rory's love interests.

For the longest time I never got recognised for *Gilmore Girls*, but as the show lived on, and DVDs and streaming allowed people to watch things multiple times, I did start to get recognised. The first time it happened was ten years after my time on the show, when I was getting married. The woman who did my wife's makeup came over to do a trial run and asked my wife if I had been on *Gilmore Girls*. Around the same time, on a flight to Las Vegas, the flight attendant kept saying she knew me from somewhere and it didn't occur to me that she might have recognised me from television. Somewhere in the middle of the flight she came back and said she had figured it out, and that she had loved my work on *Gilmore Girls*. For ten years not a single person recognised me, but now people are watching the series over and over, and *Gilmore Girls* has this second life.

Working on *Gilmore Girls* helped me get on to other shows because I had a professional credit on my resume. I didn't really end up working as an actor though in the long run. I got sidetracked with political work and it wasn't long after that that I came to realise that being an actor wasn't really my dream, it was my mom's dream for me. My heart wasn't in it. I started to look into other work and never really stuck with acting. But for that year it was really cool. *Gilmore Girls* was a big deal at the time and it felt cool as hell to be a working actor in Los Angeles because so many people struggle for that. When you tell people you are an actor they roll their eyes and ask, "how's that working out for you?" which equates to "are you getting any work?" To be 21, in Los Angeles with credits on a network show, was a great feeling.

When the revival news broke, my friends all joked about me coming back. They had hilarious theories about how Rory would go back to Yale to find a missing sock and my character would still be standing there in the laundry room. I told everyone I was outraged that William wasn't coming back, and that this was a disgrace, but I was just kidding. I didn't have any real expectations to come back. I thought the idea of bringing it back was great though.

I practice law, and write screenplays now. I realised that I love movies, stories, and television. I started writing, on a whim, in my late 20s and realised how much joy it gave me. The screenplay that I just finished is a science fiction action movie set in the future, and involves a female police officer without a father figure. The one I'm working on now is set in the 1950s and the father disappears. Single mothers, and women without father figures is a recurring theme in my writing. I love stories, and thinking of these things in my head. I never thought I would be a writer. It seemed excruciating. But, I don't think I really realised what writing was. I now understand it to be the construction of ideas, which are then communicated on paper. It turned out to be a real joy in my life.

My life in law came about shortly after my time on *Gilmore Girls*. There was a big presidential election in the United States, between George W. Bush for re-election, and John Kerry. I felt very strongly about that election and very much wanted Kerry to unseat Bush. I started doing grassroots work for those campaigns. Those elections took place in November of 2004. Even though John Kerry lost the election on election night, I felt very strongly that I was right where I was supposed to be, doing exactly what I was doing. I was supposed to be there, trying to affect the outcome of the election. I had never felt so strongly or passionately, and thought I might want to work on political campaigns or government. The conventional way to get into that kind of work back then was to go to law school. I looked into it and started studying for the LSATs. I actually loved studying for that test. I loved the process, and how it made me think. I had never taken school so seriously before. I took the exam, applied, and got into law school, and things went from there. Now I'm just a run-of-the mill attorney but I love what I'm doing, where I am working, and the kind of cases I work on. I've been doing it for over ten years now, and this is my life now.

The show means a lot to people emotionally and is a big deal to a lot of people. Not every show has this depth of followers. People are sticking with his show and not leaving it behind. As a fan of things like *Star Wars*, I get that. Some things just never really leave your consciousness. I think the relationship between a child and their mother is sacred and it's one of the most beautiful things that exists on this earth—that bond between a mother and a child, and that's what is at the heart of the show. At its core, the show is about healthy, but complicated relationships between mothers and their children which is so important to so many people. I'm not sure if too many other shows nailed this. It's Rory's relationship with her mom, and Lorelai's relationship with her mom, and the importance of those relationships, and how they define everything you do. My relationship with my mom defined my life, and really, my relationship with this show. When I think about *Gilmore Girls,* I remember the joy and excitement I had calling my mom and telling her I was going to be on television. I remember calling her from the sound stage for the first time. I remember the thrill she had watching me on television, and seeing her dream for me come true. I have two little girls now and I'm always talking to them about my mom because I want them to know how important she was to me, and how she defined who their dad is.

Rini Bell

Lulu Kuschner

I got an audition for *Gilmore Girls* at a time where I was going through a phase of wearing a lot of flowers in my hair. When I left the audition room, Brenda Maben who worked in the costume department said to me, "I knew you'd get it. You just had that look". So, that was a lovely start to my time on the show. It was a good audition. Amy was in the room and I had been in a few times to read for other parts—usually Rory's school mates. I was excited to get the role of Lulu, but I didn't realise at that point that the role would be recurring. It was offered to me as a one episode deal, but then they just kept calling me back in.

I was aware of the show before I got the part, because it was so well known. I wouldn't consider myself a fan of the show, only because I wasn't home much, so there wasn't much time to watch television. I also try to avoid watching shows before I go in for them, because it kind of taints my view of the character, and doesn't allow me to bring my own personality to the audition. More recently—now that the fan base has become a bigger part of my life—I actually did sit down and watch the whole show because the fans were interested in plot points from it, and knew it better than I did. I wasn't able to keep up with discussions that weren't about my character, and I wanted to be able to participate, so I had to educate myself.

On the first day, I remember the director was Matthew Diamond who was a dancer in Janet Jackson's Rhythm Nation video. I was so excited because I knew exactly who he was. Lauren Graham was so kind to me. I was this little nobody showing up and she said I was adorable and looked really well rested. Those small comments gave me so much confidence. I really appreciated her little random kindnesses toward the 'nobody's', because it made such a big difference to me. My first scene was in Luke's Diner which is so cute because it's part of the fake town so it's like being in Disneyland. It was just Sean and Scott in the scene and I sort of recognised them, mainly Scott because of little bits of the show I had seen. They were all so nice to me. Everyone kept saying they were so glad that Kirk finally had a girlfriend.

My favourite episode to shoot, and the one that always stands out in my memory is the episode where Kirk drives through the diner window in this big car. It was like being a part of an action movie, and that was exciting for me. There was real adrenalin and an explosion.

That same day Taylor was up on some crane overlooking the town when the explosion happened, and it was just a fun episode. Every single episode was so fun. I loved Lane's baby shower, where I was sitting with Rose Abdoo (Gypsy) and Sally Struthers (Babette) decorating baby onesies. We got to be really silly, so that was a lot of fun. I loved all of the episodes that featured a town meeting, because all of the crew would be together at once. Some of them had crazy personalities, so it was a lot of fun when everyone got together.

Sally Struthers was always a hoot to work with. I remember one day when we were sitting around waiting for our turn to shoot, she decided to show us everything that was in her purse. She had a really big bag and pulled out all kinds of punch tickets, cookies, and the thing that stood out to me the most was an extendo fork. It was really funny just watching her. She is a constant entertainment. Another time, we were both in hair and makeup, sitting in the trailer, when she started talking about little baby chicks at Easter, and telling us how if you put one in the microwave it will get really big and explode. I was horrified, until I realised I had missed some of the conversation and she was actually talking about Peeps.

Working on the show was always pleasant for me because I came in periodically and it was always such a pleasure and I was always so excited. It was always a good experience. When I heard the revival was happening, I was excited but didn't think I would be in it. I was living in New York at the time, and I got a call asking if I wanted to do the show the following week. I was excited and it was a nice surprise. I was in a scene with everybody, and the gazebo was back on set. It was a really good vibe, but it was hard to know how to handle the nostalgia. I wasn't prepared for the shock to my system. Some people looked older and some did not, but really everybody seemed the same. There was a lot of talk amongst the cast about who was married, who had had babies etc. It was a lot of fun.

While working on the show boosted me professionally in terms of visibility, *Gilmore Girls* also gave me some nice friendships. Valerie is incredible at keeping in touch with people to a degree that I would argue is insane. She would always invite people to her house to eat ice cream, and I would usually go. Since the revival, the fan festival has been a much easier way to keep in touch with people. Aris Alvarado (Caesar) hooked me up with my acting class. Rose is always performing. Stan Zimmerman (a writer and consulting producer on *Gilmore Girls*) does lots of plays and puts us in them. It's a pretty decent part of my social life. It's on and off, but nice to develop that feeling with everybody and that sense of the community of the show that we all share in.

I have been attending the fan festival dedicated to the show since the start. I was living in New York and a couple of people emailed me about these events that felt a little sudden and out of the blue. Jennie, the organiser, emailed me and I thought I don't know who this person is but she said Kelly Bishop is the only one who is going to do it. I said yes, not knowing what I was getting into, because Kelly had agreed to do it. I couldn't say no because it sounded too interesting. I remember the car coming to pick me up, and being so nervous about it. It turned out to be wonderful of course. It all felt very unknown and surprising. But, it was a very pleasant surprise. I really enjoy doing the fan fest now. I love the feeling of this recreation of our little world.

When I connect with fans I hear a lot of things like "my mom and I used to watch it together". The mother daughter relationship is so relatable, but not particularly common on television, especially at that time. It was so well done. That first season, I felt like the beginning was the most touching part. It was so sweet and really nicely done. The show really beautifully told a little love story, and not the conventional kind, but one between a mother and her daughter. Nothing else like that on television comes to mind. And of course, there is a nice contrast with Emily and Lorelai's relationship which gives real depth and balance to the show. On top of that, the success of the show comes down to the little world that has been created in it. Everybody loves Stars Hollow.

Lynda Scarlino

Buff Otis

My entrance onto *Gilmore Girls* was relatively simple, and uneventful. The casting director called me to invite me to come and read for the part of Buff Otis. I went in to read the line, imitating what they said they wanted, and was lucky enough to get the role. I had seen the show before, but I hadn't seen all the episodes. As soon as I got the part, I watched it to refresh my memory and to make sure I understood the tone. I actually liked it so much that it inspired me to finish it after my day of shooting. So, being cast in the show made a fan out of me, in some ways.

On my first day on set, everybody was so friendly. Lauren Graham (Lorelai) came over and introduced herself as soon as I got on set, and asked me to do my line. I sat with Sally Struthers (Babette) and Liz Torres (Miss Patty), and spent most of my time with them, drawn in by how nice they were, and how much fun they seemed to be having. Sally was gossiping about everybody. She was really funny. She was telling me sexual things about Arnold Schwarzenegger, and seemed to have dirt on everyone.

Lauren Graham came over and introduced herself to me and asked me to do my line so she could practice imitating it later on in the episode, in another scene she had to do. The cast was so warm and accepting. This is rarely the case for me, when I come into a show as a "dayplayer", to shoot one episode. I also get cast in a lot of soap operas, and in those shows, I often feel very isolated because they all know each other, and I am only there for one day, so the regulars don't make an effort to talk to me. In contrast, my experience on *Gilmore Girls* was so nice.

Of course, I was hoping that my part might turn out to be more than one episode, but dayplayers are always hoping for that, in every part. What amazed me was that even with only one line, so many people remember my role on that show. I used to work once a year in a mystery show, playing a detective. One time, someone in the audience looked right at me while I was on stage and said, "your enthusiasm…shocks me!" I had to try and stay in character, so I have always remembered that instance.

Since then, people have come up to me a lot and quoted that line. It's hard for me to believe that one line in a show of so many seasons had such an impact on people. Most people think it's very funny, and they enjoy such an outlandish response.

At the time I was on *Gilmore Girls,* I was on a professional "roll", so to speak. I got a recurring role on *Everybody Hates Chris,* and on *Six Feet Under* all in the same year as my appearance on *Gilmore Girls*. So, it was a very lucrative year for me professionally. The environment on *Gilmore Girls* made such a difference to my experience. I felt welcomed as family, which was not the case on other sets I worked on.

What makes this show unique, was not just my experience of being welcomed into the cast, but the storylines. The story of *Gilmore Girls* is so unique. It changes all the time, and while all the characters are different, and facing different challenges, they mesh together so well. It was an honour to work on that show, and to be remembered for my line on it.

Julie Dolan

Anna

My first encounter with *Gilmore Girls* was when I was called to audition for the role of a friend to Luke's sister Liz, but, my history with the show technically goes back a bit further than this. I went to high school with Daniel Palladino. Daniel and I did theatre together at St. Genevieve High School in Panorama City and we were really good friends. Of course, after graduating we lost contact. Every now and then we would check in. Things like, "how's it going?", "Happy

Birthday", etc. There was no Facebook back then, and no cell phones, so it was harder to stay in touch. There would be occasional phone calls, and we stayed in touch that way. So I was excited when I got the audition to be on his and Amy's show.

Before *Gilmore Girls* I auditioned for a movie called *The Man Who Invented the Moon.* Sean Gunn (who plays Kirk in *Gilmore Girls*) was in it, and John Cabrera (who plays Brian in *Gilmore Girls*) directed it. It was also cast by Mara Casey, who was the casting director on *Gilmore Girls*. It was a lower budget movie, but, as an actor, you go in and audition for everything, and I auditioned for everything that was run out of the Screen Actors Guild. I remember driving down in the heart of Hollywood and I went in and read this scene with Sean. I didn't know who he was because I wasn't watching *Gilmore Girls* religiously. He and I just connected. I got cast in the movie and it was a great experience. Sean's brothers were on set with us and we all got close. It was such a great experience and the movie did well.

Mara was impressed with my performance and asked to bring me in for *Gilmore Girls.* I had also done casting director workshops with her. These are where a casting director will come into a room with about 25 actors and give you scenes, and they will watch you read for them. It's not really an audition, but it gives them some idea of who is out there, and available for work. I had done one of these workshops with Mara and she remembered me from the movie and brought me in for *Gilmore Girls.*

When I went into the callback I went into the room with Daniel and Amy Sherman-Palladino and a couple of producers. It was odd being in an audition room with my high school friend, and his wife, auditioning for their television show. I remember seeing McKenzie Phillips at the audition and I thought if she was reading for my part she was for sure going to get it. I'm not sure which role she auditioned for, but I got the part of Liz's friend and was really happy about it.

I had to prepare for the role. Actors like to lounge around in their words but it's so fast paced on *Gilmore Girls* and it just works. The comedy comes from the fast-paced timing, the brilliant writing, and the commitment to playing it real. That's the Palladino style: faster, funnier, louder. You have to catch up with all the other actors who have been doing that for a long time. I was aware of the show already, but when I got the part I started watching to get the style of the show. It helps to have that knowledge so when you get on set no one has to teach you anything. You just show up, and know your job.

At the time, I was playing keyboards in several cover and tribute bands. My band had a gig on December 18th, 2004 and I got a call from my agent saying that I was shooting *Gilmore Girls* the same day as the gig. I told him I had a gig, and he said I had to do it. It was a night shoot too, and my first gig, so I had to cancel it. My acting career came first. That night shoot was the firelight festival, when Liz and her friends came back from the high school reunion. It was a lot of fun to film.

On that first day, I remember driving on to the Warner Bros lot. When I got there, I was told to park in the big parking structure there and was asked if I know where Stars Hollow is. They directed me, but the directions were complicated. I walked through the set of the backlot, and all of a sudden I turned the corner and I saw the gazebo. There were cameras everywhere, and everybody was there. It was this bustling film set, and I just thought, this is awesome. My sister was in the industry, and a sound man approached me as soon as I got onto the set and said, "You're Judi Dolan's sister!". I felt immediately welcome. Then, of course, you have to check in with the first Assistant Director and they take you to your trailer. After I dropped off my things in my trailer I went to hair and makeup and then got lost trying to find my trailer. I was knocking on the wrong trailers, on the wrong set, and wasn't sure if I would make it back. I finally ran into Dan

Palladino and he pointed me in the right direction so I got dressed, and walked back to set with Dan. That was my first day of shooting.

A year later, my agent said I had been booked for *Gilmore Girls* again. I hadn't auditioned for it, so I thought it was odd. I called Dan and asked, "did you do this?" He said he was directing the episode, and wanted to put me back in as the same character. He did that four or five times, over several seasons, so I would just pop up here and there. It was just amazing. I never knew if I would come back on the show, so it was always a nice surprise when I got a call and asked to be back on. It's kind of fun as an actor when that happens because it makes you feel that they trust you. You've already done the work, and you know who your character is. I felt like I was being given a gift every time I was called back. After my character became recurring, I started getting all this fan mail from fans of *Gilmore Girls*. I do the voice of Princess Leia for a lot of animated *Star Wars* and I go on the road to do conventions but people often know me from *Gilmore Girls*. It is so heartwarming that this character has sustained for so long. It was really a great experience. Sean Gunn and I are still friends to this day. We still see each other on the convention circuit, and Dan and I are lifelong friends. It was a fantastic experience.

Probably my favourite episode to shoot was the episode when Kathleen's character Liz was getting married to Michael Deloise's character TJ. We were in Luke's Diner and we—her best friends—had organised a stripper for her. We were there for a couple of days, shooting with the same group of girls, so I was happy to be on another episode. By that time, we knew each other and there was a real sense of family. When you are on set for 12 hours, sitting with them, acting with them, and getting to know them, it's easy to become close very quickly. That's why when people work on a series it becomes your family, because that is who you are spending all your time with. You get to know them, you share your secrets with them, and you come to depend on them.

The stripper scene was so fun to film because it was a round table of all the girls talking about guys, and about TJ, and then the stripper came in. By that time I was more settled in, and familiar with the other girls in the group. I was more familiar with how they worked, and how the director worked, so it was more comfortable.

The guy who played the stripper in that episode was an actor, but I also clearly identified him as a dancer. I was a dancer myself for years: tap, ballet, and jazz. I worked in a theme park as a dancer in the kids shows. I wore costumes for *Rugrats, The Land Before Time, The Flintstones,* and *Rocky and Bullwinkle.* That led me to getting cast on kids primetime television shows. I was able to dance and act in a costume, and I had done television as a regular person, so I did 69 episodes of one series, and 50 episodes of another series. I then got cast in *Beverly Hills Cop 3* with Eddie Murphy. Since the movie was based in a theme park, I was cast as one of the characters in the theme park. I was initially cast in the film as just a character to walk around the theme park, but I wanted to show the director, John Landis, that we could dance in costume. I organised a meeting with him, and did a tap dance. After the meeting, he came up with the idea to write a scene where some of the theme park characters would be dancing on stage, and Edie Murphy would come up onto the stage and dance with us to get away from being chased. It was so thrilling to have a whole scene created just because I was prepared to dance in costume and show him what I could do. I still get residuals for that film.

My other acting jobs didn't have the energy and family vibe that *Gilmore Girls* offered, on that warm, inviting Stars Hollow set. While there was definitely that sense of family, everyone on the set had a job to do, and was serious about doing that job well. Amy had a budget and she had to stay within the WB's guidelines and get the job done as quickly and efficiently as possible. This meant that if someone screwed up their lines or their blocking, the whole set would have to stop, cut, and redo the shot. This often leads the cast and crew to go into overtime, so there was a tension there around budget constraints, and a pressure to stay on schedule. On this show there is also a lot of what's called 'coverage'. The same scene will be filmed multiple times in different ways—close up, master shot, over the shoulder—and the actors had to be on top of their game and know their lines, and blocking to nail it every time.

On the sidewalk outside Luke's diner they have tables and chairs to sit in while you are waiting for the scenes to start. I remember sitting in one waiting for them to call the actors. You have to be ready. If they have to look for you because you have to go to the bathroom, or to craft services to eat, then that also creates tension. Actors sometimes get a bad rap. We have a lot of lines to learn and if someone is constantly trying to talk to us and we are trying to learn our lines to please the studio and the directors, we will often brush them off to focus on our work, and that does often result in getting called a snob, labelled unfriendly, or something similar. The reality is, if we don't do a good job, we won't get hired again, so we are focusing. That's the beauty of having a trailer. It's somewhere to go and study your lines and not get distracted.

I remember a scene with Lauren Graham (Lorelai) where she had a lot of dialogue. It was one long speech that was really fast and I was standing right next to her when she was saying it. She did one take and then missed a line, and so she repeated the whole dialogue to herself to make sure she had it down. If someone had talked to her right then, it would have broken her concentration. As well as all that concentrating, you then have to let it go and act natural once the camera rolls, and you have to remember where to move. There is a lot of stuff going on in actors' heads that they need to remember, and focusing on their craft has to come first.

Initially, I wasn't aware of the impact of *Gilmore Girls* on the fans until I started getting fan mail. It was amazing to me that they knew who I was. Some of these fans had bought the boxed set and gone through the credits, writing down names and contacting everyone in it. When I joined the convention circuit as Princess Leia, fans started bringing screenshots from *Gilmore Girls* for me to sign and wanted to talk about my role on the show. This is 15 years after the show. At that point, I realised this was going to last me a lifetime. I'm doing a convention in a couple of weeks and they are advertising me as a *Gilmore Girls* character. While the box set changed things, streaming has changed things even more, and information available on the internet such as IMDB has made it so much easier to track actors down.

When the revival was announced I texted Daniel Palladino and told him I was available. He was busy. Him and Amy did *Bunheads*, and then *The Marvelous Mrs. Maisel* in New York, and they never looked back. I didn't want to overstep my bounds. Not everyone went back. They had specific reasons for doing the revival, and had specific characters they wanted to bring back, so it wasn't my place to try and impinge on that. Friends of mine did get asked back—including Aris Alvarado who played Caesar—and I was so happy for them.

Gilmore Girls was such a success, and continues to have this amazing following, because of the relationship between Lorelai and Rory. The single mom and the daughter and the best friendship that they had was really appealing. It was also how we got to watch Rory grow up in the situations they were in, owning the hotel, the grandparents and those family situations. Of course the comedy of it was also an appealing element. The comedy was fast paced, quick witted, and happened in real situations in life that people can relate to. People wanted to sit on the couch, and watch another family go through these things and see them come out of the other side. Of course the community in the show is also so appealing. Stars Hollow is a small community where everybody knows everybody and everyone is different. There are odd people, different roles, crazy people, and mean people. It encompassed all of that. I think people can relate to it.

Now, I continue to work as an actor, and I'm in several rock tribute and cover bands playing keyboard. I have done a lot of voice overs for video games, animated series', commercials, a lot of little movies, and some other television series'. I have done a lot of Princess Leia projects and that has taken off. I am still friends with Kathleen Wilhoite who played Liz, Aris, Sean (Kirk) and John (Brian). John did a series called *The Holmes* and we worked together again on that. Sean also had a play reading at his house so we all went over there and read for it. We are all one big happy family. We call each other up, and are just there for each other. Kind of like the *Gilmore Girls*.

A.J. Tesler

Rob/Bo

I was originally cast in *Gilmore Girls* as a student in the spring break episode. We shot the episode down at the Sea Sprite Motel on the beach. I had been called in to audition for the show a couple of times, and hadn't gotten those roles, but casting directors Jami Rudofsky and Mara Casey were keen to find something for me on the show. I was excited when I went in for that last audition and finally got the part.

For that episode, I was so far in the background, my parents couldn't even see me when they watched it. I can't see myself either, but I can hear my voice. After that episode, I got a call that the show wanted me back for a different role—a bellman at the Dragonfly Inn. There was a space for a moving set piece in the Dragonfly Inn scenes, because Michel couldn't be everywhere at once. The same was true of Sookie in the kitchen, so they brought in David Greenman to be one of the moving parts in the kitchen scenes. My role was to be present when Michel wasn't, and to move the action along in scenes at the Dragonfly. I filmed a total of seven episodes, one on location, and the rest on the soundstage that was the Inn.

It was always nerve wracking trying to be word perfect, especially when working with such long scripts. I had very few lines and shooting was always so efficient, so I was very conscious of being fast and getting it right the first time. Despite these challenges, everybody on the show was so encouraging, and nice to work with. It was such a treat to work with Lauren Graham (Lorelai) and Melissa McCarthy (Sookie). They were both so warm and so welcoming. Yanic Truesdale (Michel) was nice too. They were all sweet, wonderful people, and were very complimentary to me when I was a young actor, just starting out.

The highlight of working on *Gilmore Girls* for me, was shooting the episode with the Zydeco band. The actor who had been cast as the leader of the band—Tahmus Rounds—really played the washboard, and had great stories about his time touring in the Blue Man Group.

My most challenging time on the show was an episode we had to shoot after I was still recovering from eye surgery. My eye was supposed to have healed by the time of my next episode and it hadn't. It was quite visibly bloodshot. They ultimately decided not to shoot me too close, as it was obvious something was going on there.

My last episode was the funeral for Michel's dog. I had one line and then sat around the rest of the day, waiting. In that scene I was sitting next to a beagle, a poodle, and a pug. I must have been waiting on set for 12 hours. When the episode aired, it panned from the beagle to the poodle and then cut right before the camera got to me. I had sat on set for the entire day, looking sad at this doggie funeral, only to be cut out. That's when I decided to look into making my career focused around entertainment instead of acting.

Despite this, I had a really nice time on the show. I'm genuinely thrilled there are fans that are just as invested in *Gilmore Girls* now as they were then. It feels cool to be part of something that has been such a cultural touchdown for so long.

After the show I founded the Independent Television Festival, which is now in its 15th year, and have produced and directed feature films, shorts, and television. My directorial debut was *Magnolia's Hope*, a documentary about my daughter's struggles with Rett Syndrome. I have two children now, and have become very active in the advocacy space for Rett syndrome. I also recently just directed a feature called *Hero Mode* with Sean Astin and Mira Sorvino which came out in 2021.

Gilmore Girls was a great show. That wholesome relationship between mother and daughter was an important one because it defines people in so many different ways. It's a show that mothers like to watch with their daughters because they get something out of it—even if it's just a broader understanding of life's ups and downs, and what people go through. The show really found its footing in talking to multiple generations of women in a way that felt authentic to how women communicate and relate to each other. It was ahead of its time in terms of its voice because we are still now trying to find stories that feature strong female characters in a real way. This show was doing this 20 years ago. A strong, female, single mom character, and a daughter who grew up to be a strong female character wasn't a thing that was on television back then. It was always about the men. I think the Palladino's did a fantastic job of telling the story in such a distinctive and powerful way.

Tara Platt

Shelly

My husband Yuri and I were both actors, who moved to Los Angeles for auditioning. My agent at the time had an audition for *Gilmore Girls*. I was extremely nervous but also really wanted to be on the show. I was already a fan of the show, and one of the things I loved about it was the pattern of talking a-mile-a-minute. I tend to do that myself—I talk quickly, and I always have something to say, so that

Gilmore Girls rhythm appealed to me. When you are auditioning for a show you tend to rewatch it, because you want to refresh your mind about how the angles work, and be sure you understand the tone of the show. You also want to be sure that you can fit into the cadence and rhythm of it.

    I got the audition, and I was super excited to go into the casting room. I had met the casting directors at a workshop once before. There are workshops in this industry where casting directors will come and work with you, and it's a great opportunity for actors to get a bit of feedback, and work with those casting directors who are casting for the current shows.

    The lines I was given for the audition were for the scene that I was eventually cast in. This is not always the case for auditions, but in this instance I was able to audition for my exact part and scene. I got my lines and worked on them, and was really proud of myself because I had given myself the goal of really creating the space. In the scene, I give a presentation of this teacher that is really revered and I am really presenting to everyone that had come to the book signing. Because of this setting, I decided that I wasn't going to pick one person and aim my audition at them. I was going to do it for the room. So, I did, and I got a callback, and I did it for the room again at the callback. This time there were about 15 people in the room and I actually got some laughs during my scene, but I thought, I'm just gonna take it to mean that they were responding to what I was saying about the character of Asher Fleming. Afterwards, I felt that the audition had gone really well and was thrilled that I had booked it. I got the scene sent to me, and it was the same scene that I had done for the audition. I showed up on set and they were shooting really quickly. I hadn't done a lot of television work at that point, so I wasn't familiar with how fast or slow these things normally go because I didn't have a point of reference. I was directed to a soundstage where they would be filming the scene and when I got there I was amazed because they had constructed a whole library on the sound stage. On screen, it looks like it's filmed in a real library but it had been built by the production crew.

When I got there, Michael York (Asher Fleming) hadn't arrived yet, so I got to watch another scene being filmed where Rory is talking to Paris in the library, by a bookshelf. In this scene, the two of them are supposed to be watching the scene that I was about to film. Because of the way that television is shot, you don't need everybody in the scene all at once because you are filming things like close up shots, and counter shots. You only have to shoot the section you are shooting, so you don't need all the actors on the other side. So when Paris and Rory were talking, the front of the room where Asher talks was empty. So, I got some time to hover and watch everything take place, and it made me feel like, "I can do this!" At that stage I was still new, and it really helped my nerves to watch that scene filmed before mine.

After watching them do the scene, the director came over and said, "you're my girl?" I wasn't sure what that meant, but I enthusiastically said yes! The director said Michael will be here in a minute, so I started running the lines in my head, and trying to mentally prepare myself to do a good job. Michael came out and was very nice and polite. We started shooting, and I was a little nervous. After one take, the director called me over. He said, "you did a great job, but…I want you to make Michael blush." I didn't even know how to react to that—being asked to make this acting veteran blush.

> *"Me? You want me to make Michael York blush? What can I possibly say to make Michael York blush!?!*

I had no idea what I could say to him. The only thing I had said to him was "hello", so I have no sense of history with him. I considered asking him on a date, but then figured that wouldn't make him blush. I was panicking in my head. There's a part in the scene where I whisper something in his ear. This time, when I leaned in to whisper something, I said "I'm not wearing any panties", and he had a visible reaction. After a few takes, I think he started to catch on that I had been told to make him blush, because I had been changing things up and trying different things to make him blush.

The biggest challenge was the feeling that I had to hold my own next to this veteran actor. I didn't want to look like I was green standing next to Michael York. In that scene, I am announcing his book signing and I was supposed to be the president of his book club so it needed to look natural. Overcoming my own humanness and nerves was difficult. I didn't want to let my nervousness get the best of me. Especially after the director told me to make him blush. If anything, I was blushing.

Growing up, we never had a television. My dad got rid of the T.V. when I was little. Because of that, I don't always turn the T.V. on to watch something, so I'm not really the right audience for the work that I do—not that I don't enjoy shows, but it's not my 'go-to'. I tend to pick up books and read instead.

My decision to become an actor actually started as a child, when I decided to be a neurosurgeon. My dad was training to become a doctor, and when I saw how much schooling he had to go through, I decided maybe I could just play a doctor. I went and saw a lot of theatre with mom as a child, and we went to a show that had a large chorus of kids. I thought it looked like so much fun, and just wanted to be a part of it. Mom told me it would be a lot of work, but I could do it if I wanted. She had done theatre in college, so she talked to me about what was involved, and I agreed to do it. She found me an audition, for a play called *Wait Until Dark*. It was kind of like a crime drama, and the cast is all adults apart from one child. It takes place in an apartment where someone breaks into a blind woman's home, but it's a dark apartment, so the person who breaks in, and the resident are on equal footing and there is a stand-off. The child character that I auditioned for was the upstairs neighbour, who sees what is happening in the apartment downstairs. I ended up booking the job, and that led me to do more and more theatre including musicals. I went on to go to college to get a degree in theatre, and I studied at the London Academy of Theatre as part of my training, getting my Bachelor of Fine Arts at Rutgers University. Then I moved to New York, and started auditioning for television, film, and theatre. I booked a couple of soap operas but I was also auditioning for student films and independent films. I met my husband Yuri in a student film, where we played love interests. We ended up eloping and moving to Los Angeles, so when we got here, we started doing television and film. Yuri actually ended up on *Gilmore Girls* himself. I booked *Gilmore Girls* a couple of years before Yuri did, but we were both auditioning for any work we could get. At the same time, we really needed to make a living, and we weren't sure how to do that without temping and waiting tables our whole lives. At that time, I had this epiphany. I said to Yuri, "Who is in cartoons and commercials? Who voices the characters?" It was so funny that I would think of it, and the person who grew up watching cartoons didn't, but at that point we realised that voice work might be how we make a living from our acting skills. Once we made that switch, we started working quite quickly. Our career in voice over soon took over, while we were still auditioning for television and film. Our IMDB pages now have large amounts of voice over work interspersed with television and film appearances. I booked a feature film with Halle Berry called *The Call*. Yuri and I still do acting in any, and every, form—theatre, television and films. We are just actors trying to act in any medium we possibly can—whether that is in front of a microphone, a camera, or a live audience. That's also the reason we started our own production company and our own publishing company. At the heart of it, We are storytellers and we want to be storytellers, and if we aren't in someone else's story, telling their story, then we want to create and produce our own stories and bring those into the world.

Booking *Gilmore Girls* was a helpful credit to have on my resume, and it definitely helped my demo reel. Having that on there meant people could see that I had actually done on-screen work.

There's nothing wrong with one-liner roles, but sometimes those roles don't show off your skills. Showing people how you act and react in a scene is harder to show with smaller roles. For the longest time I had the *Gilmore Girls* scene at the very front of my acting demo reel because it was with Michael York and it was a notable, popular show on the air. Now that the show is older, it's further into my reel, but I was really grateful for it for a long time, for its ability to showcase my acting work.

I have had several instances of people reaching out to me and saying they recognise me from *Gilmore Girls*. People in the fan community for the show are very kind—they have a warmth about them and a sense of camaraderie. I have noticed that if someone comments about *Gilmore Girls*, a lot of others will join in. There's a real sense of community within this fan base which does not apply to all fan bases. In my experience, it's always been very warm and lovely. *Gilmore Girls* fans have a familiarity and memory for the show that is kind of amazing.

Gilmore Girls is a show that has really clearly defined characters with really specific needs, and wants, and desires, and relationships. The audience really can't help but get invested in it, because they care about the outcome of what happens to these characters. This show created strong characters and it's very easy to either put yourself in those shoes or know someone like that and so watching it is so enjoyable. It was easy to relate to who these characters were, and easy to understand why they were doing what they were doing. You start to think of them as friends or someone you care about. And—just like in life—you want to know how things are going to pan out for them. As an audience, we also can't help but put ourselves into the storylines. We watch, asking ourselves how we would feel, or how we would act in that situation. Television in a way, is like holding up a mirror to our own lives, our own loves, our own experiences, our own humanity.

Chris Flanders

Shel

When I got the call for my audition on *Gilmore Girls,* I almost didn't go, as my fiance's sister was having an engagement party. My fiance told me that I should go to the audition, so I'm glad I did because if I hadn't, I might have gotten onto the show later, but I wouldn't have gotten the part of Shel.

I was not a fan and regular watcher of the show before my audition, but I knew what it was. When a new season of a show would come out, I would tape the first episode, and then set it aside for two weeks. If the show got cancelled, I wouldn't watch it, but if it stayed on, I would watch it to familiarise myself with the shows that were on the air. This gave me a basic knowledge of the shows I would be auditioning for. So, I had seen the pilot for *Gilmore Girls*. As an actor, it's very difficult for me to watch any shows for leisure. I pull things apart in different ways—the storylines, the accents, the way people pronounce things. I hear, and see it all, and I am always evaluating everything. It drives my girlfriend nuts.

I had known one of the casting directors for *Gilmore Girls*—Jami Rudofsky—forever. Jami and I met in graduate school. I got my MFA from the University of California San Diego and she had been the babysitter for the heading of the acting programme's children at that time. I came in and did the audition. They said it was great, but asked me to do it one more time, faster. At the end of the audition, they told me that if I was called back, I would need to pick up the pace even more. They don't do callbacks as much anymore, but back then you might have to go through a series of callbacks to get a part. My callback was actually later the same day, on the Warner Bros lot, and I ended up getting the part.

My scene was filmed on the Warner Bros lot at night. My episode was towards the end of the season—the second or third episode before the end. Usually by the end of the season the cast can be pretty tired, and feeling really 'done', but I didn't get that sense on the set for my episode. I told the makeup lady that I was engaged and she must have mentioned something to Lauren Graham (Lorelai) who asked me about it. She was very chatty and nice, and very sweet.

Melissa McCarthy (Sookie) was lovely as well. I remember everyone being very nice, and very friendly.

I also chatted with Scott Patterson who played Luke. He told me he was going to rent a house in Malibu for the summer as a vacation house for his family, where they would spend a couple of months out on the beach. I thought that was a really wise use of money. When you are an actor you are barely home, so I thought it was great that he was going to invest in this vacation time when he was between shooting seasons. He was definitely the least actor-y. He was a pro baseball player before *Gilmore Girls* so he was kind of a jock, and quite stoic.

I played classical guitar in college and around 2001 I picked up the electric guitar. I always bring a guitar with me onto set because there is a lot of sitting around and waiting, so I like to take the opportunity to practise during those times. I was playing Jimi Hendrix's *Red House* in my trailer, while I waited to get called for my scene. When I finally got called, my scene took only a couple of hours to shoot, but it was a fun little scene. That show had tons of those fun little scenes because the writing was so good, and it was great to be a part of one of them. I had friends that had worked with some of the main cast members and had reported very negative experiences, but that was not my experience at all.

I have a great recollection of my time on the show because I have kept notes throughout my career. I'm great with faces but I can't remember people's names for the life of me. I note down everything—auditions, what I read, the date, the casting people, and the role. If I book the job, I note down what I got paid for it, the episode I was in, and the director. I keep notes of every show I have done, and everything I have read for. It's just a way to keep track over the years, and have something to refer to when I prepare for auditions. It's been a helpful system for when I get in the audition room, because I can remember names that I might have otherwise forgotten. I also note down feedback I was given, and the tone and pace of each show. The producers of a show usually have the whole script and know the tone and pace of the show, but auditionees don't have all that information. Most shows have a style to them and *Gilmore Girls*—and other work by the Palladino's like *The Marvelous Mrs. Maisel*—has a specific style to it. If I get a call back to a show, I like to be prepared. I keep notes because you never know when these things are going to come in handy.

My time on *Gilmore Girls* has led to some random things over the years. When my wife and I got married we went to Costa Rica on a 'booze cruise'. My wife told some young girls on the cruise I was on *Gilmore Girls* and they all went nuts. I also met a fan who sent me a letter asking for a signed headshot. Years later he reached out to me via Facebook and was going to be in *Los Angeles*. I was working at Paramount, so I got him and his mother a gate pass with a private tour of the studios. I have given him three or four tours over the years when it's worked out. Each time I've been able to walk him on to different sets and show him things you wouldn't see on an actual tour. It's kind of a fun *Gilmore Girls* fan connection.

Gilmore Girls continues to be popular because it's so unique. I remember in grad school, having a teacher who invited us over to watch a 1940s movie at her house—*The Philadelphia Story*. It was full of snappy repartee, and I loved it. It was fun, quippy, and I thought it was great watching. It was all dialogue and innuendo, and that's how *Gilmore Girls* is. Most television—even if it's well written—is not like this. The Palladino's have of course done it again with *The Marvelous Mrs. Maisel*. It's so verbose, and specific in its writing. The Palladino shows are also full of quirky characters. My character of Shel was one of them, but every episode had an oddball. My girlfriend watched *Bunheads* and there it was again—those oddball characters, and that quirky tone. There's also a nostalgia to the show. It takes you back to an identifying time in your life.

I have fond memories of my time on *Gilmore Girls,* and it was fun. Sometimes small parts aren't that interesting, but this one was memorable. I remember how nice everyone was on set, and not all shows are like that. Everyone I dealt with—from the costumers, to casting, to the leads—were as sweet as could be and I think that probably comes out on screen. I've been on a few tense sets, where everyone is waiting to get out of there, but this was not one of them.

Alan Loayza

Colin Mcrae

My *Gilmore Girls* journey started when I had met with casting directors, Jami Rudofsky and Mara Casey. My first meeting with them was at something that's called a 'General Audition' or a 'General Meeting', which is when your agent or your manager tells different casting directors about you, particularly if you are newly signed with them. I was fairly new to acting and I hadn't met them before, so my manager set me up with them. The general meeting was basically a day that they take to sit down with five or six actors and have conversations with them—with no scripts, and no roles in mind. It's just a space to have a conversation so that they can see who's out there. I think these meetings are usually held in the casting director's downtime, and just helps them to plan and be thinking about what talent might be available for upcoming work. So, that was my first step onto the show. I met with them, and the three of us really hit it off. We were laughing so hard. It was kind of an instant connection with the three of us and I was starting to wonder if we were going to make something happen here. Before I left the meeting, they said something very nice to me. "We haven't even seen you act yet, but we already know you are going to be right for this show." It was very nice that they felt that way, just from having a conversation with me.

After this meeting, they brought me in for every role, and I didn't book any of them. I went in and auditioned for about five different roles, including the role of Marty at one point, and several other different boyfriends. There was a stage where they were kind of putting different guys in Rory's view to see what stuck and so I kept hoping to land one of those parts. After a couple of years, I was feeling worn out with the process. I was tired of going to these auditions and not getting a part. I'd be called for an audition for *Gilmore Girls* and think, 'okay…I'm going to drive all the way to Burbank, and they are going to tell me I haven't been chosen for this role, and then I have to drive all the way back home." So on the day that I was called up to go in and audition for the role of Colin, I was annoyed. I had an attitude when I walked in the door for my audition. So I walk in, and Amy Sherman-Palladino knows my name. She's never hired me, so this should seem flattering and cool, but it wasn't, because in my head I was screaming, "Are you gonna hire me, lady!??!" Mara and Jamie were there as well, which was weird because they were my friends by that point, and I had seen them a zillion times because they are really good to me and kept bringing me in for every role.

What I didn't know at this audition, was that this was the role I would come to have. This was the role that was calling to me. The role of Colin was perfect for me, and for my mood on that day. Of course, that's often how these things work. As soon as I think I'm not going to get it, I get it. When I left they said to me that this role might not be a big part. They weren't sure at that point how many appearances Colin would have on the show, and it could be just the one. There was also some concern that the show might get cancelled around that time, because of how long it had been running. They had been trying to bring me in for bigger roles which was nice, but Jamie and Mara were so keen to get me in, that they decided just to do it.

They brought me in for Colin and I just nailed the attitude. I remember Amy saying "perfect. That was perfect!" and I knew I had brought that attitude that she saw in the audition and done exactly what was needed. That first day we shot Colin's first episode where we treated Marty like garbage by the coffee stand. It was a really weird experience for me because I knew I was playing a mean guy. It's a scary thing to do when you're starting out acting, because people really start internalising that—look at Joffrey Baratheon from *Game of Thrones*. People hate that character. I read my lines and thought, 'Oh, god, this guy's a dick'. I know how to play that so well, but, if I'm too effective, people start writing things about the character online. Not long after my episode, I came across a blog on *Gilmore Girls* and I read this one quick thing about me. It was horrible. The writer of this blog hated me so much—they hated the character. They started getting personal about my looks and characteristics that were more related to me than the character of Colin. After that I decided that I wouldn't be reading any more reviews, or looking online at the feedback that Colin got.

I'm completely the opposite of Colin in a lot of ways and I tend to be hyper aware and cautious of not being 'that guy' in life. I once played a role in a gothic stage play where I played a teenage kid in drama class, whose Dad treated him like complete garbage. And, as the abused sometimes do, he went on to abuse his girlfriend and ended up getting her pregnant when they were both only 15. The boy I played the character of didn't want to have anything to do with the baby, and was just an awful guy. Of course, as the play goes along you see that his Dad is the one who made him that way, which kind of justifies the behaviour of the son. It was one of the coolest roles I have played, but I remember after the show, my friends and family would come up to me, but nobody else would. The other cast members, and people who came to see the show used to sneer at me. And this was a role—a character. I'm not that person. It made me feel like I was doing a good job—I had done what I was supposed to do so effectively that people couldn't see me as anything other than the character I was portraying. I think that experience has always stayed with me, and when I came to approach the character of Colin I didn't want it to take years to shake off that negativity. But Colin isn't so dramatic and dark as that character was. He was self-centred, but harmless for the most part. Eventually, I felt like there was a likeability to be found in Colin and I tried to give shape to that because it became clear that Colin was going to be in it for the long haul. Colin was supposed to be three episodes only and it turned into two seasons and a Netflix revival. It was fun—a lot of fun. It was a blessing.

Gilmore Girls was showing on the WB at the time, before it became the CW. It was the heyday of teen shows in the early 2000s—Party of Five, Charmed—there were so many shows directed at the high school and early college age group. *Gilmore Girls* was in that landscape, but bubbled up and became its own thing and became like the flagship show for the network. But to me, I was a young guy in my 20s getting out of college from theatre school, wanting to act in all kinds of things, and I had a lot of ideas about what roles I might want to take on, as a young male actor working in the industry. *Gilmore Girls* just wasn't on my radar at the time. When I got the role, I wasn't even that familiar with the show. I knew what it was, and I understood the rhythm and the quick clip pace, but I didn't really understand it. It hadn't drawn me in at that point. At the table read for my third episode. I was watching Lauren Graham (Lorelai) spitting through this chunky monologue. She had this funny line—kind of a dirty joke—which she said really fast out of the side of her mouth, and it was just a throwaway. She just kept on going. At that moment I think I understood what the show was. I understood its density, and the layers of it. I realised then that the lines are ploughed through, and that the rhythm is the language of this show.

After the revival I signed up to attend the fan festival, and at that point I realised that I would have to watch it because the fans attending would know the show (and my character) better than I do. I knew they would remember my episodes better than me—they would remember my lines better than me. I remember someone asking me at the fan fest about a line and I couldn't even remember it. So, I sat down and watched it and realised after watching the pilot that I had missed the hook of the show, which was Lorelei trying to get Rory into school and not having the money and having to crawl back to her parents, and her parents blackmailing her to have dinner every Friday. I had no idea that that's what the show is about. I thought the show was about Lorelai having had Rory too young. Yeah, that is the show but the real show—the real mechanism, the real structure of the show was that she had to go to dinner every Friday no matter what. That's how she's able to send Rory to school and I thought that was kind of a simple, cool little mechanism. Now, I love the show. I get it. I totally get it.

When I did my watch through, I skipped season 7. The Life and Death Brigade were absent from that season, and so was Amy. Out of respect for Amy, I just decided not to watch it. I always tell everybody I relate with Emily, which is so weird. I think Lorelai makes a lot of dumb decisions. I think she makes a lot of choices that are very impulsive. She's in the right for a lot of it, but sometimes I find myself wondering why she had to go and do something that created drama, or caused a problem. Emily is right for a lot of it too. She might be older and crabby, but sometimes she is right and Lorelai isn't, which adds to the complexity of the drama.

What made this show different from other work I have done, was the family that I acquired through working on *Gilmore Girls*. While you spend a lot of time with the people you work with, on this show we spent a lot of time together outside of work as well. It was a good vibe all around, and that's why we are all so close. There are no hard feelings or anything between most of the people that I was spending time with, and it was just such a great feeling. In fact, I met with Brenda Maben, who worked in the wardrobe on *Gilmore Girls*, out in Paris. We got some lunch and went to a museum and hung out. She's very cool. She's a very carefree lady.

Gilmore Girls was also a great experience because the actors were really good. Being on set with good actors—just doing anything professional on that level—is always a treat. Especially for me, coming from theatre school, auditioning and doing smaller parts. While I was doing those things, I was waiting for a part to come along that put me into an environment where I was working with talented, trained actors, and that's what *Gilmore Girls* was for me. They really cared about good actors on that show, and it felt right. Everybody was really sharp, and wanted to do the work. There was nobody just 'phoning in'—everyone was taking it seriously, wanting to make the show good. These were all people who cared about the craft.

There were a lot of fun times on that show—a lot of good memories. The most fun to shoot was the episode, *You Jump, I Jump, Jack.* That was a big episode, and is a lot of people's favourite episode. It wasn't shot at the Warner Bros lot like most episodes. The studio is still wonderful and fantasy driven. Walking around Warner Brothers is fantastic. But we did that episode at Griffith Park, and the Disney ranch which is where they shot things like *Pleasantville* and a lot of beautiful movies with picturesque lakes and trees. Our trailers were brought up for that episode as well as all the crew and it was a wonderful time. Kenny Ortega was the director and he is a directing giant. What I mean by that is he has directed things like Olympics opening ceremonies, and Michael Jackson tours. So, having Kenny directing that episode felt like working with royalty. We also had all these toys and big cranes, so that was fun. In the episode, the Life and Death Brigade is camping, or 'glamping', and in a way it was like camping while we shot the episode. One night I remember we were all hanging out at the top of Griffith Park, playing guitar, singing, and hanging out with cast and crew members. When I left the set, I couldn't believe that it had been work. It just felt like a chill hang-out session with some really great people. That was one of the best days I've ever had.

Another really fun episode was the episode where we go to Logan's to play cards. Now, that was a fun day. We were sitting there for eight hours, just playing poker with a big camera on a crane and our faces kind of moving around. There were a lot of jokes and laughs that day, a lot of silliness. Alexis and I kind of bonded over the fact that we are both white looking Latino Americans. She is a very chill person. We went to the movies to see *Team America* and we drank beers in the theatre. That was hilarious. On another day we went out for Cuban food.

We all got along, we still do. Of course, there were some 'diva moments', but not really by the leads, and they weren't a big deal. In most sets there are those kinds of moments. If they did happen, we would just roll our eyes and laugh—it was never anything too serious. I tend to get frustrated at people holding up the set for a little thing. I'm a much more self sufficient, behind the camera guy. I'm all about teamwork and getting dirty to make that beautiful shot and that lens frame over there look great. Everything else on set could be a mess, but I'm going to work to get that one piece looking nice. After all, that's the illusion that we are trying to create on a show or a film.

The other thing that makes my time on the show stand out from my other experiences is the fans. The show never dies. There aren't a lot of shows out there that keep getting bigger, long after they have aired. The revival was years ago and we are still talking about *Gilmore Girls*. It's still playing on everyone's televisions and laptops in the background. Fans watch *Gilmore Girls* inbetween everything, and keep talking about it, and that's special. Obviously, it's a cult classic—it has a cult following, and a big one. I'll be out in public and be recognised for my time on the show. It's nice to be part of one of those shows that's going to live in people's memories for a long, long time. I like being a part of that. I liked being a part of a show that makes people feel so good.

I work in film, so I'm always constantly analysing what makes the thing work. *Gilmore Girls* has so many different elements to it, that work. There's something about the speed—this is actually something that's very surface level, but there's something about the speed of what they're saying. It's not only fast, it's dense. Because of the density of it, every time you hear it, or say it, there is something new to get out of it. Of course, fans have watched it so many times, that they have memorised all of the little things. I think there's something that's interesting about the nostalgia that this show holds because it's starting to get a little dated in some ways—especially some of the references. The show is peppered with so many references from that era, and the era before. But, that's what gives the show its density. There is so much to get from it. I also think that the actors' performances are comforting—their voices, and the storylines. It is a dramatic show and these dramatic storylines drive the plot forward but they aren't scary. The drama in *Gilmore Girls* is safe. It's easy to leave on. I also think there is something to be said about the relatability of the three main female characters. It's a great show for moms who relate to the drama. They relate to raising kids, having a relationship with their own mother, getting along, and not getting along. It's relatable. Single moms love this show—I see single mom fans all the time. They are raising their kids alone and naming their kids Rory or Lorelai. It's just had such a huge cultural impact on people.

The other contributing factor in why this show doesn't die is because of Netflix. I've been watching a lot of reaction videos on YouTube—it's kind of been my guilty pleasure lately. Most of them are created by millennials who have never seen some of the best movies of our lifetimes—things like *Schindler's List, The Shawshank Redemption, Back to the Future, Star Wars*—all the biggest things. And they're doing it with television shows, too, including *Gilmore Girls*. These videos have been made possible, or at least easier, by the series being added to Netflix. John Cabrera who plays Brian on *Gilmore Girls* has just done his own reaction series on Clubhouse which has been quite popular with the fans. A lot of new fans are discovering the show through Netflix, and so it continues to grow its fan base all the time. I feel like 50-60% of people who start it will get into it and see why it's so popular. Of course, the revival was a Netflix series, so in a way Netflix breathed new life into the show—both the original run, and the revival.

By the time the revival was announced, I was working at Buzzfeed as a producer. Buzzfeed makes a lot of lists for their content, and a lot of the lists—as many fans will know—are about *Gilmore Girls*. One particular list, "20 Definitive Men of Gilmore Girls" included me, and I just thought, "This is crazy! I've made a Buzzfeed list, and I work here." It was kind of neat. *Gilmore Girls* was added to Netflix along with other shows that were being digitised such as *Full House*. When it was added, Buzzfeed started writing all these articles about *Gilmore Girls'* original run. At that point, I never saw the revival coming.

Then the ATX festival happened, where the *Gilmore Girls* panel took place and everyone started buzzing about whether some sort of reboot was in the works. I remember hearing internally at that time that Amy was thinking about bringing it back, but I figured the odds were slim. It had been so many years since the show had finished. When it was confirmed, I didn't initially know I would be asked back. I was crossing my fingers, of course, but when I didn't hear anything, I figured I wasn't being called back in. A few days later, I got the call that they wanted me to come back in. I hadn't done any acting work in a while. The last thing I had done was acting in a video game. At this point in my life, I am mostly behind the camera and I had to dig really deep into that old 'Colin' headspace. Acting is my real love though, so when I got called to go back to it, I was excited.

My first day on set at the revival was the shot with me on top of the building, with Alexis and Matt golfing. It was the first time I had seen both of them in years, so up on the rooftop, we had our reunion, and it was like no time had passed at all. I met Alexis' husband on the roof too. The revival was the first time I was really able to explore Stars Hollow and the Gilmore world. That's when it felt like I got to be a part of the family even more—not just one of the Yale guys. My role as Colin had previously taken place in a different world than the one that Miss Patty, Kirk, and all of the Stars Hollow characters inhabit. Whenever I read things about the show it's always Stars Hollow and its people that the fans want to meet and hang out with. The revival finally gave me a chance to be a part of that legacy, and connect those two worlds by bringing the Life and Death Brigade to Stars Hollow.

In a way, *Gilmore Girls* gave me a place to start my career. I was at the tail end of auditioning by the time I got the role of Colin. I hadn't given up, but I was burned out and was starting to feel that I should push pause. I felt like I spent most of my time auditioning, memorising pages, and then sitting around waiting for it to be my turn to do those pages. After *Gilmore Girls* I took a long break from entertainment before coming back and getting behind the camera. I started developing a show that my friend wrote into a television show. I met with a production company to pitch the show. I wrote and directed a pilot while I was on *Gilmore Girls* with some actors that I knew, and with a director who was pitching for different networks and trying to get them on the air. I decided to use my leverage from the little people I knew in the industry to get it done. Someone almost bought it but I was too new, so it didn't go anywhere. That was my first attempt at that. We had agents and met with executives at different networks. It was a great experience.

The greatest reward from the show came from the friendships that I have created. I've made friends with the fans, cast, and crew. Those relationships are more than just surface level. In tough times, those people have really been there for me. Nick Holmes who plays Robert, and Tanc Sade who plays Finn, will be my friends forever, and I am also good friends with Nick's dad. They have all had a big impact on me. There are only a handful of shows out there that feel like a friend, and *Gilmore Girls* is one of those. It is bigger than life, and I don't see it ever going away. I will have that forever.

Lee Shallat Chemel

Director and Co-Executive Producer

I was working as a freelance director, and was offered a gig on a later season of *Gilmore Girls*. That's when Amy Sherman-Palladino and I met. We really got along and she liked the way I did things. I listened to her and how she wanted it done. I tried to get the tone and the feeling of the show. I hadn't watched the show before, but I did go back and watch several episodes before directing. There was no streaming in those days, so I asked Amy for her favourite episodes, and which ones she considered the best of the best. I enjoyed it immensely. The writing was so engaging and spontaneous.

When you are a freelance director your agent just sends you on jobs. As a director, I would then spend several days doing preparation. This included looking at the script, the locations, working with the assistant director, prepping when and how you are going to shoot—what angles, working up a shot list, and then the next week you start shooting and each day is set up and you work through your schedule. The aim of your job is to get to the first cut of a film or episode, called the director's cut. When I became the co-executive producer on *Gilmore Girls*, my job increased exponentially because I did the same job, but then also handled rosters, set up the season, and did the producer's cut. I also had to do a lot of the editing—cutting, and reducing time—as well as casting sessions. These new responsibilities were on top of my usual responsibilities as director. There was a huge amount of work. I had two kids in grammar school at the time, so it really felt like a lot.

The first day of filming for me was a big show with a lot of the cast members in it. The episode included a town meeting, so everybody was there. I was so glad to be doing it and I was having a good time and felt really confident about it. Before shooting, I would have a meeting with the main writer. I would articulate how I was thinking of doing it, and we would chat about it. By the time it got to the shoot, I was nervous, because I wanted to understand each actor and how they worked. I wanted to be able to communicate in the right way, and give directions where needed. Lauren and I had a very similar sense of humour and I quickly realised how to work with her. I was able to pick up very quickly how everybody worked. I was very happy that I felt like I blended well with how the show ran.

There were some really fun moments with one episode early on, when the car crashed into Luke's diner. Filming that scene was a huge deal, and it came with a lot of unique challenges. We were going to tear down part of that structure for the scene, but that structure had been on the Warner Bros studio lot forever. It was part of a lot of different shows and movies and we had to get a lot of permissions for that. There were really big lights needed for that shoot, and I had to storyboard the scene very carefully, because we could only shoot it once. The car had to be safe, and while the stuntman did the actual crash, Sean Gunn did all the approaching driving, so lots of set up shots were done, and the crash shot was done last. The Director of Photography suggested we put a camera inside from the diner point of view, looking toward the window as the car crashed into it. I was not happy about letting a camera operator work inside the diner while the car came crashing in, so we put the camera up on sticks without anyone manning it. Things were going well until—in the middle of the shoot—one of the big lights exploded in the heat. That's how hot it was that day, filming outside in the California sun. Thankfully, nobody was injured, but the incident did cause us to shut down filming for about an hour and a half while we replaced it and cleaned up the mess. The scene was otherwise planned so well and for just the accident part we had three cameras rolling. They built a little ramp so it forced the car up towards the window. It was great because the kinds of things I direct don't often have a lot of stunts so it was really fun and everyone had a great time. The final shot looked good and worked out perfectly.

Season 6 turned out to be the last season for Amy. She was upset, I think, when I told her that I wanted to stay. It was her expectation that my loyalty would mean I would not want to do the show without her, and sadly, this ultimately led to a falling out between us. I had to make the best decision for myself professionally, and for my family. I was having a great time and enjoying myself on *Gilmore Girls* and I didn't want that to end. Amy had created a wonderful show and had given me a job that I didn't want to leave.

I became executive producer in the last season and the really challenging thing was that Amy, for the first six seasons, had been the main writer. She influenced every single script. Even though she had assigned writers, she went over every one and rewrote, giving it her own sound. In season 7, it was up to the new table of writers and executive producers to step up to the challenge, because the person who had so much control and influence over so much of it was gone and that was a real challenge for everybody.

By that time, Lauren and Alexis were getting tired. It's a long haul, and a huge job over a long day. One of the shooting protocols for the show dictated that for the wide master, we would shoot as many takes as necessary until the scene was word perfect, even though there would be numerous closer shots for the scene. So I changed that requirement and let directors decide when to move into closer coverage. I did that in hopes of mitigating the exhaustion of the cast and crew.

The last episode was another challenging one, because we had to create a lot of rain. We built a large tent for Rory's going away party, all setting up for Luke and Lorelai to kiss. However, Lauren Graham and Scott Patterson weren't getting along, so the shoot didn't go as smoothly as planned. It had been a tough year for everyone, and they just weren't feeling it. I knew we were going to have to do a big shot for the kiss because Luke and Lorelai were 'end game' and everyone was waiting for it. We had a crane to do the big 'pull up and back' shot. I had a chat with the two of them beforehand, emphasising that it was imperative that they sold this. I was up on the crane with the camera operator and just as we were pulling up, they stopped kissing, before the shot was over. I told them they had to make it work, and make it last until I yelled 'cut!'. We had to do three takes before we got it.

We knew during season 7 that the story had to be completed that year. The news came about half way through the season that whether it would be re-signed or not was up to Lauren and Alexis, and their willingness to return. It was my understanding that Alexis definitely didn't want it to go any further and Lauren was trying to figure it out. If they wanted to continue, it would go forward, and if they didn't, it wouldn't. After Christmas it was announced that the show was done. The network would have definitely done another year or two if the girls had committed to it. After Christmas the writers had to come up with storylines that would take the show to its conclusion.

I have so many good memories of my time on *Gilmore Girls,* but a few specific episodes stand out in my mind. I remember having a really bad case of the flu and we were shooting out on location. I was really sick and I didn't want to give it to anyone else so I sat in my car with a walkie talkie and a monitor, directing from the car. What was really lovely was how everybody did such a great job, rising to the occasion because they knew I was sick. It was a really long walk and talk scene with a lot of dialogue and the cast were great, and so wonderful. It was so nice to see them come together and help me out.

I loved episodes in the little antique shop. Emily Kuroda who plays Mrs. Kim was so much fun to work with. I loved her so much, it was really fun shooting in there because you could shoot over dusty things in the foreground and it was really visual. I also loved the episodes that we shot down at the University of Southern California. Years later, my son went to that school and graduated in 2015, so that place has great memories for our family. Another great episode to film was the episode with the 'knitathon'. Costumers Valerie Campbell, Brenda Maben, and I all knitted things for that episode, because we were experienced knitters. I tend to knit on set while I direct. I make sweaters for babies, or for my family. Valerie was really helpful if I ran into a knitting problem, advising how to fix it.

After *Gilmore Girls* I spent a decade doing a show called *The Middle,* and was in the same job for ten years. It too was a wonderful show and I enjoyed my time on it. *The Middle* had some overlaps with *Gilmore Girls*—it was a family who are trying to make it even though they don't have a lot of money, and it's character driven like *Gilmore Girls.* The Middle was also filmed on the Warner Bros lot so it was great to have a permanent work 'home' for so many years. We shot a couple of scenes in 'Stars Hollow' on that show, and it felt weird being there when Stars Hollow wasn't anymore. There were some other crew members who had worked on *Gilmore Girls* that came over to *The Middle,* so we talked about memories when we were there. Working on these lots that have been around for years makes you feel that you are truly a part of motion picture history, when you work in them. I have shot on that square so many times, across so many different shows.

Overall, working on *Gilmore Girls* was wonderful, and very fun. There were many times when it was challenging but it was really a great opportunity for me to be an executive producer. Working with Lauren was great, and we got along really well. Over the years, people have been really excited when I told them I was a director on *Gilmore Girls*. I'm always surprised at how much love there is for this show, and how it keeps generating. Its success is undoubtedly owed to the idea of a single mother raising her daughter. It's a healthy relationship, with love, but with issues that need to be worked out. Having those strong female characters with charm, but quirkiness also worked. The show was edgy, with sharp wit and intelligence, and all of the cultural references made it a delight to watch. In addition, Stars Hollow is a fantasy town that made a great setting, and appealed to so many people. It's idealised in a way. Every character there has a basic goodness. Even the 'bad' people have a charm. Stars Hollow is a nice place to go to, and *Gilmore Girls* is a nice place to go to. It's a place that you want to spend an hour in.

Nick Holmes

Robert Grimaldi

Being on *Gilmore Girls* was one of the true privileges of my life. I was a fan of the show before I was on it. I loved the *His Girl Friday* style dialogue—rapid fire, and full of extremely random and obscure references. The dialogue is full of material pulled from movies, music, and literature and picking them up and finding out what they all mean is fun. I was always entranced by Lauren Graham and Alexis Bledel's chemistry, which was exceptional. On this show, it's impossible not to like the lead characters, but the ancillary characters are also really excellent. If the show was just Emily and Kirk I would still watch it. The world they created on *Gilmore Girls* was filled with such vibrant creatures that it's hard to tear away from it.

    I had originally auditioned for the pilot, for the role of Dean, but didn't get the part. The script was so cool and interesting that when it aired I had to watch it to see how it turned out. I loved it right away. I tried for years and years to get on the show, going back and auditioning for the role of Jess too. It took me a long time, but eventually I was cast as Rory's fellow Yale student, and Life and Death Brigade member, Robert.

    My first day on set was one of my most memorable experiences. The shoot took place at Griffith Park, which is the Los Angeles version of New York's famous Central Park. A section of the park was shut off to the public for filming the Life and Death Brigade glamping scene in the episode, "You Jump, I Jump, Jack". The set was over 200 yards long, and was magical. It was a huge professional production like I had never seen before.

    I was to report there at 9pm at night, and the shooting would go into the night. I immediately decided that I did not like Tanc Sade who plays Finn on the show, because he was so charming and handsome, and seemed so comfortable on the set. I was not comfortable. I was nervous, and was trying very hard to feign confidence. Of course, we are great friends now. Matt Czuchry is the most charming person, and I liked him right away. He had a guitar and was noodling around playing songs. The paintball scene in that episode was the highlight of my time on the show. It was shot at the Disney ranch, and I got to shoot a paintball gun at men in tuxedos while flying through the air. I knew then, that this was surely a once in a lifetime opportunity. My role was originally only one episode, so I didn't know if I would be coming back. When I did get the call that the character of Robert would be recurring, it was a brand new kind of magic.

Being cast in *Gilmore Girls* was very validating. Prior to that I had been doing commercials, so it was my first television show. I had a cute, boyish face and a distinctive voice, but I think ultimately my ability to speak quickly was what got me the job. After I came back for the episode, 'Pulp Friction', I started plugging #TeamRobert on social media. In a way, I was just doing whatever I could to make Robert seem more important to the story than he actually was. Team Robert ended up taking off, and there is now a Facebook fan club, and t-shirts that promote Team Robert as a fandom of its own.

Being on the show had more of a personal impact on me, than it did professionally. It changed my personal life in a huge way. My community of people that I have in my life is largely from the *Gilmore Girls* community. Sean Gunn who plays Kirk is one of my closest friends, and is one of the really significant people in my life. He's very important to me and very good to me, and I can't say enough good things about him. My first feature film was a weird little horror movie called *The Thirst: Blood War* with Rini Bell (Lulu). She is still in my life and it's been great to see her at the fan fest each year. Because of the friendships I have made, and how significant those are to me, I would say that *Gilmore Girls* was one of the most important events in my existence.

I was thrilled when I heard about the reunion episodes, as both a fan of the show, and an actor. I was making dinner with Sean Gunn just after I had heard about the Palladino's plans to make *A Year in the Life*. Sean is good friends with Amy Sherman-Palladino and Daniel Palladino, and he had a feeling that I would be coming back for the revival. I was very excited when this was confirmed. One of the best things about coming back was that I got to film in the Stars Hollow town set. The Life and Death Brigade were a Yale group, and they had no business in Stars Hollow—all of their scenes were at Yale, or its surroundings—so that was my first day shooting in the town square. It was all done up magnificently, and it felt like a genuine privilege to be there. Though I haven't heard anything official about any further revivals, I think you would be hard pressed to find any of the ancillary cast who wouldn't love to be involved again because it's so good. We were all really proud of it, and I think we would all sign up again. I certainly would.

There's not a place in the world that I have been where I have not been recognised for *Gilmore Girls*. It's just one of those things because people who watch it, rewatch it. I don't even look like I did back then when I was cast on the show, but I still sound the same and often get recognised for my voice. *Gilmore Girls* is everywhere.

Gilmore Girls has influenced me creatively in just about every manner imaginable. The relationships that it cultivated and the experiences that I have had have been hugely influenced by the show. It warms my heart to think of it. I also love being a part of the fan community, because I am a fan of the show myself. The #TeamRobert fans are also a wonderful group of people who do alot of things to help each other out, and are just there for each other. That's not because of me, or my character Robert, it's because of *Gilmore Girls*. The fans are a strong community. It's a thrill to be part of that kind of community.

Artie O'Daly

Seth

I'd only been acting professionally for about a year when I had the audition for *Gilmore Girls*. I remember being in the waiting area with all the other actors who had been called in for the episode. They were casting quite a few parts since it was the debut of the Life and Death Brigade, so there were a lot of people there. I looked around to see who else might be reading for a 'nerdy' part, since the role of Seth was basically the nerd of the brigade. I saw one other guy who might have been my real competition. The outfit he wore was so spot on—he just looked like an inventor. I had brought my glasses to try and look 'brainy', but I wasn't sure if it was enough. So when I went in, I made sure I did something no one else would think of, so I'd stand out to the producers, and hopefully get the part. The audition consisted of the exact lines that I delivered in the episode. At one point in the 'You Jump, I Jump, Jack' scene, I'm on the ground, watching Rory and Logan jump off the tower. When that part of the audition came up, I had to pretend that they were actually 80 feet in the air. So I looked way up, gasped when they jumped, watched them fall intently as they sailed down and landed safely, and then shared unscripted sighs of relief with the people who would have been around Seth at the event. Of course no one was actually there, but that bit made the people in the room laugh, and I think that's what sold them on casting me for the role of Seth.

    I had to go to the set before my actual shoot days for a wardrobe fitting and approval from the director. However, everyone was off on location shooting the Life and Death Brigade evening scenes, so I was picked up in the Stars Hollow town set to be taken out to the park where the filming was taking place. The town was completely empty of people, but fully decorated for the fall. There were pumpkins everywhere, and the town was covered in orange and yellow leaves. It was like stepping from the California heat into an autumn snow globe. It was so cosy and beautiful. I'll never forget how warm and inviting it all looked. And now that's exactly how I view the show.

    I wasn't yet a fan of the show when I worked on it. My boyfriend at the time was a huge fan, so he was very excited that I was going to be on it. After hearing him talk so much about it, my first impression was that it was a pretty big deal to get to meet Rory Gilmore. I've since become a major *Gilmore Girls* fan and especially love watching it during the fall, so it's interesting to me that my first memory of the show is tied to the fall season—waiting in Stars Hollow to be picked up.

On the first day of the shoot, I was terrified that they were going to send me up to the actual 80-foot tower. When I pulled up in the van, I could see this giant, looming structure and became really nervous because I am genuinely afraid of heights. I didn't know how I was gonna tell them I didn't want to go up there. It wasn't until later that I saw they'd built two other much shorter towers for us to shoot on, thankfully. The only time I actually interacted with the main tower was when I first climbed down the ladder to go meet Logan and Rory. I had to climb up the ladder high enough so that my feet wouldn't show in the frame and then wait up there for my cue to enter. Any time they had to retake the scene I had to climb back up the ladder and hold on tight and wait. Up and down, up and down. Kenny Ortega, the director, would shout out, "Sorry, Artie! Back up the ladder!" It was hilarious, and a good workout.

I was only in the one scene, although it was shot in three separate portions over two days. But, getting to be a part of what has become such an iconic part of a fan-favourite episode makes it one of the best things I've ever done. Plus, now that I'm a fan of the show, it blows my mind to see myself existing in Rory Gilmore's world.

Once my episode aired, I started watching the show on DVD, and then bought them all. By the time the show finale aired, I was fully invested. I was devastated when they announced that the show was finishing. When *A Year in the Life* aired, I rewatched all the original seven seasons to prepare, and then binged the new episodes over Thanksgiving. Of course, there is a whole community of fans who are as devoted as I am. People are constantly rewatching the show, and the fan community is still very active.

Gilmore Girls is great, because of the world that it has created. Stars Hollow, and the Gilmore universe is a small world of people who are all very different, yet all exist with each other in a beautiful way.

They fight frequently, but they work things out because they still care about each other. None of the characters are perfect, yet they all try to do their best at any given moment. It's a utopia. On top of this, you've got the best actors saying the best dialogue with the best art direction and costumes. That kind of cornucopia is going to stand the test of time. I also compare *Gilmore Girls* to a good book you don't want to put down. Each episode is a chapter, leading into the next. You can pick it up at any time and get transported into a world of cosiness, intelligence and heart, and see regular people living regular lives in a really lovely way.

Stars Hollow is my happy place. When I am stressed out, I imagine myself living there. Part of me wants to move to Burbank so that I can live in the backdrop of the 'Stars Hollow hills' that are visible above the town on the show. I've attached myself to *Gilmore Girls*, and attached myself to the town, and its people. I create my own web series *Bad Boy* and will often incorporate *Gilmore Girls* into the plot lines or jokes in one way or another. Whenever I am on the Warner Bros lot, I still make a point of walking through Stars Hollow. The show has lived on in my life. I get why the show lives on and is still so relevant to people. Perhaps it hasn't had an impact on my future roles, but it has certainly had a personal impact on me, much as it has had on the people who continue to be fans of the show today.

Elisabeth Abbott

Rosemary

I'd been acting in Los Angeles for a couple of years, doing lots of commercials and a few independent films when my agents sent me the audition for *Gilmore Girls*. I wanted it so badly—but you can't think that way when you're auditioning. You just need to show up, do great work, and then forget about it. The casting directors—Mara Casey and Jami Rudofsky—always made auditions fun. For the callback, Amy Sherman-Palladino herself was in the room, which I was not expecting. It was clear that she was incredibly cool, funny, and invested in every aspect of the show, but she wasn't at all intimidating. When I got the call that I had booked the episode, I called my mom, squealing. She was always happy for me when I booked something, but I knew she'd be particularly proud of this one. I thought it was just going to be one episode, but it eventually turned into four, and I was thrilled every time I was asked back to play. That's what it felt like every time: being asked to come and play.

I loved the show from the beginning. I was in college at Northwestern University when it premiered and didn't have a television, so my mom would mail me VHS tapes with episodes she had recorded so I could watch them with friends. Whenever I was home from school, my mom and I would watch it together. I'm sure this has been said by every fan on the planet, but *Gilmore Girls* felt like "our show." We were an only daughter and a single (divorced) mom, so the Rory/Lorelai relationship resonated for us. It also felt like the fast-talking, feminist screwball comedies from the 1940s that my mom and I both loved and watched on repeat.

I played Rosemary, a friend of the Life and Death Brigade at Yale. Rosemary was (along with Riki Lindhome's character, Juliet) totally comfortable in Logan's rich-party-kid scene. They weren't exactly frenemies to Rory; I think they liked her a lot, despite their constant sarcasm. Rosemary and Juliet served to contrast with Rory, who at that time was feeling conflicted regarding class issues, and confused about her purpose at Yale, and in life. We were also around simply to banter with the Life and Death Brigade guys (which was a true joy every time, whether the cameras were rolling or not).

My first day on set was for the Chinese restaurant scene in season 5, episode 15. I was a little nervous. Matt Czuchry (Logan), Alan Loayza (Colin), Tanc Sade (Finn), Wayne Wilcox (Marty), and Alexis Bledel (Rory) had all filmed together many times before, and they seemed like such a cohesive group. Riki and I were meeting them all for the first time. I knew that the dialogue had to be spot-on and super-fast (obviously — it was *Gilmore Girls*!), but what if we couldn't get it to click right away? Almost immediately, my nerves faded. My boyfriend at the time (now husband) knew Matt from an acting class, and he had been right: Matt Czuchry might be the kindest and most welcoming person on the planet. He, Alan, Tanc, and the rest of the group made us feel right at home.

If you can't tell from my effusiveness so far, every moment I spent on the *Gilmore Girls* set was a favourite moment. A couple of great memories that come to mind are the night shoots we had for season 6, episode 1, and season 6, episode 8. Those were both big social scenes set in the pub. Two things made this episode particularly fun to shoot; Firstly, we were all in jailbird costumes. Secondly, we were filming into the wee hours of the morning with a ton of background actors. Both times truly felt like being at a party. On one of the evenings we were shooting, someone set up a karaoke machine off-set, so the cast and crew got pretty silly when we weren't actively working. I also loved getting to do an Aaron Sorkin-esque walk-and-talk scene in season 6, episode 19, directed by Amy herself. Getting to reference Woodward and Bernstein especially tickled me, since I had been a journalism major at Northwestern.

It was so cool to work with the iconic Kenny Ortega (who directed season 6, episode 8). It was a big challenge not to ask him about his experiences working on *Dirty Dancing, Pretty in Pink*, and *Newsies*. I wanted him to think of me as a professional, so I didn't ask. But now I sort of wish I had.

Now, I'm a licensed psychotherapist in Los Angeles—in fact, my office is one block away from the Warner Brothers lot in Burbank where we filmed *Gilmore Girls*. I work primarily with individuals working to heal from trauma, anxiety, and depression, as well as folks who work in the entertainment industry. As a trauma specialist, I empower clients to discover their own resilience. Being a therapist isn't as different from being an actor as one might think: they're both about sharing stories with vulnerability, listening to and understanding other humans, and helping folks to feel less alone.

I think there are several reasons why *Gilmore Girls* continues to grow a cult following. First, it's just a great show. The fast pace, the cultural references, the beautiful look of it—but really, it's the characters. The population of the magical town of Stars Hollow has all of these archetypes we know and love—I firmly believe, we all know a Kirk. I also had a dance teacher named Miss Patty. Returning to that town felt like coming home every week for a lot of us. On a deeper level, it's a show that prioritised women's relationships: mothers and daughters, ride-or-die pals, rivals turned steadfast friends. There weren't a lot of shows that so consistently passed the Bechdel test in the early 2000s, so this show was a trailblazer in many respects. The women characters were allowed to be complex and often unlikable, but also eminently lovable. There is so much to relate to in these women, and I think they all represent parts of ourselves. I know I see more of Paris in myself than I'd like to admit.

The *Gilmore Girls* fan community is an active one. This is clear to me because of all the sweet messages I receive. Acquaintances, strangers, and even clients in my psychotherapy practice will often say, "So I was re-watching *Gilmore Girls*...."

I love being a tiny part of such a beloved show.

Devon Sorvari

Honor Huntzberger

My character doesn't come in until season 5 of *Gilmore Girls*, so the show had been running for a couple of years when I got the chance to audition. I was already a huge fan, which meant I didn't have to do any special research, like I would have if I wasn't familiar with the style and tone of a show. When I got the audition, I thought "pinch me!" I was more nervous than usual because I loved the show so much. Despite my excitement and nerves, I went for it, did my best, and got the part.

What I liked about the show was the humour and the heart. I loved the mother-daughter relationship. I loved the style—where they had all this complex, dense dialogue, but they made it seem so effortless. I really related to that style, and I was also super excited to do a show where everyone talked fast because I talk way too fast myself.

I remember loving the character of Honor because she was a fun "blue blood" type, and I felt that was something I knew really well. I'm from the East Coast (I grew up in Massachusetts and New York) and my family has a long history in New England so I thought it would be a good fit for me. As I got to know Honor better, and as her character was developed over more episodes, I started seeing that she was not as much about her blue-bloodedness, as she was about her perspective on the world, and her crazy inner life. She's quite hilarious, actually.

Originally Honor was a one-episode character, with the possibility of recurring. I remember getting the call that I got the next episode and I was completely over the moon. I wasn't sure at the start if there would be more, but I was hoping. Logan was such a significant part of the story at that time, and I was lucky they fleshed out his family life, as that meant more episodes for me.

I had very little television experience at that time, so the only work I had to compare this role to was acting in theatre. Some actors argue that the work is the same, no matter which medium, but I couldn't disagree more. I found on-camera work very nerve-wracking. I'm sure it has to do with not having four weeks of rehearsal, like you do in a play. It was "Ready, Set, Go!" It was a challenge, for sure, but a fun one. My innate wackiness seemed to be quite welcome in the character. I was weird, and they went with it. The more quirky and interesting the take, the more they seemed to like it, thank goodness.

Gilmore Girls impacted my journey in an interesting way. It made me stay in Los Angeles a lot longer than I intended. Before I got the role of Honor, I was considering going back to New York, but when I was called for another episode, I stayed in Los Angeles until my character's storyline was complete. These episodes were, of course, spaced out, so it kept me in Los Angeles for some time, and I am still based here now. Right after *Gilmore Girls*, I met my husband. So maybe if I hadn't been on *Gilmore Girls*, I wouldn't have met him. Another thing to love about the show.

These days, most of my work is in narrating audiobooks in my studio in Santa Monica. That's not what I initially came to Los Angeles to do, but I absolutely love it. I'm also part of a theatre company here which has become like a family, so I am grateful that Los Angeles eventually became my home.

I don't feel like I have the time to be a superfan of anything, so I am always really impressed with people who remember every episode. I don't have the attention span to become as committed as some of the *Gilmore Girls* fans that I have met. They're an impressive and delightful bunch. The reason people love this show so much is probably the same reason that I love it—it made me feel smart, while engaging me emotionally. I loved when I would "get" one of the witty references on the show. It made me feel like part of a really cool club. *Gilmore Girls* was unique in that way, I think.

Although I haven't been to an in-person fan fest, I loved doing the virtual one in 2021. I was in Palm Springs, at a friend's house having a "Covid Bubble" vacation, so I logged in to the festival while pool-side, with palm trees surrounding me in the background. Honor would have approved.

My most memorable episode to shoot was "Bridesmaids Revisited," where Honor was getting married in this gorgeous, full-skirted wedding dress. I loved it, but it came with its challenges after hours on set. Valerie Campbell in wardrobe—who is at the heart of the whole *Gilmore Girls* family—had to carry the train of the dress as I walked around the studio lot, or it would have gotten dirty very quickly. This even extended to when I needed to use the bathroom. She would carry my train into the bathroom, then arrange it on my lap so it wouldn't touch the ground, and then when I was done, she would have to come in and help me untangle myself from it, and keep it off the ground again. Poor thing. Luckily, Valerie is a total superhero.

The scenes where I am smoking were a bit of a challenge, too. I am a resolute non-smoker, and would have preferred not to smoke for these scenes, but I didn't have the nerve to ask them to change it, so I just did my best. I was acutely aware of what an amateur smoker I must have looked like. Although, come to think of it, I came across an online list of actors who smoke in real life, and my name was on it, so that was a bit of a shock. I was so sure I had done it really badly, and yet, I must have convinced someone. Another piece of funny online content that I came across was a meme where a fan made fun of the wig I was wearing in my wedding episode. You know you've made it when someone makes a meme of your "fright wig."

A few important relationships have blossomed from my time on *Gilmore Girls*. Valerie still hosts huge get-togethers at her house many years after the show wrapped, and I think it really kept the Los Angeles cast members together. I'd never met Nick Holmes (Robert) while doing the show but he was great to interact with at the virtual fan fest and he has become a new *Gilmore Girls* friend. I am still friends with Devon Michaels (Bill) and Emily Bergl (Francie Jarvis). Oh, and not that I met him, but Leslie Odom Jr. was in one of my episodes, so I like to joke that I am "*Hamilton*-adjacent."

When the reboot was announced, there was some online speculation about whether Honor would come back. I thought it was unlikely, but it would have been a lot of fun to be back on the show. I would have cleared my calendar. Having watched it, I realise that the story arc involving Logan's character doesn't really call for his family to make another appearance. I have some ideas about where Honor has gone in her life since *Gilmore Girls*. After living the high life, with all the money and connections, Honor got bored and has rebranded, and re-dedicated herself to social justice. This has been aided by her family's deep pockets. We aren't sure how Mitchum feels about that, so we don't talk about it. We just sip our martinis. I bet fans could come with good alternative future realities for Honor too.

Out of all of the things I have done, I think people love this the most. It was one of my favourite jobs, because this show has such incredible fans. It has the longest lasting, and most far-reaching family of any project I have been involved in, and over time, seems to be leaving a long trail behind it. I felt really lucky to be on the show—like I lucked into a giant loving, squishy extended family. I felt really fortunate to have had a seat at the table.

Dave Shalansky

Harry

I was doing sketch comedy on the sunset strip in Hollywood when I got the part of Harry on *Gilmore Girls*. One of my friends from New York, David, was a writer, and had come to see my comedy show one night. He brought his girlfriend Rebecca with him, who was a writer for *Gilmore Girls*. She put in a good word for me, and it led to an audition.

Gilmore Girls was a very specific, stylised show that was not like anything else on television at that time. At that point in my life I was 32, a bachelor, and living in Los Angeles. I had not seen the show when I got the audition, and I wasn't really friends with anyone who was in its key demographic. As an actor, you are trained to do research when you are going up for a role, so I borrowed the seasons on DVD from a friend in acting class, and got the idea very quickly—they speak really fast, and it has a captivating style.

I was a stage actor, with experience doing commercials, and had just acquired new representation. This new manager had called me with the audition for *Gilmore Girls* and told me that he wasn't sure how many episodes it was for, but that it was definitely going to be a recurring role. He was excited for me, and ended the call with, "Let's book this thing."

The audition was held 'cattle call' style, and was full of the quirkiest actors you would see around town at that time. Every type was represented in that room—tall, skinny, nerdy—all of it. I didn't think I was in the right demographic, but I went in anyway. The scene was a 'walk and talk' monologue, and after I did it, I was told I would be coming back for the callback. Callbacks are normally another day, but in this instance it would take place in two hours time. I got some feedback to prepare for the callback. I was told to read as fast as I could, not to even take my eyes off the page. As a stage actor, who was used to beats, and pauses, I thought this was craziness.

I spent those two hours getting coffee, walking around the Warner Bros Studio lot, and reading the lines as fast as I could. When I got back into the audition room my friend's writer girlfriend was there, and I suddenly got really nervous about the speed I was told to read with. I looked down at the paper, and just read it as fast as I could. In hindsight, I think they already knew that I was what they were looking for, but they wanted to check that I could speak in that *Gilmore Girls* tongue. After I left, my manager called to say that I had booked the job.

Between getting the job, and going in to shoot, I watched more episodes, learned the back stories of the characters, and talked to friends about the show. My manager reminded me that if I did good, I would get more episodes, which made me really nervous. The pressure to do a good job was mounting. I teach acting now, and I talk to actors in my class about this experience. It's a real lesson in nerves, and the power that we have to go further if we deliver well. I felt super prepared for the job, but I had two pages of dialogue, and a lot was riding on this.

Once I got to the set, the wonderful director—Jamie Babbitt—was so embracing. She had been in my audition and she was very encouraging. She introduced me to the whole cast and crew. Alexis was super friendly. She was very calm and collected. We shot my walk-and-talk scene at a real office within the Warner Bros Studios lot. I think it was the accounting department, and it was cleared for the day so we could use it as the newspaper office for the Stanford Eagle Gazette. I was a big fan of *The West Wing* which was famous for those walk-and-talk scenes, so I was excited that my first scene on this show was going to be that style. The scene was shot with Rory and I walking forward, while a man carrying a camera walked backward in front of us, filming us walking, and talking.

In a scene like that, everything has to be in place to do it correctly in one take. You have to walk from point A to point B, lighting and camera has to be right, and every word has to be said accurately. There are no wide coverage shots needed for this kind of scene, but you do have to land on your marks, and say your lines correctly. This seems easy, but it's the hardest thing for an actor to do because there is no edit. You can't cut to a different shot if you make a mistake. That's one of the reasons that a lot of theatre actors were hired for this show, because they are used to having to get it right the first time. On this show in particular, every word had to be exactly as Amy Sherman-Palladino wrote it, and I imagine she has carried that through to *The Marvelous Mrs. Maisel.* This show was known for being 'word perfect'. It was a unique role because the main focus wasn't my acting, it was drilling the words into my brain until I could spit them out exactly as they were written.

We rehearsed it, then the lights were set, and it was time to shoot. The first take, I nailed it. For safety, we went over it a few more times, but I was feeling on cloud nine. Alexis could not have been more supportive, and kind, and Jamie was fantastic to work with as well. I felt proud of myself after that, and was feeling good about how it went. The next day, I got a call from my manager to let me know that I had been written into the next episode, and would be coming back to shoot next week. The script arrived in an envelope at my apartment, and I ripped it open and read it from cover-to-cover. I had been assigned another walk-and-talk scene, which made me feel really confident that I had made a good impression with my last one. However, things took a turn at this point.

At this time, I was a green film actor. I had been given this great television role with the potential for it to grow and I got cocky. I rested on my laurels. For the next episode, I didn't do my acting homework. I didn't watch the episodes, I didn't chat with people about the show, and I didn't go through my techniques. I trusted that I knew it well enough, and that on the day everything would be fine.

I showed up for my shoot and it was Friday—my birthday. It was also Halloween, and Amy Sherman-Palladino was directing. I had heard through the grapevine that when she directs it's a little bit more disciplined. She's more focused and knows exactly what she wants from everybody. So I wanted to honour that. My call time was noon which was quite late for television. I saw the shot list and there was a ton of work still to get through before the weekend. My scene was last and supposed to be shot at 6 P.M. I had time to memorise my lines and work on my scene but instead I talked to people, ate, and generally just relaxed. I wasn't focused on the job I was there to do, I was too cocky. While this didn't work out well for me, the lesson that I learned on *Gilmore Girls* was great, and changed my career forever.

By 6 P.M. we weren't even close to shooting my scene, and it was a Friday, so there was no coming back tomorrow. Everything had to be finished before we left for the night. It was 9.30 P.M. when I finally got called. It was Halloween night, and people wanted to go home to their kids. I figured, if I do this properly we can have the shot wrapped in half an hour and go home. I don't know if I was just exhausted, or had drank too much coffee, but my words did not come out correctly. We did the rehearsal and I made a bundle of mistakes with the words. I went away for 40 minutes and had a break. When I came back, I still wasn't getting it right. The tension was starting to mount amongst the other cast and crew members, and I became anxious and panicky. We did six takes, and I didn't get any one of them right. Amy Sherman-Palladino came out and asked me what was going on. She knew I had nailed it last time, and was aware that everyone wanted to go home. I gave it one more college try, and still didn't get it right. Two hours later, we finally got to go home. Nobody even said goodbye to me when I left. I felt like I had let the whole team down. I cried all the way home that night.

I tormented myself for a week before my manager called back. I had been written into one more *Gilmore Girls* episode, with only a line or two. It was clear to me that I had been written out. For about two years after that, I completely lost my confidence in audition rooms. I learned a big lesson about the business: When I get hired, I have only one chance to make an impression, and when that door comes-a-knocking, I better be prepared. Luck is when preparation meets timing. On *Gilmore Girls,* I got the timing but I wasn't prepared and I lost my shot.

Two years later, I was in a bar in Silver Lake, Los Angeles, at a birthday party for my friend David whose friend Rebecca got me the part on *Gilmore Girls*. She was there, and we got to chatting. She told me that I wasn't written out because of my work. It was only ever a three episode part. She said I had done everything right, and that I wasn't the first actor to struggle with getting the lines word perfect. I was one of dozens of actors who had the same experience on the show. I had spent two years hating myself over something that wasn't true. There was another lesson for me there. I had to stop taking things so personally.

Gilmore Girls boosted me professionally, since having a three episode arc on such a successful show looked great on my resume. Casting directors always loved *Gilmore Girls* alumni because if you could handle an Amy Sherman-Palladino script, you could handle any script. I am still an actor now, and have just wrapped up a great part, playing Henry Kissinger in a Paramount Plus limited series about the making of *The Godfather*, called *The Offer*. I also teach acting, directing showcases and films at the school. It's a great job, and the school I work at (AMDA) hires working actors, so if I need to go to Los Angeles for a job, I can. I have shot *Grey's Anatomy*, and *How to Get Away with Murder* while I have been teaching, and AMDA have been very supportive.

Gilmore Girls was such a precise genius that tapped into themes and wonderful story arcs that had not been told in that way before. It dealt with relationships, single motherhood, and family in a unique way. Amy was able to balance brilliant writing that captivated and was music to your ears, while sustaining and balancing something very believable and real. The show was stimulating the viewer's brain and emotional core at the same time. I think the development of characters also worked. Alexis Bledel growing up on that show allowed for people to attach themselves to something that they saw in themselves as well. It's like a really good play. You gravitate toward it, you cry, and you laugh. The subtler writing doesn't hit as much in other shows. With Amy's brilliance, that musicality pulls you in. I had a small part in it but I am very proud to have been a part of the *Gilmore Girls* world.

John Kapelos

Orientation Leader

When I came to be on *Gilmore Girls*, I was represented by an agent that already represented another actor on the show. Someone had been cast in my role as the orientation leader, but had dropped out and I was offered the role. Since I was coming in as a replacement, I didn't need to audition. I do remember being very excited about working on the show, as a fan of it. I liked the show so much, and thought it would be a lot of fun to work on. I had never auditioned for the show before, but I had worked on the Warner Bros lot.

My episode was shot in the evening. Amy Sherman-Palladino was a really good friend of a friend of mine, so I already knew of her. My friend used to attend amazing parties at her house, and would tell me how much fun they were. Daniel Palladino was also at the shoot, so I got to meet them both. I don't know if the scene was entirely written to their satisfaction as there was a bit of fussing with the script during my shoot. I got the feeling that they were not particularly happy that day with some things that were going on behind the scenes. However, they were nice, cordial, and friendly, but not warm and fuzzy. There was a degree of professionalism and preoccupation about them. I mentioned my friend and they acknowledged that, but ultimately, they were there to work.

Daniel was the director for my episode, and he was quite particular with me. I'm not sure if I exactly fit the bill for what they wanted because I was a recast, and of course, I hadn't auditioned. I'm a 'Chatty Cathy' so on any set I look forward to getting in there and talking to people, but I soon learned that it wasn't a very chatty set. The first scene we filmed was a classroom scene which had a fun dynamic. I was older than everybody, and my character had a prison guard type personality. Overall, it was a cool experience.

I have worked on television shows in the past where the producers have underestimated the fans. *Gilmore Girls* is a real exception when it comes to fan loyalty. I think as much as fans love a show, they can, strangely, hurt its progress. However in the case of *Gilmore Girls* the fans are very smart, and quite resourceful. In a way, I think the fan response has worked well for the producers of the show. Fan demand certainly seems to have played a part in the decision to reboot the show. I've always thought fans were short-sheeted by producers. Some of the shows I have worked on have done well for two or three seasons, and then changes are made such as having the writers replaced. When shows are altered like that, small plot holes start appearing. Whenever new writers are brought in, they are oblivious to these small inconsistencies, but fans are not. Season 7 is a good example of this, when the Palladino's left. There was a palpable difference in the show in their absence. It's always folly to replace the show runner. On any television show, that is a move that is fraught with peril.

When I came onto *Gilmore Girls*, there was a sense that this was a really successful show and that these people were at the top of their game. *Gilmore Girls* ran like a robust, humming machine. There's no doubt that these people are massively talented. That's why Amy has gone on to have so much success with *The Marvelous Mrs Maisel*. None of these shows would have happened without Amy and her creative brilliance. When all is said and done, *Gilmore Girls* is kind of cool that way. It's unique. There aren't too many shows like it. That's the one thing about Amy's voice. It's a very male dominated field, and Amy breathes fresh life into her shows, and into the industry. I was glad when they got another shot at their final season, and did *A Year in the Life* the way they wanted to.

Yuri Lowenthal

Sous- Chef Carl

    I had auditioned for *Gilmore Girls* more than once before getting the role of Sous-Chef/Carl. Most of my work is in voice acting, so I was already a member of the 'loop group' for the show, which was a team of people that did chatter in the background. Our job was to record chatter to fill in audio backgrounds in things like diner scenes, or street scenes—anywhere you might expect to hear background noise. When they are filming, for example, a scene in Luke's Diner, all of the extras in the background are mouthing without sound because they don't want to talk over the principal actors' lines. To get the background noise, they then bring in a loop group to fill in the background. This is a much more controlled way of adding sound to the background. This sound can then be dialled up or down individually, to create the soundscape that is in the background of the scene. I was already part of that loop group so I had already worked on the show in the background before in front of the camera.

Being in a loop group is similar to normal voice work when you fill in people's mouths with sound. Sometimes it would be very specific. For example, there might be a couple in the background who are talking, so they would ask two people to come up and 'act' as those people and have a conversation that will cover the sound for those actors. When you listen to a show, if we have done our job right, you won't hear any of it specifically. Adding this sound makes it seem like there is a whole world around the scene.

I worked with a group that was working on several other shows, and *Gilmore Girls* was one of them. I knew the director of the group through the voice acting community. When you are putting a loop group together you want a variety of people to bring together a background sound full of blended chatter. Sometimes, a loop group will have more specific needs. For instance, they may need younger voices, or speakers of other languages. Usually a group is made up of a core number of actors who show variety and versatility. At that time I was part of the core group for my loop group. The pay for loop group work is quite good, so it tends to be a cutthroat and sought after position. I kind of fell into it but most people who once were in it, held onto their positions with their claws.

When I first came to Los Angeles I was only doing on-camera work. I fell into voice acting when I realised that these television and film jobs don't come as easily as I had hoped. I wondered what else I could do to make a living and that's how I started in voice acting. I still do television and film occasionally. So it's all acting but sometimes it's a little job here and there. I started in theatre, then went into television and film, and then found voice acting. I now do all of those.

I was actively auditioning for television roles at the time that I got *Gilmore Girls*. It was really hard being in a loop group and auditioning for roles because the loop group needs you to be available all the time, and on call. That's why I didn't stick with loop groups over time, because I struggled with the scheduling and exclusivity of it. For some actors, because of the money, health benefits, and eligibility for SAG AFTRA, loop groups are a great choice.

I was really nervous on my first day at *Gilmore Girls*. It was early on in my television career as far as those types of roles go. Kenny Ortega was the director for my episode, and having him direct reminded me of being in the theatre in a way. It was intimidating being around Kenny, and being on set but one of the people who put me most at ease that day was Melissa McCarthy (Sookie). I cannot say enough nice things about her. She was so genuine, so wonderful, and so warm. Even though she was the hot shot in that scene she never acted like she was any more important than anyone else on set. It made me a lifelong fan of her work, having had those brief experiences with her.

It was a bit surreal when I got onto the set that is the Dragonfly Inn. On television, it looks like a real place, with the sun shining through the windows. In reality, the rooms are on a soundstage, and the sun coming through the windows is lights behind the window, beaming into the set. The reality sets in that this isn't a real place, so it was a nice 'peek behind the curtain'. If the crew are doing their job right, it looks like a real place on screen, which of course the Dragonfly does.

On my first shoot, it was nice to see that the actors don't always get it right the first time. They are the stars on the show, they are professionals. I was nervous that I was going to mess up. I remember Melissa got jumbled up on her words, and that was when I realised that this is part of the process—making mistakes. It was comforting to see how other actors come in and they might be nervous even though they are stars of the show. It was a learning experience across the board for me.

It felt great to be cast as a character with a name. Up until that point I was used to playing roles like "waiter", but this was Carl and it felt special to have that credit. I didn't know initially that I would be coming back. The role was just for one episode, so it was a great surprise to be called back in again. In my second episode, I had to do multiple takes because I didn't speak fast enough.

The quick snappy dialogue was probably what made the show a success. It felt alive and almost hyperrealistic. It definitely stood out among the other shows of its type. The fan community lives on, which is how they could bring it back for another Netflix season. That doesn't happen often. It's a very special fan community that can bring a show back from the dead.

Almost all of my work now is voice work including commercial voice work, animation, dubbing voice animation, and video games. I initially thought I wanted to be a movie star, but being flexible in those early days allowed me to enter this amazing and magical voice space. I've been the Prince of Persia, Peter Parker, Bucky Barnes, Ben 10, and lots more. I've gotten to work on cartoons, video games, and gotten to work with a tremendous community of actors who are in movies and on television. With video games it's become full circle in a way. I started out doing theatre, moved into film and television, and am now working on motion capture, so I do a lot of acting in a suit with reflective dots on. It's almost like doing theatre again. As a kid I never would have thought that I would be Spider-man in a video game. It's super magical and I love what this career has become.

Devon Michaels

Bill

My journey to become a part of *Gilmore Girls* started about four years earlier when I was brought in to meet the casting directors Jami Rudofsky and Mara Casey for another audition. It was what's called a general meeting, where they don't have a specific role in mind but are looking at what actors might be right for the show. My agent said they should meet me, so I went in and read for them. I remember very vividly that after I read they said I had done a good job but would need to go faster. I did it again, with a quicker pace, but they told me I needed to do it faster still. I didn't quite have the full picture on the tone of the show at that point and how many words its actors squeezed in. It wasn't until much later that I understood how the speed of the dialogue in *Gilmore Girls* affects what the characters are saying and how the scene is interpreted. I didn't get a role as a result of that first meeting, and for years I pretty much thought I had blown my chance to be on *Gilmore Girls*.

Four years later, though, Jami and Mara brought me back in to read for the part of Bill. It was a guest star role with three scenes in the episode 'Just Like Gwen and Gavin,' playing a member of the Yale Daily News team. After my initial audition, they asked me in for a callback with the producers. Unfortunately I had already scheduled a flight back east to see my family for Thanksgiving. It was too late to cancel or change my plans, so I taped my audition and sent it to my agent to pass onto the production team at *Gilmore Girls*. This is done all the time now, especially since the pandemic, but it was much less common back then, so I didn't have super high hopes for getting the part. Still, I was determined to do the best I could. I had done more research this time around, watching the show and asking people about it, so I was more prepared. I recorded the lines with my girlfriend at the time on a yellow couch in my apartment, including a personal note at the start thanking whoever was watching for letting me record the callback. Sure enough, I'd just arrived at my sister's house in North Carolina when I got the call that they wanted to book me for the job. It was really nice because I got to tell my family in person while everyone was there. It was a pretty great feeling.

At that stage, I was booked for just one episode, but my character went on to appear in nine. I later found out that the production team had always planned for Bill to be a recurring character, but that was still a mystery to me at the time. I had already done quite a few guest appearances on other television shows such as *The West Wing* and *Without a Trace,* so I knew something about the general culture I was stepping into. When you're a day player and just briefly joining a group of people who have been working together for years, it can be a little daunting. Most shows have a unique dynamic, so there's some quick adapting you have to do when coming in for these guest star roles. And you learn to accept that the bonding experience may be fleeting. When I stepped onto the set of *Gilmore Girls,* however, it became clear pretty early on that this was not quite the same. There was an extra affection, right from the start. My first impressions were all really positive and I found out right away that the writers had loosely based my character Bill on one of the people on the writing team.

My first scene was early in season 6, so of course a lot of the cast and crew members had been working together for years. The DP (Director of Photography) at the time was terrific. It's always a good idea to get on well with the DP, since he or she is in charge of making you look good or at least knows the most about the way the camera is capturing you. We liked each other right from the start. I was consistent with my performance, and he was clear about how each shot was going to be—how wide the angle was, etc., which really helped me to fine tune my performance on the fly. There was an all-around really great vibe on the set.

Right from the beginning, I also formed a bond with Liza Weil, who plays Paris. Our trailers were pretty close to each other, so we started chatting and really hit it off. She's a super cool, super smart person with a great sense of humour. Our characters may have clashed, but behind the scenes we really had a lot of fun.

Something that was different on *Gilmore Girls* was that the show didn't do close-ups. It's just not part of their shooting style. This was a slight technical adjustment for me, as most other films and television shows make use of these shots. This took a bit of getting used to, because I almost had to treat the show like a stage play. Because the camera was never too close, I didn't have to worry much about being too big and could play things up a little. The *Gilmore Girls* style in general was meant to be a little heightened—not as much as a multi-cam sitcom or a Nickelodeon or Disney Channel show, but still heightened in its own way. I have a long background in theatre so it was a fun chance to embrace that.

My favourite episode is probably 'Friday Night's Alright for Fighting' since it gave me the most to do and really established my character. But, if I had to choose a favourite scene I'd probably go with the one I did a couple of weeks later in 'A Vineyard Valentine.' Apparently the episode had some time to fill, which was rare for *Gilmore Girls*. Most episodes of the show had 75 or 80 page scripts instead of the industry standard of around 50 or 55, so normally editing the episodes down for time was in order. This one must have been running short though. I wasn't scheduled to work on it at first but was called in at the last minute because they'd added a scene at the Yale Daily News office with Rory mostly on the phone. There was nothing else going on in the scene, and the producers probably felt that it needed more, so they decided to have Bill there talking to Rory. It felt great to be specifically requested to fill in that space and round out the scene, almost like being the paintbrush an artist is inspired to grab to finish their painting.

Aside from my notorious sweater vests, the yoyo I used back in 'Friday Night's Alright for Fighting' has become one of the most recognized tropes of my character. When we were preparing to shoot that scene, the production team was noticeably worried about me knowing how to perform the trick. The cat's cradle was specifically in the script, and it was my third episode playing Bill so they couldn't exactly recast it if I couldn't physically pull it off. They called my agent and asked if I already knew how to play with a yoyo and specifically if I knew how to do the cat's cradle. When I got to the set, they had the props guy ready to teach me some more, and Valerie from wardrobe also helped out. I really worked at it to get it right and was actually pretty proud because I got to the point where I could complete the trick nine out of ten times. When we shot, we did about ten takes, most of which I got right. Of course, the one they chose for the final cut, however, was one where I failed pretty spectacularly. I knew the comedy element had been prioritised, but I see a lot of comments online about how I don't know how to use a yoyo, which is pretty funny.

Another highlight I remember was when all the Yale Daily News actors got called in to do some Automated Dialogue Replacement (ADR) and we got to work together after one of our episodes. ADR is used when the audio quality of a scene needs to be improved after it's been shot. In this instance, we were doing it for the episode where Rory's father Christopher had taken us to the fancy restaurant with the crème brûlée. Since we had not shot the scene on our usual set, the sound didn't come out perfect, so they brought us all in at the same time to replace some of our lines. We all met up at the studio and just had the best time getting a sneak peek at the episode with each other. The whole Yale Daily News staff had a great energy together. We got on really well both in and out of the studio. The engineers played our stuff on the big screen while we re-recorded certain lines for the microphone. It was a great day, getting to hang out and play those scenes again.

That restaurant scene was one of the more challenging scenes to shoot in general. It's very difficult to get coverage shots of a large group sitting around a table like that. We had to have a lot of camera setups to pull it off. To get all the angles we needed, they set up a different 'fake' table that had the camera peeking up through the centre so they could shoot our faces and get more interesting coverage.

When I realised that the Yale Daily News actors would probably not be continuing on the show, it was obviously a disappointing moment. The episodes were sometimes produced out of order, so I think the ADR session on our penultimate show turned out to be the last time we would all be together. When we first shot that scene in the restaurant, I thought my character was going to continue on in the series because there were some lines where I got drunk and confessed my love for Paris. The dialogue made it clear that seeds were being planted for a specific story arc between Bill and Paris. When we did the ADR for that scene though, those lines had already been edited out, so I knew that meant I probably wouldn't be returning.

Being on *Gilmore Girls* changed how I was perceived by my agent and by most of the casting offices in town. On a business level it showed I could be a recurring actor, not just someone for single episodes. That opened up opportunities to be considered for larger roles, including series regulars on other shows. I was brought in for more pilots, and for major movies which I hadn't really had much of a chance to do before. This was an exciting shift but at the same time a double edged sword. I was no longer being brought in for the smaller roles that can be easier to book. Instead my hat was thrown into a more competitive ring with people who were pretty well known—famous names who had way more film and television roles under their belts. I got brought in for a series regular role on *The Big Bang Theory*, but lost the part to Johnny Galecki who had been on *Roseanne*. It's an interesting dynamic because on one hand I had made a step up, but that put me in a place that was hyper competitive. Then the writers strike hit, shortly after *Gilmore Girls* finished, so it was not really the best time for me to be at that level. Just when I had the most heat on me as an actor, all of a sudden the business went to sleep for a year. By the time we came out the other side, a lot of that heat was forgotten and I had to start over with more single episode opportunities. Some of these were great, like playing Timothy Moore on *House*. It felt good to be back in the trenches again, but it was disappointing that I hadn't been able to take full advantage of the momentum *Gilmore Girls* gave me.

Aside from all the career oriented ways playing Bill affected my path in the business, it would be a crime not to mention the amazing support I've received from the show's unique fans. I'm not exactly an A-list celebrity—my IMDb starmeter barely dipped below the 10K mark for one week back in '09. But television is a bizarre phenomenon, and *Gilmore Girls* in particular has made such a profound impact on so many. Millions of people I've never met have seen me in a sweater vest spouting know-it-all speeches in their living rooms. And, thanks to syndication, DVDs, and the nation's latest pastime of repeat binge streaming, I still get recognized about once a month, mostly by restaurant hostesses or friends of my teenage nieces.

One fun story stands out from when I was visiting Italy a while back. I had to go to the U.S. Consulate in Florence to sign something about my apartment in New York, where there was a dispute with the huge company that had just bought my building. Aside from interrupting my vacation, the whole thing made me kind of nervous. But thanks to *Gilmore Girls,* what could've been a really stressful administrative chore suddenly turned into a warm, family-like moment. The clerk behind the bulletproof glass was a huge fan of the show, recognized me immediately, and invited me back into the protected area to take pictures with her and her co-workers. It was a rare taste of celebrity treatment, and such a bright memory.

In more recent years, I've had the pleasure of attending the fan festivals. Getting to interact with all kinds of people all in one place to bond about this shared love for something that's warmed their lives has honestly been a highlight of my life. I have so many truly great moments of connection, and encouragement, and even some new friends.

Gilmore Girls has a sense of home that not a lot of shows have. Television in general is about people wanting to spend time with other people in their living room. Audiences want to watch something in their pyjamas and feel like these characters are in their home and part of their life. *Gilmore Girls* does such a great job of embracing that. When streaming developed, and the show got added to Netflix, it became an even bigger phenomenon that still hasn't quieted. People grab onto that feeling of home and never want to let it go. *Gilmore Girls* has become a home for so many people, and I'm proud and grateful to be a part of that.

David Greenman

Fred

My journey on *Gilmore Girls* started when I met one of the casting directors, Jami Rudofsky. Jami confused me for another actor Jon Wellner (who was also on the show), and came over and started talking to me. Jon and I are similar actors, and have a similar look, so we quite often get confused with each other, and it's become a bit of a running joke. At the time, I didn't even know Jon, so I found him online and we became good friends. Meeting Jami in that fashion was actually a much better introduction to a casting director than the standard way an actor would meet one. After our chat, she called me in for an audition on *Gilmore Girls*. I thought I had done well at the audition, but the feedback they gave me was to talk faster. That was the only time I had ever been told to talk faster in an audition. I did it again faster, when Daniel Palladino told me to recite the lines once more, even faster. On that third read through, I didn't even feel like I was acting. I was just racing through the dialogue as fast as I could. I booked the job.

At that point, the job was just for the one episode. You always hope the job will become recurring but don't expect it, so it was nice when I got called in three more times to shoot for season 6 and 7.

The role I auditioned for was Fred, the sous chef at the Dragonfly Inn. Even at that stage, I thought it was interesting that they named characters. It speaks to the world that they created. So often when you are auditioning. you are waiter #2, or something like that. It was nice to feel like I'm playing an actual person, not just some chef with a couple of quippy lines. I felt like I was a person in this town, and my part was important. Other people who I have met who had smaller parts on the show existed in the world even if they didn't have their own storyline. That's fascinating really, because most shows have different extras every episode. *Gilmore Girls* tried to make Stars Hollow an authentic place by inhabiting it with characters that were seen multiple times, as if they really lived there. I don't know if the average fan would recognise me, or my character from my four episodes, but I still appreciate the effort, and holistic view that was put into building the Gilmore world.

Before my audition, I knew the show was popular but I hadn't watched it. I didn't know what I was walking into, on that day of the audition really. I would have been less surprised about how quickly I had been asked to talk, if I had seen the show beforehand. The first thing I thought when I walked on the set was 'wow'. That kitchen set in the Dragonfly Inn was stunning. It is one of the things I still marvel at, even though I have been in and around the industry for 20 years. The work that they do in production design is so immaculate and detailed. The fruit was stunning—there were bowls of fruit, and nuts, and pans and utensils. Things were laid out in a way that felt both lived in and a little bit ethereal which was a quality that *Gilmore Girls* had. It was also the first time I had walked onto a set with four walls. Most shows are open, but this one was an actual room. If the crew needed to access something, they moved the walls, and then put them back. There was a lot of time and effort put into ensuring the room was perfect. Sitcom sets have much less detail. While the Inn was filmed in a sound stage, I did get to shoot in the town square once, though it wasn't for *Gilmore Girls*. I did a shoot in a fake marijuana shop for the series *The Mentalist*. I played the manager of the pot shop, which was in the Stars Hollow town square.

  I was the only guest actor in the scene that day. There were a lot of extras but I didn't really have anyone to chat with until I was walked onto set. I was working with Lauren Graham who played Lorelai.. When we were waiting off set I got to chat with Melissa Mcarthy who played Sookie. I didn't know who she was at that time, as I didn't watch the show. She was delightful and welcoming. Actors are not always that way when you are guesting on a television show. It is a glamorous job to be on a television show, but also a hard job and it can be a bit of a slog with dialogue to learn, and long hours to keep, and the job can be incredibly taxing. So, it was rare to be treated with genuine warmth.

  I also had a lovely experience working with Lauren. She was very helpful with blocking, making sure that I was in the right place in the scene. This scene had a lot of extras and it can be challenging navigating a lot of people. She came in and knew what she was doing and what needed to be done. We ran through the dialogue a few times, and got the job done. It was over pretty quickly. That was a very easy shooting day. It was impressive and it was fun. I had some humorous dialogue and got a vibe for the show and the energy it brought. One of the things that adds to the charm is the speed that is so quippy and sharp. People latched onto it because they got it. It made people feel smart because they could follow it and be a part of that. It was fun to see that, and be a part of it.

The hardest episode to shoot was my fourth one, but it was also the most fun. I was filming with Melissa (Sookie) and Jackson who were both very nice. I also worked with Yuri Lowenthal who played another chef named Carl. It was a complicated scene and the director wanted to do it all in one shot. It was myself, Melissa, Jackson, Yanic Truesdale (Michel Gerard) and Yuri. We all had overlapping lines, and it was a long panning shot where we all tasted soup. It was the last scene of the day and Melissa had a show at Groundlings that night so we had to get it done and get out of there. Inevitably, when you have that much dialogue and you have to deliver it that fast, someone is going to mess up, and in this instance, one of us messed up every time. We had to do 26-28 takes, so it got pretty tedious but it was also funny. That was a fun day because everyone was so nice and funny, and working so hard to make this cool scene work. That's what makes acting exciting—when there is a little more of a challenge.

My third episode is probably the most memorable, because I got cut out of it. I had a scene with Lauren and Melissa again. After my dialogue which opened the scene, I picked up a dish of something and carried it off. When the episode aired, they had cut the start of the scene off, probably for time. It's hard as an actor not to have your feelings hurt, but while it was a cute opener, it wasn't necessary to carry the story forward, so I understood their decision. Funnily, you can still see the side of my head when I leave the scene, so I still got credited for my work in that episode, and I still receive royalties for it.

I stayed in touch with the casting directors after the show, and with Yuri and A.J Tesler who played Rob/Bo at the inn. Los Angeles is a weird town because we all move on to different projects and we all moved on with our lives. People book jobs out of town too, so you tend to just drift in and out. I went to see Melissa's Groundlings show and chatted with her afterwards.

The second episode was difficult, technically, because I had to bang pots on cue to agitate Lorelai's character who was hungover. Banging a non specific loud noise with a pot, on cue, is actually really difficult. I remember thinking that everyone was mad at me for not banging my posts well. In general, the more chaotic a scene was, the more challenging it was. Of my four episodes, that was definitely the one where I didn't totally feel like my best work got to shine. However, all of my experiences on this show were positive, and a lot of fun overall.

It doesn't shock me that there is a devoted fan community for *Gilmore Girls,* and I think the birth of the internet around the time the show was starting, probably contributed to that. I think the show touched a generation of people because it tapped into emotion but was fun to watch. It's quippy, fast, and funny. It had the energy of a comedy but the soul of a drama and that really appealed to people. I think it was one of the first shows to bridge that hybrid nature. It was an hour long show that was funny but dramatic. It was smart and it could bring viewers in on different levels and they could enjoy the mother and daughter dynamic, themes of classism, and small town, amongst other themes. These are all things people can relate to.

I started doing *Gilmore Girls* off my run on *General Hospital* and then afterwards I started on *Bones* which I recurred on for three seasons. I started writing in 2012 for film and television. I hit a point where I was feeling creatively fulfilled by that and not by acting anymore so I just kind of moved away from acting and it felt okay to do that. Now I write. I am mostly focused on writing features. I help my wife who is a producer and she has her own organising business. I direct and produce videos for her business, and I'm hoping to have a career as a writer and to direct.

Tahmus Rounds

Buzu Barnes

I auditioned for *Gilmore Girls*, and when I heard I got a callback, I was really nervous. The part was for a cajun band leader. While I am a musician, I don't play the washboard. I also didn't have one, so I went and bought a real washboard from a thrift store and put wire around it so that I could wear it. I have always been a Hank Williams fan, so I performed *Jambalaya (On the Bayou)* for my audition. I was hitting the washboard with my nails, not realising at that time that you are meant to use metal finger picks. It didn't end well. By the completion of the song, my hands were in a bloody mess. Regardless of my hands, I felt like I had nailed the song and felt good about the audition. I heard the next day that I had booked the job, and I would be playing Buzu Barnes. There's a terrifying time after the audition where you keep going over your audition in your head, and wait for the phone to ring. It was great news when I heard that my hard work (and messed up hands) had paid off.

When I got to set, the crew and cast were really efficient. I was only coming in for the day, but I was impressed at what a well oiled machine the show was, and how fast they worked. The cast were well rehearsed and ready to work. When you approach the building, and the sound stage that you are going to be working on, you walk in like it's the first day of school and hope that somebody is going to like you. Thankfully, someone comes up to you as soon as you arrive and walks you through it. They set you up with a room, tell you who to report to, and make sure you are comfortable. Once I was ready, the director came in with Daniel and Amy Sherman-Palladino. They were very kind and made me feel that they were very glad I was there. That was really nice because sometimes on set there is a sense of "just get on with it", so I have always remembered how kind they were.

I was really nervous about doing my part well, and doing it right. I was cast as the leader of a Zydeco band, but the others cast in the band were from an actual established Zydeco band, so I felt a heightened sense of responsibility to do well. On the day of filming, I was given finger picks to play the washboard, after the production crew became aware of what happened to my fingers at the audition. The finger picks protected my fingers, and made the percussion sound louder. There was a real sense of family among those who worked on the show regularly. Even though I was coming in as a dayplayer, everyone was very kind, very nice, and awesome to work with. I was uptight and cautious, but they were relaxed, and encouraging.

While my musical skills were not usually focused around a washboard, I did do musical theatre in college, and I do play four stringed instruments like the tenor guitar, and the ukulele. One of the highlights of my musical career was getting to play Hank Williams in a live musical production called *Hank Williams: Lost Highway*. The show included more than 20 of William's songs and ran at The 6th Street Playhouse in Santa Rosa for a month. I was also the founder of a Hank Williams band and it was really great fun. Playing music is just as much fun, if not more, than acting.

Before *Gilmore Girls* I was living in Chicago, and travelling in a show called the Blue Man Group. Our show was a high energy rock show, and was truly an incredible theatrical experience. A friend of mine in college got into the Blue Man Group early on when it only had three members. My friend became one of the first replacements of one of the three original members. As they saw the show expanding, they started running auditions and my friend reached out to me. I didn't get in for the first show I auditioned for because it's a particular style and skill set. However, they gave me another chance a year later for the opening of Chicago in 1996, and I was in.

It was eight shows a week, and was very intense. I felt like I couldn't do much else in my life. All my days off were spent resting. Eventually, after four years, I just wanted something different. I was a California native and living in Chicago for four years was fascinating —and I loved everything about it—but I longed for the 'Cali' weather, my family and friends, and my old stomping ground. I wanted to come back. I have a lot of friends in the Blue Man Group who are still in it and I keep in touch with a lot of them. They are a great group of human beings.

I believe that any time you get to meet someone and do your craft, or your work, you establish a bit more good will within the acting universe. My role on *Gilmore Girls* gave me a boost of confidence to book a nice guest starring role in a top show and be able to call my mom and say I'm going to be on television. That was really gratifying. Every single job makes me look forward to the next one. I think acting is a tough business, and when I was first starting out I was afraid. People quit, get chewed up, and spit out. It can be really rough on people, especially the time in between jobs. I have known friends who get depressed and it can happen to the best of people. But I think if it's something you really love, and you are able to stick it out and maintain a simple lifestyle I think acting can be a worthy profession, regardless of your status as an actor. Whether you are a George Clooney, or a guy like me, living a middle class lifestyle and feeling like life is good, if three people saw my work and got something out of it, then they made my day a little nicer. We have all relied so much on entertainment in the pandemic and made the world look at it a little differently. It's gained an importance to humanity because people realised they really do need entertainment when times are tough. That's one of the things I love about it.

    I love that shows that existed before streaming have these new lives breathed into them by the fact that they have been uploaded to streaming platforms, and people can go back and watch them from beginning to end. It's a wonderful aspect of streaming. *Gilmore Girls'* very fast talking, great writing, and fast paced clip has done really well with the next generation of viewers. I have nothing but fond memories of my time on *Gilmore Girls*. It was exciting for me to get to play something as zany as a Cajun Zydeco guy.

Ryen Hermann

Alexandra

My Dad was my best friend. I find it very cathartic to see his presence live on, in *Gilmore Girls*. I feel incredibly lucky that I can sit down and watch him whenever I want to, and listen to him whenever I want to. I always tell people that if they love someone, record their voice, or record them on video, even if it's just doing the most mundane things. After my father passed away, I was pregnant with my twins, and grieving his loss. At that point I hadn't watched the whole show from start to finish. My wife and I watched all seven seasons of *Gilmore Girls* and it was an incredible experience. It's a gift, in his absence, to be able to watch him on screen, hear his voice, and see him moving around, like I remember him.

I'm really removed from the film and television industry. When I was growing up, Dad worked in Los Angeles, but lived in a small Connecticut town. This gave us the normality and consistency of attending a regular school, in a small community, while Dad still worked in the film business. Dad was really low key when it came to red carpet events, and other glamorous occasions. He was first and foremost, a family person. If he could come home and spend time with us, he would. He gave his acting his all, but he would forgo a part in a film or a television show to be at my graduation, or a piano recital for my little sister. My brother is a chef in Los Angeles, and my Dad would often bring his friend to go and eat at my brother's restaurant. He wanted to support us in all of our endeavours.

Living in a small Connecticut town became a valuable resource on the show in some ways. Amy Sherman-Palladino would confer with Dad often on upcoming plot points, and, as a result, there are episodes where my experiences in school are covered. Sometimes I would be watching an episode, and I would see Rory go through things that I had just gone through. For instance, the prep school, and how out of place Rory felt. I grew up in a small town and was switched into a private school. My transition to a new school, and my experiences of trying to fit in and do well mirrored Rory's in a lot of ways. Of course, this inspiration for the show wasn't always limited to my experiences. Little spats between Emily and Richard also mirrored arguments my parents had.

The first time I came to the set was for the episode where Rory plays golf with her grandfather. That was also the first time I met Alexis Bledel who plays Rory. She was incredibly shy, and was still getting her feet wet in acting, since *Gilmore Girls* was her first real television gig. I spent a lot of time going back and forth to Los Angeles while Dad was on the show. I went to boarding school, and then college, so sometimes flying to the set would be the only opportunity to spend extra time with him. The golf scenes in that episode were shot on a real golf course. I was hanging around with my Dad when he told me to go and make friends with Alexis. I didn't want to go over and force myself on her, and I told Dad that, but he insisted. He said she was probably feeling out of place, because there was nobody else around that was her age, and she was "surrounded by fat old farts". So, Alexis and I chatted, and became friends. When I was in Los Angeles, we would hang out, and she reached out to me when Dad passed away.

    Alexis later said that my Dad was the first person who made her feel at ease on set. He was very down to earth, funny, and would talk to anyone. He had a cool, kind of hip wit about him even though he was older. He could hang with the best and the youngest of them. I immediately loved the premise of the show, and knew it was going to be good. The thought of a 16 year old single mother was still taboo then, and people where I was from would still have turned their noses up if that happened in our town. But, the idea was something that younger people could relate to. Plus, the show was funny, and female dominated. There weren't—and still aren't—a lot of shows that address these topics in such a relatable way. Visiting my Dad on the set for that episode was great. I loved meeting the cast, and watching my Dad in action. It was the perfect introduction to *Gilmore Girls*.

    After that, I would often go onto the set. Dad had a great connection with Kelly Bishop, who had come from a heavy theatre background. She was very welcoming, and a real professional. We used to joke that Kelly was his other wife. She would come to visit him when he was sick, and they were great friends. While this was not a jumping off platform for her, she was happy to be a part of something different, and supported and encouraged those new people for whom the show was a launching pad. In the film industry, it's quite common to run into people that are jaded, and demanding. There was not a single person who came across that way, and who wasn't kind on *Gilmore Girls*—from the catering staff, to cast, to hair and makeup. There was no ego or entitlement to be seen. For a lot of actors, *Gilmore Girls* was their first main acting gig which brought a freshness to the show. Everyone was happy to be there, to be working, and to be part of a team of people who were so respectful of one another. The main cast were grateful, and kind, and it was really refreshing. Overall, it was a lovely set to be on.

The *Gilmore Girls* family was a humble group. They would put together events at their homes, and would invite everyone. I remember standing in Valerie Campbell's kitchen one night and Melissa McCarthy (Sookie) was there. She would always refer to me as "the tall blonde Amazon". She used to say, "could you get any taller? Or blonder?" Everyone was so down to earth, and chilled out. They were hanging at each other's homes, and drinking beers. It was such a tight knit bunch.

I didn't really understand how popular *Gilmore Girls* was when it was on, because I didn't really sit down and watch films or television shows that Dad was on, with him. I would sometimes watch the episodes on my own, but I didn't make a big fuss about it. I was very cautious about telling people my Dad was an actor. I was raised with the belief that being an actor was equal to all important jobs like being a policeman, or a teacher. Dad never wanted to draw attention away from other people. Since we didn't really talk about Dad's acting work, and he didn't either, I just didn't understand what a big deal it was.

I remember being on set in the second or third season and Dad and I were being driven around the Warner Bros lot. I had promised a friend at school that I would bring her something from the Warner Bros Studios gift shop, and asked Dad if he could take me there. He suggested that he find something from the *Gilmore Girls* set to give her, but I didn't think she would want that. I just didn't realise how significant the show was. While we were driving around the lot, we saw a tour taking place, and people in the tour group started screaming and pointing, "That's Richard Gilmore!" He tipped his hat and waved, and I was shocked. I assumed the only popular people were the two *Gilmore Girls*, and maybe their love interests. I was stunned that fans would be so interested in my Dad's character. That's really what was so cool about this show. While it was about the two girls, and that key relationship, so many other characters defined the show. People related to all these other characters that really supported the foundation of the show as a whole. It's a show where every character is important, not just the main ones. My Dad tapped the driver and asked him to stop the cart, because he could tell the fans were about to run over. The man driving the touring golf cart radioed through to our driver and said that the fans would love to come and get an autograph, which just stunned me. I was so removed from the whole situation. I was going to school on the East Coast, coming to visit my Dad at his work, and fans were running over, addressing him as "Mr Gilmore". My Dad agreed, of course, and gave them all an autograph. I looked at him, and said, "Your show is really popular.". He just looked at me and said, "I told you."

Dad had a huge appreciation for fans. As well as meeting and talking with them on the lot, he also used to write fan mail, by hand. When people wrote into the show, he didn't just send back autographs, he would sit down and write them letters, sometimes over several days when he had time off set.

Dad had really strong comparisons with his character Richard. He was not judgemental the way that Richard can come off, but there were very real glimpses of the real Richard Gilmore in my Dad. He was relatable, witty, mischievous, and fun. There were also strong similarities in the way that he felt people should present themselves. He wanted people to commit to their cause, to their craft. If someone wanted to be a writer, then he encouraged them to figure out how to be a writer, and would support them in that. It didn't matter if he agreed with someone's dreams, or career pursuits. If they were dedicated and passionate about it, then he would support them. However, in return, he would also expect to see the hard work it takes to make it happen. Richard, and Dad were both committed to their work, and wanted to pass that strong work ethic onto others. He was everyone's biggest fan, and he was loyal. Once he made a connection with someone, that connection was made for life.

Dad disliked shortcuts in life. He felt that there was value in the lessons that come from waiting, and doing the hard work. As much as he would not want to see someone struggle, he also felt that struggle could be a gift, and a part of the process. A lot of people want a quick fix, but he saw value in the learning that takes place when people don't get that instant gratification. I think Richard took that same approach with Rory and Lorelai. There was a sense of him being there, but not rushing in to save them. He would help them figure it out, but he wouldn't jump to their rescue. They had lessons to learn, and things to figure out and he made space for that.

One point of difference to Richard's character was that Dad didn't care where people came from. There was no blue-bloodedness in his beliefs about people. He didn't care if people lived in a beautiful home, or went to Yale. He had the utmost respect for blue collar jobs, especially if people did them well. His philosophy would be that if life handed you a job as a bartender, then you make it your mission to become the best bartender you can be.

Even the more minor aspects of Richard's character mirrored characteristics of my Dad. He liked beautiful double breasted suits, and he enjoyed dressing up. He entered a room the same way, and he spoke to people like Richard does. He felt that the important things in life are the things you can't buy—manners, language, poise. Dad, like Richard, was also not up with the latest technology. He had an appreciation for more traditional ways of doing things. For the longest time, Dad refused to have an IPhone. He held onto his old school Motorola flip phone, but kept losing it. When he did, the phone company would tell him he could choose any other phone for free, because of the cost of getting another old flip phone, but he resisted. When he did finally upgrade, he refused to use emoji's, and shorthand language. If I texted him "R U OK?" he wouldn't respond. He would wait for me to rewrite the text with the correct grammar and punctuation. When I took the time to use my education and proper language, he would give me the same respect. Dad believed in being thoughtful, and measured with language. He hated sayings like "what's up?" and people taking unnecessary shortcuts in their speech. I think there's a real crossover there with Richard.

Later in the show, I decided for about a second that I wanted to be an actor. I wanted to pursue performing arts because I was dancing and loved acting. I was living in New York at the time, and was acting in a theatre group. I was on the WB set one day during the filming of a cafeteria scene and I asked Dad if I could be an extra on the show sometime. I just wanted to be someone who sat at one of the tables, or on a park bench in the background. I wanted a taste of the industry, and I was also hoping to get my union card which would entitle me to the benefits which come with being a member of the Screen Actors Guild (SAG AFTRA). Logging acting hours as an extra would get me one step closer to this goal. Dad had a chat with Amy and told me that he had set up a screen test for me in New York, and Amy would look at it. I was a bit taken aback, since I had only asked to be an extra. When I went home, I did the screen test, and got a call that I would be cast in the episode "Bridesmaids Revisited", as one of Honor Huntzberger's Bridesmaids, named Alexandra.

I had done theatre, and a couple of commercials when I was younger, but this was the first real television show I had been on. I was nervous because I was thrown in with actors who were much more experienced than I was. One of the other bridesmaids in my episode was an established soap opera actress, and one was on television with a major comedian. I also felt like a giant next to these petite women. I am six feet tall, so when they fitted us for our dresses I wore slippers, while the other women wore high heels. Valerie Campbell in the wardrobe department was really supportive and made sure I was dressed accordingly. I thought it was hilarious that the sweatsuits came in a size that fitted my six foot tall frame, but I was grateful.

I didn't tell the other women in my episode who my Dad was because I wanted to stand on my own two feet. At one point, he walked onto the set and said, "Hey, kiddo!" He told me he was really proud of me, but I was trying to tone the encounter down. I had earned the role on my own, and screen tested for it, so I didn't want anyone to feel like I had taken any kind of shortcut onto the show.

During that episode, there is a connection to my life, as there were so many throughout the show. One of the other girls delivers a line about a prep school called Brearley. Brearley school is an all-girls private school in New York where I went, and it just reminded me that *Gilmore Girls* had stepped into my life, or maybe it was the other way around.

Everyone on that episode was amazing, and it was so fun. Alexis was really excited that we would be in an episode together. The bridesmaids all had lunch together and hung out, and it gave me a great taste of what life would be like as an actor. At that point I was very seriously considering that as my career path, but I wasn't sure if I would go into film and television, or theatre. After that episode I decided that I would go back to school and do my masters, and get into interior design. Though life has taken me in different directions, I am still really happy that I got the opportunity to do that episode. I worked on something beloved, and I love that I have that episode to show my kids one day.

When Dad passed away, a lot of the cast and crew took it very hard. We didn't have any connection with the industry by that time, and I was taking care of my twins who were only two months old. Dad had already had some discussions with Amy about the reboot, and had expressed a strong interest in coming back to reprise his role as Richard Gilmore. Unfortunately, he died a year after he was diagnosed with brain cancer. I was invited to the premiere red carpet event for *A Year in the Life* so I organised a friend to come over for the night to help my wife who would be alone with the twins for the first time. I took my sister in law with me, so that I would have some support if things got difficult, emotionally. My Dad had been gone a year by that time, but I don't think I had really fully processed his passing yet. It was heavy, and hard for a lot of the cast members too. Some of them had come to his memorial, and contributed to a film memorial that we made for him.

None of us knew when the revival episodes came out, how they had been written, or what role my Dad's character would have. When I watched them for the first time, I couldn't believe the parallels between what I saw on screen, and my Dad. Richard's library looked like it had been taken directly from our life. He had a library at our house, and if you couldn't find him anywhere, he would be up there at his big desk, doing work. That is still where I go when I go home. It's the place where I go to be close to Dad—in his library, sitting at his desk. When Rory ended up in Richard's office, at his desk writing, I cried buckets. It was uncanny. My sister in law and I stared at each other, silently questioning if what we were seeing was real. It was as if the writers had watched what we do when we go home—visiting his library, sitting at his desk, touching his things. Rory's grief represented ours.

The way that the whole Gilmore family navigated Richard's absence mirrored our journey through the grief of losing my Dad. It was eerie. I felt like Amy had studied how we processed his death, and then put those experiences on the screen. We really didn't grasp the significance of Dad's presence, or the impact that he had on our lives until he wasn't there. I knew he was important, I knew he was my best friend, and I knew he was the number one thing in my life. But, it wasn't until he was gone, that I realised all of the areas of my life that he had previously affected in some way. It was surreal to be watching other characters navigate that new reality, in a fictional setting.

I thought it was really wonderful how they had honoured him. Amy could have very easily written Richard's character out, explaining in the script that he had passed away and the characters had moved on since then. The show was about the female dynamic, and that was a strong current that had run throughout all the seasons. Instead, she had chosen to take almost an entire episode out of only four to really focus on the loss of the father figure, and how his passing had affected all of the women in the show. They captured a legacy, and I was unbelievably touched, and proud. It was hard to watch, but I was really grateful, and felt blessed and honoured to watch it for the first time with all of the cast and crew.

My wife and I went to one of the fan festivals for *Gilmore Girls* and took our twins. I ran a quarter mile with my twins in the stroller, for my Dad. It felt crazy to be on stage for the panel and realise that this whole convention was just for the one show. I don't know if other sitcoms have fan festivals like that. These annual festivals are something that has been put together by the love of the cast, crew, and fans. People are showing up out of love, and loyalty. It's mind blowing. I got the most incredible reception when I went. They presented my and my mother as special guests, and we walked into a standing ovation that brought me to tears. I was so stunned at how much love there was for us. People shared their stories of what *Gilmore Girls* means for them, and it was amazing to see how much the show had impacted them. It was a true honour. The fans are real people. There is humanity in the world and it shows up in the *Gilmore Girls* fan community more than anywhere else. There aren't many shows that so many people can tap into, soak into the love of the show, and then trickle it back out again. Dad would have gone every single year if he could have. He was the kind of person who would stop in the middle of a meal to chat with a fan. He valued the ability to transform a moment for someone. He loved how television could take people places, and cherished being the vehicle for that. That's why he still loved theatre—because he could go out the stage door afterwards and meet people. He loved *Gilmore Girls* because fans were so drawn to it, and affected by it.

After the premiere of *A Year in the Life*, I asked the show if I could have the giant portrait of my Dad that was featured in the revival episodes. It was oversized but I thought it was amazing because it really epitomised what a dominating figure he was, and allowed for this lingering presence of such a dominant character in the show. It was a great way to place this figure in their lives which would give a real tangible presence. It was not an easy thing to do to bring light to such a loss and shift in dynamic, while still having the characters and the storylines address it. I thought it was brilliant on Amy's part to have the unspoken elephant in the room, on the wall in such a commanding way. I thought the painting raised a lot of questions about loss—how to be surrounded by it, and what to do with it.

Gilmore Girls was a fantastic show because it wasn't afraid to deal with uncomfortable things like death, and loss. It wasn't afraid to go there, and explore the more difficult facets of life. Those things are always relevant, and they were explored on the show in constructive ways. Sometimes the ending was not happy ever after, and that's reality. Sometimes the couple breaks up and doesn't get back together. Sometimes people have to grieve a loss, because that person isn't coming back. Take Rory's situation in the revival: is this the right time to have a baby? Did she have it with the right guy? This is a tricky topic that won't ever date. It will always be relevant, and I feel lucky, and blessed to have been a part of it.

Ronnie Alvarez

Connor

I had an unusual start on *Gilmore Girls,* which began when I was travelling in South America with my sister. We were leaving Peru or Argentina, and when we got on the plane, my sister and I were not sitting together. Instead, I was sitting next to two women. I was tired, so I was minding my own business and passing the time. At some point I thought I should try to be friendly, and at least say hello to these two people sitting with me. So, I asked them how they were, and it turned out they were Americans who both spoke English. We got talking and it turned out we were all from Los Angeles. One of the women asked me what I did for a living. I told her I was an actor, on holiday in South America. They were casting directors who had been to Machu Picchu for leisure. I didn't want to keep bringing up work on holiday, so I didn't ask them what they were casting for. We finished up our flight, and said goodbye.

Several weeks later, I was back home when I got a call from my agent telling me I had an audition. I got to the Warner Bros lot and while I was waiting, the casting assistant came to get me, asked me if I was ready to go into the audition room, and then told me that she had heard all about how the casting directors and I had met. I had no idea what she was talking about. As she opened the door for me to go in, I saw Jami Rudofsky, who was one of the women I sat with in the plane.

She held up an invite for a play I had just been in. When I am in a theatrical production, I send invitations out to all casting people, just to let them know that I am working, and staying busy. It was an invitation to the show with my business card, and picture and she had gone along after receiving my invitation. I proceeded with my audition and it went well. I felt good about it. Jami gave me an adjustment—it was very minor and she said my correction was perfect, and that I would get a call back. I came back a day later and I walked into the same room and now the director, and the producers were in the room as well. I did my part and they loved it. I booked the job, and that's how I became the Yale student and tutor, Connor.

Initially, I was booked just to do that one episode. They called me the night before my first day on set to say there was a 6 am calltime. I was told I would have a car parking space reserved right next to the soundstage. Sometimes you have to park in a building or a lot and walk onto the studio lot, so it was nice to have a spot to drive into. I got out of my car at the studio and Brad Pitt was walking right towards me. He had his coffee and his cigarette in his hand. During one of the breaks, I went outside and George Clooney was playing basketball with the crew. I later found out they were shooting *Oceans 11* on the lot.

On that first day, the wardrobe people were very supportive, kind, and encouraging. They congratulated me and welcomed me to the show. They said I must be someone special, because everyone who comes on this show goes off to do big things. Brandon Routh, who went on to play *Superman* did *Gilmore Girls* first, as did Seth MacFarlane and other very visible actors. When I got on to the set, the dialogue coach George Bell came up to me and asked if I wanted to run lines with him. Once we got to shooting, my work was done quite quickly, but it was fun. That scene with Paris in the Yale tutor's room was so funny to shoot, and to watch. I tried to play the frazzled tutor as Paris was laying into me. It's always great to work with good actors, and people always remember that scene.

After the first episode I shot I got phone calls, and messages, all from women who were excited that I was on the show. They wanted to know what it was like, and asked if I had fun shooting the episode. I got a few dates out of that. Being on the show was also good for my resume. Once the character had a name and I got offered the second episode it really legitimised my credit. I booked more jobs after that and continued to be an active actor. I went to dance class before the pandemic and a girl behind the counter said she saw me on *Gilmore Girls*. People still recognise me from the show, and send me messages about it.

One day, almost a year later, the phone rang and it was my agent. Casting had called him and said they wanted to have me back and offer me a recurring role. This felt like a little feather in my cap, because the scene I would be filming was with Edward Herrmann. He was an accomplished stage actor with a booming, resonant voice and I had a lot of admiration for him. I knew I had to bring my A-game in this scene with Edward, and had a lot of fun filming it. After being given a name, and getting two episodes, I had hoped to get more episodes, but the show got cancelled.

I still act, working on commercials, voice over, print, film—all of it. I work on stage as well on screen. My acting teacher taught Leonardo Dicaprio and Hilary Swank. Actors get their 'vitamins' on stage, so I try to do a play at least once a year but I'm very picky about what plays I do because they are a big commitment. But, I do it for the experience and will probably always be on the stage. I hope in the future I do even more. On my bucket list, of course, is to do a play on Broadway.

Gilmore Girls is popular because of the mother-daughter relationship. That relationship is universal. Anyone can relate to that in some capacity. My experience of the show though, will always be highlighted by working with Edward Herrmann. He was so giving, and encouraging. It really felt like he was cheerleading for me.

Lou Saliba

Ronald

    I had a bit of a history with *Gilmore Girls* before I actually shot an episode. I had met one of the casting directors—Jami Rudofsky—at a casting workshop. She called me in for an audition for *Gilmore Girls* for the role of the court bailiff in season 6, episode 1. The scene involved Rory going to court for stealing a yacht, and the role had some lines. I didn't get the part. I was a bit disappointed, so when Jami ran another workshop, I decided to go along and use this next one as an opportunity to show her what I could do. The workshops are often seen as quite controversial, because there is a 'pay to play' aspect. You enrol in the workshop and pay a fee, with the hope that it will lead to work. I paired up with Pip Newson, who had played Glenda, an interior decorator on *Gilmore Girls*. We did this scene that rocked the room, it was so funny. It was a scene from *Gilmore Girls* in the hospital room when Sookie had her baby. I played Jackson and Pip played Sookie. The writing was brilliant. After that casting workshop, I got another audition for *Gilmore Girls* to play Rory's therapist at Yale. I didn't get that part either. I had felt that the audition went well, and I think the casting directors had too, because even though I wasn't right for that part, they immediately called me in for another audition for a role as a reporter, which I also didn't get. The next audition I was called in for ended up being the one where I finally booked a part. It was my fourth audition on the show, and I was happy to finally get on. I would be playing Ronald, a fellow student in Luke's swim class.

I knew a little about the show before I got on, because I always tried to watch a bit of each show that was on. I would usually schedule myself to watch the pilot of the whole fall lineout, to be prepared for shows I might audition for. The industry has changed a lot over the last 10-15 years, and shows premiere across the whole year. You have to watch each one as an actor to know the style because you never know what kind of auditions you might get. I knew the pace of *Gilmore Girls*, and knew the casting directors through those workshops.

I always find it funny that nobody asks actors at auditions if they have certain skills. I once got a part where I had to drive really fast down a dirt road in a Mercedes without hitting Tom Selleck. Nobody asked me if I could drive. I did *Modern Family*, playing a dad who was a basketball referee, but nobody asked me if I knew anything about basketball. For *Gilmore Girls*, I was cast in a pool scene, but nobody asked if I could swim. I can swim, but nobody ever asked. My scene was shot in one day, on location at a swimming pool at the Glendale YMCA.

The scene was funny to shoot, and the director seemed to be happy with my work. I knew who Scott Patterson was, and it was fun to work with him. Between takes someone would come and put us in robes, and I would chat with Scott Patterson and Mia Cottet who played Susan while we were waiting. It was a very pleasant experience. It was really enjoyable. I got to eat lunch with Will Schriner, the director. I had an overall positive experience and I would never have guessed that someone would have hired me to be in a pool scene so it's kind of funny in an ironic way. I was really comfortable.

The Palladino's were gone by my season, so I didn't get to meet them, but from the top down—from the director, to the crew—everybody that was associated with the show was so nice. I've never had a bad experience working with cast and crew on a television show, but *Gilmore Girls* people, in particular, were lovely to work with.

In my opinion, *Gilmore Girls* was successful because of the casting, and the writing. If you can do that fast paced, funny writing on a show where people love the characters, it's always going to be good. I can certainly recognise a great show when I see it. How many shows are there that depict a mother daughter relationship that is so positive? There weren't too many shows around at that time that had great roles for women, and strong female leads.

Austin Tichenor

Dr. Goldstein

    I got the part of Dr Goldstein in *Gilmore Girls* after my third audition for the show. Auditioning for the same show multiple times happens a lot in this business, especially if the casting directors like you. In my case, I think they did, but I wasn't cast for the first two because I wasn't quite right for the roles. I had previously auditioned for the role of the priest that came to talk to Rory over dinner in season

6, episode 7, but Michael McCarthy got the role. I knew Michael, and thought he was much better suited to the role than I was.

Before I was on television, I was a drama major in college, and got my MFA in directing. I went into theatre, running a theatre in New Hampshire before moving out to Hollywood. My wife was touring with Second City—an improvisational theatre troupe—writing and performing shows. When I was in Los Angeles, I got hired by the Reduced Shakespeare Company, and started touring with them. The Reduced Shakespeare Company has been called a "trio of modern Marx Brothers". It consists of three of us, who perform fast-paced comedies that deal with serious topics, in a condensed or 'reduced' way. After four years of touring the world, my family and I decided to move back to Los Angeles and I would try to find some acting work.

I had known one of the casting directors for *Gilmore Girls* for a long time because Jami Rudofsky had been involved with *Felicity* and *The Practice* which I was on. The first thing they tell you on *Gilmore Girls* is that you have to talk as fast as you can. I was advised before my audition to talk really fast and not to take any pauses. Amy Sherman-Palladino likes the dialogue lickety split, and this is also evident by the dialogue in *The Marvelous Mrs Maisel*. After my audition I hadn't gotten 100 yards from the studio before I got a call telling me that I got the role of Doctor Goldstein.

When I was living in Los Angeles I played a lot of doctors and lawyers, so this role was right in my wheelhouse. *Gilmore Girls* wasn't a show that I watched, but I knew what it was. A lot of people were talking about it, and a lot of my friends had been on the show as guest stars.

The day I shot my episode, the vibe on set was great. It was very professional. It was good money, and it was great to work on a hit show. I felt more pressured than usual in my time on the show because the words had to be perfect, and fast. I made sure I was as prepared as possible. Nobody wants to be *that* guy—the person who shows up and can't get it right, holding the whole set up. I had done an episode on *The West Wing* and had played a prosecuting attorney on other shows. The casting people knew that I was a stage actor, which I think gave them some assurance that I was dependable with dialogue, and able to deliver it at a quick clip.

I had a lovely moment with Kelly Bishop who couldn't have been sweeter. My scene was a 'walk and talk' where I was to leave the waiting room, walk down the corridor and through the hallways of the hospital while I answered Mrs Gilmore's questions. She was questioning my character about his credentials, and I had quite wordy responses to recite, so it was a huge take. There were about 50 extras walking around, and an enormous crew with a steadicam operator, who operates a handheld camera while walking in front of us, backwards. After the first take, they didn't like it. We went back for a second one, and were told to all go back to our starting points again. They yelled "action" and at this point, I flubbed my line, cracking under the pressure a bit. Kelly Bishop took my arm, patted it, and said "it happens to all of us". I've always remembered how gracious she was at that moment. She could easily have rolled her eyes and been frustrated and miserable with me. It couldn't have been a more lovely gesture.

There are different pressures on different shows, and on *Gilmore Girls* those pressures surrounded the dialogue. The show was known for its sharp, crisp, peppy rhythm. Walk and talk scenes are always more challenging because they have to be perfect in one take. In episodes where I play lawyers, There will be a lot of dialogue—closing arguments and long speeches—but I get several takes, because the camera switches between myself, the judge, the jury, etc. I did a few episodes of *Alias* with Jennifer Garner and I had a page and a half long speech about the effects of some super secret poison gizmo. It was a long speech full of bad news, and it was the very final shot of the day. We were coming right up to having been on set for 12 hours. They shot Jennifer Garner's reaction first, and I knew that I needed to get this right, as soon as it was my turn. They turned the camera on me, and I knew that everyone was relying on me to nail this, so that we could all go home. So, there are pressures on every set.

I didn't get called back for the Netflix revival of *Gilmore Girls*, which I think was a horrible mistake! I saved Grandpa Gilmore, and for that I think I should have been embraced by the fans! I'm kidding, obviously.

It is one of those shows that people continue to watch, and people still reach out to me when they have seen my episode. I was really excited when *A Year in the Life* was announced because our good friend Rose Abdoo would be going back. Rose is a Second City veteran along with my wife, so we were thrilled that she would be busy with *Gilmore Girls* again.

PART TWO
CREATORS

It's a Lifestyle

Jennie and Marcus Whitaker

The Fan Fest Society

I didn't start watching the series until after it ended. When the show first aired, everyone I know was watching it. I was starting college and didn't take a television with me so all my focus was on campus involvement and my classes.

Discovering *Gilmore Girls* was a happy accident nearly a decade later. I was working from home in 2009 and watching *Ellen* on my lunch break and the show had just switched from mornings to afternoons. I must have gone to check the mail or gone outside for a bit, because when I came back in, the infamous "You Jump, I Jump Jack" episode from season 5 was on my screen. I saw one scene and I was hooked.

I started saving it on my DVR to watch each night with my husband. We watched the rest of season 5, then 6 and 7. When we saw the finale it was a bit sad because technically the journey was over, but the best part was still to come, seeing where it all began. Most people logically watch shows from beginning to end, but we watched seasons 5, 6, 7, 1, 2, 3, 4 and then ran through 5, 6 and 7 to make the finale the final (before we started watching again, of course.) It was so fun that way, almost preferable now that I think of it.

Let's just say, Litchfield County in Northwest Connecticut was so close to portraying Stars Hollow that it could have been a stand in! I was in literal town hall meetings weekly, with the selectman and highly opinionated townspeople. There were no cell phones, very few restaurants (but all very good ones) and a beautiful inn that hosted me for days on end for nearly two months. Getting hit by a deer was extremely likely on the windy roads and Friday night dinners were definitely something people did. Private, high-end schools are a reality in that part of Connecticut and there were definitely locals that knew everything about everyone, a la Miss Patty and Babette. There were characters—I mean humans—at coffee shops that were semi-permanent fixtures and only one place to buy groceries in town (where I posed with a box of cornstarch).

It was, and is, picturesque and magical. I'd recommend all of Litchfield County to anyone that loves stunning scenery, quaint shops and delicious food. Obviously, we're biased but one particular weekend in the fall is our favourite, when all our friends gather there for a reunion of sorts. We do all the things you'd expect—drink coffee, eat food, and celebrate a fandom we think means more than most people could understand.

The first one was unforgettable, but then again so was the second, third, fourth and fifth. I have a very long story about each festival and I hope I get it on paper before I lose all my memories. I love replaying them in my head and my perspective is totally unique to everyone else's, who I hope is having even more fun than we are.

At the first event, fandom was at a high point, even 15 years after the show aired and none of the cast and crew could tell us anything about the revival that we would all see a month later. It was a beautiful secret they held from us and we anticipated more than they understood.

Tickets sold out the day we launched them. Media from all over the world reached out. Cast and crew members contacted us and we literally couldn't keep up with the pace of requests in the beginning. We were overwhelmed in the best possible way, by everyone. We have done lots of things, but had never put on a festival. It was truly one of the most exciting projects of my career. My husband and I have owned a small marketing agency in Austin for years, but this was something unlike anything we had done before. Instead of looking for an audience, the audience was looking for us—a marketers' dream. It was such an exciting time and we could talk about it endlessly, ad nauseam. Surely I'll tell the whole story one day.

Over the years, many of the same people have supported the event as we have all grown closer than anyone would have expected. We have cast members who have come year after year, some have even built fandoms around their characters name. Fans adore the cast and crew, and rightfully so. They are amazing humans, aside from their incredible talents. We have countless attendees we know by name that are a part of our family now, people we talk to daily and weekly, outside of the festival.

The group has grown far beyond the intended beginning. Sometimes we forget it was even about *Gilmore Girls* back then, because the community has grown beyond its name to something truly magical. We're so grateful we pursued such an unmarked, narrow path—we had no idea what we were getting into but it changed the lives of so many of us. We get feedback, often, about how people met at the festival and continue to benefit from their experience throughout the year. We're proud of that, but mostly just grateful. Grateful because the relationships have impacted our lives too and we can't imagine a world without fan fests and the communities behind them.

Covid19 changed everything, all around the globe (and at the time I'm writing this, things are still so unknown). The fan fest was no different. We couldn't gather. History will show that the world shut down in many ways, but when it came to large events—we were shut down completely even if our community was still thriving. There was no way to bring people together from all corners of the world safely in 2020. So, we did what anyone would do, the next best thing.

For us that was a virtual event. We had a normal festival schedule, over three days in October of 2020 from our home, broadcast to everyone else's home in attendance. People who had been before and people who could never join in the past. We had double the number of cast and crew, over 40 involved, plus attendees from over 25 countries. It was a great reminder of the joy the show brings to everyone who's spent time following the Gilmores.

In January of 2021 *Gilmore Girls* Fan Fest pivoted to create The Fan Fest Society. The story of "why" is much longer than anyone cares to hear, but the short version is that we wanted to start thinking about how we could, one day, create new "societies" and "fan fests" with the same magic that was there from the start of GGFF. The Fan Fest Society will continue to meet in Connecticut once a year to talk about all the things we mutually love about our favourite show, alongside cast & crew, but we hope to see new communities and new fan fests stem from The Fan Fest Society in the near future, when it's safe to gather face to face.

I think *Gilmore Girls* hits on so many classic themes that it will always be relevant. Maybe, as a fan, I'm biased, but I don't think the fandom is going anywhere, simply because the show transcends generations.

The characters are believable and easy to follow. There's no violence, there's age-appropriate death and the most tragic things that happen on the show are dramatised from rough patches in relationships and usually end up just fine. It tells the stories of countless people, which means everyone can relate to someone. Me? I'm Rory—book lover, achiever, rule follower, writer and only child. My husband? 100% Luke—can do anything, will help anyone, doesn't mind being alone, loves to fish, adores his truck and will always undeniably be the best husband and friend a girl could ask for without needing much in return.

I think that special type of Gilmore escapism will always be dream worthy. I can't imagine a day when *Gilmore Girls* isn't something someone can relate to in some way. And, gosh, maybe if that happens it'll be a period piece at worst. At best, we'll always have someone to talk about our favourite show with and we'll have a community ready to debate the inner workings of life in a town with a gazebo in the middle of it.

Either way, over the past few years I finally found my version of Stars Hollow. It's a community of people I see every fall, who are there for one another year around, no matter how different their journey has been or will be. Maybe that's why we all love the town hall meetings Taylor led. It's quite clear that the quirky group of townies all have a different story, but the tapestry of their individual personalities is the reason we all have a favourite and it's probably why *Gilmore Girls* resonates so personally with everyone.

Kristi Carlson

Author of the *Eat Like a Gilmore* Cookbooks

In February, 2001, I sat down to watch an episode of *Gilmore Girls* for the first time. It was the Donna Reed episode. As much as Rory's orange gingham dress and Lorelai's hot yet unacknowledged chemistry with Luke sucked me in, I had no way of knowing these quippy characters would continue to woo me, episode by episode, until they had become part of my DNA. I also never imagined that 15 years later I'd write a *Gilmore Girls* cookbook.

Personally, I don't watch much television. In fact, when my husband and I first met, I didn't have "television" at all. No cable. No

Direct Television. The only thing I watched was *Gilmore Girls* on old, worn DVDs. I used to turn to the show for comfort during bouts of anxiety, mild depression, and the inevitable fallout periods that come after dating the wrong kind of men.

Whenever I felt defeated, lethargic, or not good enough, watching *Gilmore Girls* was my antidote. Taking a nightly trip to Stars Hollow felt like taking a trip home, where Lorelai Gilmore was my alter ego. Even though I didn't have a kid, I related most closely to her. She and I were roughly the same age, same height. Two brunettes. We both wore lots of denim and tight tops. We had the same commitment-phobic tendencies, most likely due to us having loosely similar mothers. Yes, Lorelai is a fictional character, but I learned self-confidence from her. Seeing someone who was so similar to me act so confident and quirky was a revelation. She acted that way and people found her *appealing!* This gave me confidence to let out my own quirks. Thinking about it now, Lorelai Gilmore was the first person to give me permission to be myself.

Okay, so how did all of this turn into a cookbook?

In July, 2015 I mentioned to my then-boyfriend, now-husband, Tim, that I wanted to do something creative. My 9-to-5 job was slowly killing my soul and I needed something to counteract its effects. He thought for a moment, then rolled out with "You talk about all the food from *Gilmore Girls* all the time. Why don't you try creating those recipes?". As soon as he said it, I recognized it as the exact thing I needed. But I didn't want to simply write recipes. I wanted to create a cookbook and I wanted to do it with Warner Brothers.

For years I'd been complaining that Warner Brothers never put out a *Gilmore Girls* cookbook. Back in olden times, during seasons 1, 2 and 3, the Warner Brothers website had recipes for a handful of foods from the show. I always wondered why they didn't take that a step further and give us a full-blown cookbook. It was such a perfect idea, and it drove me bats that they never did.

That day, after talking with Tim, I wrote to Warner Brothers. Looking back, I wish I had hand-delivered a letter attached to a fruit basket or something. The lot was two blocks from my apartment in Burbank, and it possibly would have gotten me more attention more quickly. But I didn't make that effort. I took the cheap, lazy approach and emailed them. I asked about either collaborating on a cookbook, or licensing content from the show to make my own cookbook. They batted my email around between their corporate departments for several weeks. Finally, in December, 2015 I received a formal "we're not interested" response. I was disappointed, but undeterred. I wrote back accepting their decision, but alerting them I intended to move forward with the cookbook, as a fan-based project.

For the next few months I took advantage of the "one hour free consultation" offer from several Intellectual Property attorneys around Los Angeles. I called them, described my ideas, listened to their advice and weighed my options. Through years of working with bands, I had become pretty conversant in copyright law—the dos and don'ts. However, for this project I knew I needed an expert, so I paid a retainer to one of those IP attorneys. He was exactly the safety net I needed as I moved forward. As you read through *Eat Like A Gilmore*, you'll notice there are no photos and no direct quotes from the show. Even some of the recipes are called by different names, like Johnny Machete is called Chicken & Noodle Bake. The reason why? Copyright. My intention was to be respectful (and lawful!) with regard to copyright, while still producing a book for us fans to enjoy; one that *feels like* Stars Hollow. With my attorney's expert help, I feel like we accomplished it.

Another book, *The Four Hour Workweek* by Tim Ferriss, is something akin to a career coach to me. In it, I learned several of the tactics I needed to create *Eat Like A Gilmore* and make it a success. The first tactic was to test the cookbook idea to see whether or not it had legs. Was anyone else going to even want a *Gilmore Girls* cookbook? I had no idea.

By now it was 2016. Netflix had made episodes from all seven seasons available on demand for two years, and announced a *Gilmore Girls* revival for Fall, 2016. So I knew the show still had millions of fans. But the last episode of the original series had been filmed 9 years earlier! Would anyone want this cookbook? Rather than guess, and then throw a bunch of time and money into something based on that guess, I launched a Kickstarter. To me that was the easiest, clearest, most fun way to see whether or not any fellow fans would want an unofficial cookbook. My goal was $20,000. (It turns out cookbooks are expensive to make. Between ingredients, photos and printing costs, it was going to cost more than Lorelai's new roof to make it.) If the Kickstarter failed, so be it. I figured it was better to find out early on. But if it succeeded, if enough people wanted it, I was ready and willing to jump into it.

The Kickstarter launched, and I got some good responses. A bunch of my friends and a few fellow fans were excited. During Week two of the campaign, a little article came out that changed everything. A journalist and fellow fan by the name of Krystie Yandoli saw my campaign and decided to write an article about it for her employer, Buzzfeed. Her article came out March 21, 2016. The headline read "There's Going To Be An Unofficial "Gilmore Girls" Cookbook:Some people wait a lifetime for a cookbook like this." (You can still find it online.)

That one article spawned dozens of others from outlets like Food & Wine, Teen Vogue, People, Entertainment Weekly; each one talking about me, the cookbook, and the campaign. For the first time in my life, a project of mine went viral. Friends and family members were calling and texting to tell me they'd read about the cookbook in *Real Simple* or saw one of their Facebook friends post about it. Talk about surreal! The following day, my campaign hit its $20,000 goal. Thanks to Krystie, word had gotten out, and the *Gilmore Girls* fans came through. There would be a cookbook.

What's more, a few weeks later, two more Gilmore Girls fans, Sam Levitz and Chamois Holschuh, approached me from Skyhorse Publishing. After some back-and-forth emailing and a few phone calls, I had a publishing deal.

By November 2016, *Eat Like A Gilmore* by Kristi Carlson, with photos by Bonnie Matthews, was on the shelves in bookstores around the world. The following July, it reached #1 among all books on Amazon. To date, with help from *Gilmore Girls* fans all along the way, it's been the biggest, most fun success of my life. It's also given me the opportunity to meet and interact with thousands of fellow fans around the world. After a decade of not knowing a single soul who loved this show as much as I do, this book helped me find my people. Now I feel like I'm part of a sisterhood (and brotherhood for all the guy fans out there!). All because of a television show I sat down to watch one Tuesday night in 2001.

Kristine Eckart

The Gilmore Book Club

For many people, myself included, there is immense comfort to be found in a beloved television show like *Gilmore Girls*. I've always re-watched the show on a regular basis, but in times of physical, emotional, and mental strain, I've always found solace with the Gilmores and the community of Stars Hollow. Thanks to Netflix, many others are now also doing the same. New people who are discovering the show for the first time and falling in love with the characters, like I did, are keeping the popularity of *Gilmore Girls* alive long after the show went off the air. But for a Gilmore fan, that's not enough, there can never be enough. Fans are ecstatic over re-watching platforms, going crazy over Scott Patterson's (Luke Danes) new podcast, *I Am All In*, and John Cabrera's (Brian) Remarkist app that creates a community around television streaming, starting with *Gilmore Girls*. The *Gilmore Girls* fandom is here to stay. It's been 14 years since the final season ended, five years since the revival, and Gilmore fans are still clamouring for one more minute in Stars Hollow, one more moment with the *Gilmore Girls*.

Because of my love for this show, I've dedicated myself to reading all of the 340+ books on the Rory Gilmore Reading Challenge list, experiencing each book mentioned on the show for myself. Although it started as just a bucket list goal, it became a life-changing journey. Each book became an opportunity to do a deep dive into my psyche. I processed grief and healed from trauma. I found my purpose and solidified my voice. I had glorious epiphanies and devastating realisations. I identified areas I needed to change and things I had to work on. By opening my mind to whatever message each book had to give, I formed a lasting connection with every book I read. I didn't like every book, but that's not the point. It's the connection, the insights you learn that create that bond between you and the book and eventually change your life.

And so, I began to write about my journey with each book, recording every insight and moment of vulnerability, hoping that by offering myself and my life as an example, people could see that they too could use books to transform their lives.

Yes, I watch a lot of television and movies. Quotes from my favourite shows often make appearances in my daily conversations. I routinely re-watch my favorites, *Gilmore Girls* and *Grey's Anatomy* on an endless repeat, *Harry Potter* at Halloween, *Lord of the Rings* at Christmas, *Sex and the City* around New Year's. I've even used examples from *Grey's Anatomy* to discuss my plans for the future with a potential date and why, based on this example, we wouldn't be a good fit for each other. He understood immediately, no drama or painfully awkward conversations needed—thanks pop-culture! Besides, what could be more Gilmore than an extreme and varied amount of pop-culture references in everyday conversation? I'm basically a combination of all the characters from *Gilmore Girls*—even Kirk. I truly believe we've all got some Kirk-y traits somewhere inside us.

To me, there's more to television and movies than just enjoyment and the passage of time. I believe there are reasons why we become so obsessed with the latest show, why we buy sweatshirts and t-shirts with our favourite quotes, why we choose sides and declare our team of choice to the world, and if you're like me, why you choose to read every book a show mentions. But why do we do this? We get so enmeshed in these shows not just for the fun of it, but because they touch us on the deepest human level, communicate with our subconscious, and speak to us on a psychological level. We relate with their humanity, are touched by their vulnerability, rejoice in their triumphs, and share in their grief- all the highs and lows that make us who we are. These shows speak to the human experience and our hearts and souls are pulled toward that connection. I've spent almost three years studying and analysing that connection in myself, watching how television, *Gilmore Girls* in particular, affects me. How is it affecting my relationships, my self-care, my romantic life, my career, my identity?

Kristine Knows Books

Pop-culture references are an integral part of what made *Gilmore Girls* so iconic, and one cannot discuss the show without referencing the way literature was used and portrayed on the show. I've always been a reader, but would I put myself on the same level as

Rory? Could I achieve the expert literature status of a Gilmore? Some very special friends gave me my answer.

"This is Kristine. She knows exactly which book you need to read at exactly the right moment in your life," a friend once said as she introduced me to another one of her friends. I was slightly taken aback because this friend and I had only hung out once or twice and texted a little in between. In other words, she barely knew me, but from our conversations, one thing was clear to her: Kristine knows books.

I don't claim to know *all* books, but I do know books, and in a short period of time, this new friend had zeroed in on the essence of me and that was one thing: books.

It's difficult for me to remember a time when I wasn't reading. As a kid, I chose to spend time with a book instead of playing, reading so much it often upset my sister because her playmate was consumed in a book. Book fairs were as exciting as Christmas Day and Barnes and Noble was a wonderland with infinite worlds to explore. I'm passionate about many forms of art (music, television/movies, writing, dance) but there's a large portion of that passion that developed from books. The story is the foundation for everything.

Through middle and high school, and all the way through college, I excelled in anything dealing in the art of the story: English, Creative Writing, History, and Filmmaking, tapping into the lessons I had learned from books from an early age. I was good at school, but something always seemed to be missing. I loved reading and discussing books, writing and crafting stories, but there was something I couldn't put my finger on, an element that eluded me, no matter what. So I kept moving forward, always writing, always tending to my connection with books. From poems to plays to works of fiction, I did it all—testing my voice, creativity, and craft, exploring all the modes of writing.

One year, after a few years of physical New Year's Resolutions, I made a resolution to read all of the books on the Rory Gilmore Reading List, all 340+ of them. About a third of the way through the challenge, I began to notice just how much of what I was reading could apply to my life. Quotes from *Gilmore Girls* and the books I was reading kept repeating themselves in my mind until I understood why I was drawn to them. And that's why I started the Gilmore Book Club, not just to record my thoughts about each book, but to really dig into the text, my memories, thoughts, and emotions. I was doing the same analyses on books that I was on television shows, and the blog was the perfect place to combine the two of them. I've covered how to find a soul mate with *Pride and Prejudice*, self-care with *Ethan Frome*, recovering from trauma with *A Tale of Two Cities*, finding a home with *Gone With The Wind*, and so, so much more!

My reading is not limited to just books from the Rory list; I also dig into books written about those books, and authors, as well as other books by those authors. Just like Rory, I'm a researcher, and I like to have as much information as possible when I write so that I can give readers the most well-rounded essay and most genuine examples possible because that's what life is. We don't just think one-note thoughts and have one-note conversations. We pull in our emotions from that fight with our friend from the other day, our thoughts about that meeting we just attended, our dreams we just can't let go of, the television show we watched last night, and what we ate for dinner. It's all a part of us, and I want to be true to that.

But a part of being true to the way that life is constantly vacillating, is showing everything, the good, the bad, and everything too complicated or confusing to put in a category. I have to be open and vulnerable. As hard as it is to share those moments where you feel you're at your worst, there's value in that story. Sharing those moments of humanity is a strength. It's taken a lot of mental and emotional work, therapy time, and extreme self-awareness to analyse my life in such a way and pull out these deep connections with every book, but I've become a master at it. I've learned to lean into courage and away from fear, to show that being vulnerable in my writing is one of my greatest strengths.

Chronic Illness and My Gilmore Journey

When I was 13, I began experiencing pains all over my body. A few pains quickly turned into a chronic illness that completely upended my life. That illness accelerated my journey from teenager to adult with the world on their shoulders overnight. When my symptoms were at their worst—when I was at my worst—I kept it all hidden. That's what we're taught to do—show the Instagram version and not the reality. But as I adjusted to my new life and body, I also adjusted to a new mindset, one that wasn't afraid to speak my truth, or more accurately, write about it. We all have something, whether you call it baggage or trauma, and it's hard to heal that without doing the hard work of exploring, processing, analysing where we've been and how it made us who we are today. And I'm willing to go there, I'm willing to do the hard work, willing to put my story, my heart, my past out there for everyone to see.

I vividly remember every feeling I went through, I actually still go through many of them. The loneliness, rejection, fear, anger, sorrow, frustration, confusion, despair—I've been there and I know so many people out there are feeling this way. Sharing our stories, either through books or conversation, is a comfort for any time of need. It's not always easy to share, and some people may never share, but that's why I'm sharing my story, so others won't feel so alone, so they know that the *Gilmore Girls,* a host of literary characters, and I are all here for them.

This combination of joy and sorrow is what makes a beautiful story, one that will go down in history like *The Great Gatsby* of *Game of Thrones*. And that is what makes us beautifully human and exquisitely strong. We don't always like to be human, but it's an unalterable state. Our job is to understand and do the best we can, and that involves learning.

Reading and growing as a person is not always easy—it takes a lot of dedication and work, but what so many people don't realise is that it's totally doable! So think of me as your Lorelai or Rory, showing readers how to connect with literature and use it to change their lives by making it approachable, vulnerable, understandable, and full of identifiable pop-culture references. Or, if you prefer, like Carrie Bradshaw—dishing out a weekly column on books instead of boys. Because our deepest and most valuable connections are with those friends we trust, who have fun with us, encourage us, gently push us when we need it, but are also there to hold our hands or simply sit with us when life is just too much. Books and the Gilmores have done that for me and now I'm here to do it for others.

Where You Read, I Will Follow

Where you lead, I will follow… except I won't, because I'm very picky about who I follow. Since I was little, one thing was clear: I liked to lead. I'm very much like Paris in that regard. I'm comfortable being in charge, and I prefer it that way because I want to make sure that everything gets done and that it gets done well. But, when Lorelai and Rory Gilmore entered my life, I was more than happy to follow their lead.

I can't remember exactly when I started watching the show. It must have been around season 2 or 3, but I do remember loving it. *Gilmore Girls* was a great combination of 'young adult' (YA) and adult—it felt grown-up but achievable. It also worked out well that Rory was right around my age. There was this amazing dichotomy between being Rory now and knowing that I would be a Lorelai in the future, that really resonated with me—like I was being shown both sides of my personality, and my present, and future all at once.

I could name a lot of things I love about *Gilmore Girls*, but my favourite thing is how smart the show was, and how it made being smart the cool way to be. All the other shows at the time were about running with the popular crowd or about the latest crush, but *Gilmore Girls* was a celebration of smart. From Rory's bookish quotes, to Lorelai's pop-culture references, to Paris's witty comebacks—everyone had a brain full of amazing things to contribute and didn't hide their knowledge or wit for any reason.

Growing up, I was always the smart kid: known for getting good grades, being a high-achiever, and having a laundry list of dreams and aspirational goals. No other television show really reflected that as accurately as *Gilmore Girls* did. (I mean name a school show where characters actually studied—pretty rare, right?). *Gilmore Girls* was about being you, standing out, and knowing—well, everything.

I still remember the night that the final episode aired. My sister, a few friends, and I were all fans of the show and had been attentively watching the final season. The night of the final show, we had choir practice at church that ended exactly at the time the show was supposed to air. This was before live streaming, and even before recording was prevalent, so you had to watch everything live or you missed it. We made a mad dash back to Katie's house—hers was the closest to the church. We burst through the front door and down the stairs to their den, where the television was on and waiting for us. And there we sat, entranced for the next hour, desperate to know how it ended and yet holding onto a gossamer veil of hope that our time with the Gilmores would never end. But, end it did. As the camera slowly zoomed out through the window of Luke's dinner, framing Rory and Lorelai drinking their coffee (mirroring the final shot of the pilot), it felt like my connection to Stars Hollow was fading with every inch that the camera pulled back.

But, the people we love find a way of coming back to us, and so the Gilmores came back to me. Over the next decade, I watched *Gilmores Girls* whenever reruns appeared on television and then whenever I wanted, when streaming became available. I turned to the show many times for many reasons. Sometimes the world and my problems were just too much and the only solace I could find was in Stars Hollow—laughing at Kirk's latest job, tracking all the literary references, and drinking coffee at Luke's. Sometimes the wind would blow yellow and orange leaves from the trees, and I knew it was time to return to the cosiness that only Stars Hollow can bring. Sometimes I'd catch a whiff of that magical scent that only those blessed with a Lorelai nose can smell and I'd think to myself "I smell snow". In those moments, I'd have to join Rory and Lorelai in one of their walks through the first snow of the season. Sometimes, I'd endlessly scroll through all the streaming options, none of the television and movie choices felt right, so I'd turn to the Gilmores because spending time with them always felt right. *Gilmore Girls* became my comfort, my joy, my solace and the characters that were once acquaintances now became my friends and family.

When the news broke of the *Gilmore Girls: A Year In the Life* Netflix mini-series, I was thrilled. Part of me wanted the characters to be living the lives I imagined them to be living over the past 20 years, and part of me would be just as ecstatic if all the reunion showed was back to back town meetings—nothing fancy, just Stars Hollow at its wackiest and best.

Around that time, I had also started a major Gilmore project and it impacted me more than I thought was possible.

The Gilmore Book Club

I had recently committed to the Rory Gilmore Reading Challenge—an epic list of 340+ books and other literature that was referenced on the show, and I was going to read every single one. So, I sat down and marked everything I had read up to that point. Thanks to high school, college, and my usual appetite for reading, I had already read about 50 checked off—a pretty good start. With my library card as my golden ticket, I requested books from the library as often as I could, taking whatever they had available from the list so I could read as much as possible. I spent nights, weekends, and most of my holidays reading, listening to audiobooks on my commute and by the end of the year, I had finished another 45 books, some of them very long and tedious books, which brought me close to one third of the way finished with the Rory Challenge.

And then, disaster struck. A perfect storm of being under a lot of pressure at work, putting in a lot of overtime, trying to find a new apartment and packing everything I owned, and dealing with a chronic illness brought me to my knees. All of it was so stressful and overwhelming that I could barely keep it together—we're talking the incredible sinking Lorelais, minus a handsome and friendly shoulder to cry on. A voice kept breaking through all of the chaos, and that voice was part Lorelai and part Scarlett O'Hara. "I'll think about it tomorrow, at Tara." Over and over that line would repeat in my head, telling me to take it one thing at a time.

Fast-forward to my first full day in my apartment and I was devastated. I had worked so hard for this and everything was dirty, broken or missing, or I couldn't find it at all. How could this place ever be my home? Scarlett hadn't left me yet because she was detailing her arduous return to Tara and how she had to fight every second of every minute for the place she called home. I realised I had to do that too; I had to fight for my home.

And so *Gone With The Wind* and *Gilmore Girls* had taught me their first lesson. Suddenly everything was different, reading was different. All this time I had been reading for pleasure and for school, I had let the story fade after I turned the last page. But just as the characters of *Gilmore Girls* had stayed with me, so had some small part of every book I'd ever read, I just had to readjust my focus to see it. That's how the Gilmore Book Club blog was born. Not only was I committing to reading all the books on the list, but I would write about all of them too and how they and the *Gilmore Girls* were changing my life.

I had debated starting a blog before, and several friends and family had encouraged me in that, but something just never felt right until I started writing about *Gilmore Girls* and the book list. It felt like everything was falling into place, like this is what I should have been writing about for years, like this was the project that was waiting for me and only me.

But there was something I had to address before I published these essays: me. If I wanted to really honour the books and the show I loved, I had to do it in a genuine way, which means I had to write about everything—all my fears and doubts, my traumas and mistakes, my bad days and good days, my hopes and dreams, and all my joys—everything. I'd never done anything like that before—shared my story on such a level, but if I was going to do this, I was going to do it right, or at least I was going to give it my best shot.

I was nervous about sharing all of my vulnerabilities with the world, and so much of my writing as well. But I was more scared of living with the regret of not starting the blog, of not working toward my lifelong dream of being a writer. I chose my first book, *A Tree Grows in Brooklyn*, which was the perfect way to start because it's about how books can change your life, but it's also one of Lauren Graham's favourite books. So, I wrote and wrote, did a lot of editing, and hit 'publish'. Friends and family commented on my first blog posts, but it felt a bit like I was doing all this hard work and all this writing, and no one was seeing it.

Over the next two years, I worked at growing my audience: learning new methods, putting new ideas, or ideas I knew about but hadn't been able to implement, into place, and setting aside time to grow my community. It took a while, and believe me that was frustrating, but I clung to the fact that I was finally writing what I felt what I was meant to write—what no one else but me could write—and believed that people would see truth in my work and find something that resonated with them and that would be my success. That is what is happening now.

Readers have reached out to me saying they've wanted to do the Rory Reading Challenge but were intimidated by the size of the list, and sometimes the content of some of the books. They told me they were glad to have someone to talk about it with on social media, or have a resource for ways to connect with the material or get more into the Gilmore world through my blog. It's been an absolute joy to meet new Gilmore Girls fans and bond over shared favourite moments, discuss pop-culture references, and debate the eternal question: team Dean, Jess, or Logan.

My intention for the blog was not only to share my writing and my love of books and *Gilmore Girls*, but also to show people that books are such a powerful catalyst for change and that anyone can tap into that transformative power. There are so many reasons why people read, but in our formative years, a large portion of that reading is enforced. From reading comprehension in elementary school to literary analysis in high school and college—we focus on the facts we can extract from literature. We read the book, memorise the information, and regurgitate that information back on a test. And then, for the most part, we move on. We do the same process over and over again like little reading robots. And believe me, I was really great at being a reading robot. It's no wonder some become disenchanted with reading and don't continue the journey with books outside of school. I've continued to read after my years in school, but it became more about staying inside the box, not about learning and pushing my boundaries.

Part of me started to wonder how our lives would change if we changed the way we read. If we learned how to connect to books, even ones we don't like, and still benefit from reading them, how would we be different? Would we be able to recognize and process our emotions better? Would we be able to stop harmful patterns and know which actions to avoid? Would we be able to make deeper, lasting connections with each other? Would the world be full of more kindness, love, joy, and hope than before?

I'm not saying I can answer all of these questions or that reading will solve all of them, but I do believe reading plays a part in all of them.

While I don't hear from every one of my readers, I do hear from some, and those comments have been wonderful. I've had a reader say they weren't bookish in school so they thought they were stupid, but working with this new approach to reading has helped them see how smart they are and heal their relationship with books. Another reader told me that they felt seen and not alone after reading a few of my blog posts about my chronic illness journey. Several readers have mentioned that they've wanted to do the Rory Gilmore Reading list and having me and my journey with them has helped them choose books, connect with books, and persevere when they hit a bump in the road.

All of that has been amazing and makes me so excited and hopeful about the future of the Gilmore Book Club. I will continue to write about each book and my journey with the Rory Reading Challenge. My dream is to turn all those essays into a book. I also enjoy putting together smaller, more manageable book lists that focus on different Gilmore topics or inspirations, like books for all the

Gilmore guys or books I think Rory would be reading today. I love analysing each book I read and asking myself if I think the Gilmores would like it; the books I deem Gilmore will continue to be added to those book lists.

As for the future, I'm open to exploring more options like being able to host book club meetings for everyone doing the challenge or doing a TED talk on a few of the books I've found that have changed my life the most. Whatever I do, I'll be sure to bring a ton of books and the Gilmores along with me.

Larisa Kliman

Eating Gilmore

It's hard to truly convey the magnitude of my *Gilmore Girls* obsession. I could tell you that I have probably seen every episode of the original run probably 50 times (arguably more) and the *Netflix* revival episodes about five times each. I could tell you that for a few years, I watched an episode every single day. I have a *Gilmore Christmas* tree, a *Gilmore Girls* tattoo, my fair share of *Gilmore* memorabilia, I went to two *Gilmore Guys* live shows, I've won *Gilmore* bar trivia (team "I had sex, but I'm not going to Harvard"), my dog and I dressed up as Lorelai and Luke for Halloween (you read that right—I said my dog), and I made a *Gilmore*-themed island on

Animal Crossings: New Horizons (that was pandemic project #1). Other than attending the fan festival in October (which I will be this year!) or visiting the Warner Bros lot (never been to LA), I had pretty much reached the peak of my obsession.

But how did this (as Rory would call it) 'psychosis' really set in? I was first introduced to *Gilmore Girls* on rerun on what used to be called *ABC Family*. As any young teen who was home alone for the summer, I admittedly watched a lot of television. Flipping between *Guts* on *Nickelodeon GAS* (any early 00s stan would know) and *Lingo* on the *Game Show Network* eventually became tiresome, so I began channel surfing. One scene, in particular, caught my eye. Two young women were arguing about a boy and school and when the argument came to a heated close, they both turned to Macy Gray's *'I Try'* in their angst.

Somehow, I managed to catch the pilot episode of *Gilmore Girls* before watching any other episode, albeit not at the beginning. I was captivated by the relationship between the young mother and her teenage daughter, and like most fans, the quick and witty dialogue hooked me. I tried to catch other reruns that summer but wasn't able to watch the show in full because that was pre-streaming. I also was never able to really watch the show live because it aired when I was at dance lessons after school, and we didn't have a DVR at the time. I still watched the occasional episode here and there on *ABC Family* and followed along with the storyline for the most part. I knew there was drama around Jess, that Rory chose Yale over Harvard, and I can distinctly remember hearing a radio ad for the penultimate episode, "Rory, will you marry me." However, it wasn't until college that the 'psychosis' really sank in.

For most of my life, anxiety has had a mighty grip on my brain, and as you might expect, college only increased this. On a regular trip to *Half Price Books*, I spotted the warm golden yellow of the season 1 DVD collection of *Gilmore Girls*. I remembered how comforting I found the episodes I had watched, so I made the purchase. Naturally, I blew through the first season quickly, and I returned to *Half Price Books* to buy the soft blue season 2 set and the light purple season 3. If my ability to remember the colours of each season's box set this easily years later doesn't tell you how much I've watched those DVDs, I don't know what will.

When I got to season 4 (green by the way) and the college years, I felt more comfortable in my own college experience. By the end of my sophomore year, I had the entire series on DVD and had already watched every episode a couple times through. Any time life became too stressful or my anxiety was too high, I would put on an episode of *Gilmore Girls*. Lorelai and Rory became my best friends when I needed them most. The show was like a weighted blanket for me—it still is.

Netflix then announced that it was making all seven seasons available for streaming. At first, I was indifferent because I already had the entire DVD collection, but the ease of streaming and not having to get up to change out the disc every four episodes made binge-watching even easier (Hey, when you're in a state of high anxiety, even the littlest of efforts is hard). This meant *Gilmore Girls* was on a constant loop. I'd say goodbye to all the townies at Rory's Bon Voyage party while Sam Phillip's special *Gilmore Girls* rendition of '*How to Dream*' played in the background, and then almost immediately, '*There She Goes*' by the La's would be playing as Lorelai gave us the first introduction to Stars Hollow.

I was then introduced to the podcast *Gilmore Guys*. If you're reading this, and you've not listened to them, I urge you to do so immediately. Though, give them time to grow on you as they find their footing and figure out their format. As the *Gilmore* fandom surged again through their podcast, I realised that this show provided the same level of comfort to so many others as it had to me. And then *A Year in the Life* happened. For me, the revival was special. I got to see what my favourite characters were up to, hear new lines, and visit new locations. I know there are mixed emotions about the revival for most fans, but overall, I am glad that it happened. In the time since watching *A Year in the Life*, I've never really stopped watching the show. It's sort of become this joke with some of my friends where they would recommend a show for me to watch. I would get through a couple of episodes at most before I switched back to *Gilmore Girls*. Nothing else really brought me the comfort as that show did.

When the Covid-19 pandemic hit, I, like many others, turned to what was familiar and comforting. Naturally, for me, this was *Gilmore Girls*. I found myself watching it even more than I normally did. It was nice to escape to Stars Hollow when the rest of the world seemed so uncertain. As I'm sure many of you did during the quarantine, I looked for new hobbies. I dabbled in candle-making, turned into an *Animal Crossing* gamer, and tried my hand at mixology. But I wanted a long-lasting project that excited me even past the lockdown. And then I had the idea for Eating Gilmore!

Let me backtrack a little bit. One of the first virtual events that I found towards the beginning of the pandemic was an at home *Harry Potter* con, and through this, I found the incredibly talented Brad Bakes. He is a UK-based YouTuber who is cooking his way through the *Harry Potter* books. He recreates every food and drink that's mentioned—even the potions! The more I watched his videos, the more I wanted to try a similar project. It didn't take me long to think of a series that I love that also talks about food a lot. What did take me a long time was to build up the confidence to start the project and even longer to decide to share this project publicly (see above: lifelong anxiety).

See, I don't have any professional cooking experience. I consider myself to be an average home chef who enjoys cooking. I also don't have any blogging experience (unless you count *Xanga*—again, any early 00s stan would know). But as I posted more dinners on my personal Instagram story, my friend Michaela kept urging me to start a food blog. And so, one day in November (because autumn is so emblematic of this show), I pressed the publish button of my first dish for the pilot episode, Sookie's famous peach sauce that makes Lorelai declare "I want to take a bath in that sauce!"

The premise is simple, for each episode of the show, I choose a food, drink, or dish that's either mentioned in the episode or inspired by the episode. I didn't want to make every single food and drink that's mentioned because quite frankly that's a lot of food. There are also a few dishes that I am happy to skip. One that comes to mind is an octopus ice cream that Sookie mentions she tried making back in the 90s (no thank you).

There are some episodes where it's really easy to pick out what I'm going to make: Sookie's magic risotto for "The Deer Hunters" and deviled eggs for "Take the Deviled Eggs". But there are many episodes where there is so much food mentioned that it can be difficult to decide what I want to make. For example in "Nick and Nora, Sid and Nancy", Sookie makes an extravagant feast for Jess arriving in Stars Hollow. There was a lot to choose from for just that meal in that episode, but I settled on the last minute grilled cheese that she decided to make. Though knowing Sookie, it was not a simple grilled cheese. So of course, I had to make it fancy. It's fun deciding what I should make for each episode.

Now whenever I watch the show, the food stands out to me even more. I usually jot down a couple of dishes from the episode and decide later on which one I want to recreate. Sometimes I'm really torn between two dishes like for "Teach Me Tonight". I couldn't decide on ice cream in cooooones for Jess or Luke's triple the amount of chocolate brownies. I had my Instagram followers vote and the brownies won! For other episodes, I don't make food that's exactly mentioned in the episode, but rather is inspired. For "Richard in Stars Hollow", I made grapefruit margaritas because Richward was so adamant about having grapefruit every day for breakfast; although, I don't think grapefruit margaritas were what he had in mind!

My process of coming up with the recipes starts with a lot of research. I've always enjoyed reading through cookbooks. That's something I shared with my late aunt. I find recipes that are similar to what I want to make, and then, I will adapt them or use them as a starting off point. So far, there has been one recipe that the show actually gave me: Luke's special omelette in "Back in the Saddle Again" (three eggs with bits of bacon, cubed tomatoes, swiss cheese, and a dash of oregano if you were wondering).

One of the things I love so much about *Gilmore Girls* is how integral food is. I often say the food on this show is a character in and of itself. Between Luke's Diner, Sookie the gourmet chef, and Friday night dinners, food already plays such a huge role. But then Lorelai and Rory are constantly eating or at least talking about eating. So *Gilmore Girls* really wouldn't be the same show without the food.

There are some dishes that are so iconic to the show that I HAD to make them, but they definitely challenged me. Homemade pop-tarts were a dish I knew I had to make early on because if you ask someone to name a food from *Gilmore Girls,* pop-tarts probably come to their mind first. They took a lot of patience to make but were so worth it. Sookie's famous "you haven't lived until you tried" stuffed fried squash blossoms were fun, but the middle of winter made it tricky to track down fresh squash blossoms. Sookie also threw me for a loop with her chocolate espresso tassel hat cake that she makes in "Lorelai's Graduation Day". It took me five attempts to get this cake right, but it's one that I'm really proud of.

The dish I'm probably the most proud of so far is the edible pretzel basket with a goat cheese filling that I made for "A-Tisket, A-Tasket". While it took some engineering, it actually wasn't too difficult to make. I figured out my pretzel recipe and realised pretty quickly that instead of dunking the woven basket parts into boiling water with baking soda as you traditionally do with pretzels, it was better to brush the basket parts with baking soda water to create the signature pretzel texture. I had all six of my basket pieces and my goat cheese filling, but then I had to figure out how to actually assemble the whole thing. With some ingenuity, several toothpicks, and my sister's help to hold it steady, I put together the basket, ready for Sookie and Jackson to have their picnic and get engaged.

When I first started this project, I wasn't sure I would go all the way through the show, but barring anything major in my life, I have confidence that I'll finish strong with even a few ideas of what I'm going to do after I finish this project. I've made a few friends along the way and found people that love this show as much as I do! And whether you're a Sookie or a Lorelai in the kitchen, I've tried to make the recipes as easy to follow along as possible. So from me to you, happy cooking in the Hollow!

Ariane Lariviere

GG Inspired Lifestyle

In December 2020, I did an advent calendar newsletter, where I was sending one email every day, reviewing a *Gilmore Girls* pop culture reference. I advertised it on Facebook and it became quite popular. After this, I created a blog to post my reviews online and a little while later came the items and the online store. That's how GG Inspired Lifestyle came to be.

I've loved *Gilmore Girls* since I was a teenager. I remember thinking how refreshing it was that there was no outrageous drama in the show—nobody's trying to kill their own son or make out with their brother. The everyday challenges and struggles are relatable. I'd never seen anything like it before. Even sitcoms sometimes tend to be a little exaggerated, but I found everything that happens in *Gilmore Girls* to be natural.

I have always had a knack for remembering actor names, movie titles, and book authors. One of the things I loved about *Gilmore Girls* was how often these things were name dropped, and how fun it was to pick up on all the references. It was also fantastic to see two women who were so knowledgeable about pop culture on screen. Like me, the *Gilmore Girls* are not into cooking, plants, or sports—they know literature, cinema, and a million other obscure things.

I also loved the girls for their 2000's fashion style—clothing items such as those with leopard print, rhinestones, the Spice Girls necklace, and the "cat wearing a tiara" sweaters appealed to me. I also found their mix of good and bad taste refreshing. Nobody is a perfect fancy-pants of good taste, and on the flipside, nobody's taste is all bad. Of course, taste is subjective, but in *Gilmore Girls*, there is a merging of the two. For instance, there is a fine line between Lorelai's love for *Casablanca*, and *Hardbodies*, which are both put on the same level of cinematic importance. While Lorelai can also dress elegantly, she gets away with wearing a Bunny Ranch t-shirt. And let's not forget the infamous monkey lamp. Their taste represents a wide range of interests, and reflects how complex people's tastes and interests really are.

It was also refreshing to see a grown woman on television, with a Hello Kitty clock and *Powerpuff Girls* shot glasses. I love the fact that they rewatch bad movies as their household classics. I love that they eat 'mac and cheese', marshmallows, and pop-tarts without a care in the world about the nutritious aspects or the amount of calories. Lorelai taught me that being an adult is awesome, because you get to make your own rules. There is not just one right way to be an adult. You have some responsibilities, sure, but the rest of the time, if you want to spend it seeing concerts, decorating hammers with bows and feathers, making up painting songs and ordering take-out, well, you can!

With Rory, I learned that being an introvert and needing alone time doesn't mean you are anti-social. She's an energetic, community-driven young woman. She prefers to sit by herself at lunch and read more than chatting about silly teenager stuff. She taught me, like Lorelai, that there is no one right way to be a person. You don't have to wait to be an adult to do things your way. Like Lorelai says, Rory can "do what she wants as long as it doesn't hurt anyone else." I've happily been living my life that way ever since I heard that line.

The most important thing I learned from the *Gilmore Girls* is to think for myself. Lorelai, at 16 realised she didn't belong in her parent's world, and set off on her own path. Rory did the same, concentrating on her studies and not allowing herself to be influenced by the flashiness of popularity and trends. I find trends extremely boring and I hate to be told what to do. So those aspects of the show really strike a chord with me.

Like Rory, I'm an introvert, but I love people. What I love most about my *Gilmore Girls* inspired business is packing the orders for my customers (and adding a few free goodies to them). It's also great fun organising Stars Hollow events online. I encourage people to make a day of it, decorate their homes, prepare a junk food buffet the girls would be proud of. We then get online and play games and watch a few episodes of the show together. It's a complete blast.

In my rhinestones-and-tie-dye-decorated online store, you can find clothing similar to what the girls wear, Stars Hollow festivals' souvenirs, and items like mugs and tote bags with pop culture references on them. You can also get my very special *Gilmore Girls* inspired card deck, "What Would The *Gilmore Girls* Do?"

I strive to offer items that are as eco-friendly as possible. From the sourcing to the packaging, I think every little detail so that our love of *Gilmore Girls* doesn't harm the planet.

Megan Craig

StarsLorelaiCrafts

Gilmore Girls. People who haven't seen the show think it's just another television show. True Gilmores know that 'it's a show, It's a lifestyle, it's a religion.'

I'm Meg, I'm 22 and from Leeds, United Kingdom. If you follow *Gilmore Girls* fan pages on Instagram you may follow mine (@starslorelai). I started my account in April 2020 as a little hobby and something to keep me going throughout the pandemic and the countless lockdowns and restrictions here in the UK. Little did I know how much having this account was going to change my life. I'm not just a huge fan of *Gilmore Girls*, but of actress Lauren Graham too.

Once my Instagram was up and running, I would post several times a day with different photo and video edits, creating my own themes and filters and would spend hours creating edits and finding the scenes and clips to go in them. This hobby would help my days pass by and would always make me so happy. As time went on I gained more followers, and I started to collaborate with other fan accounts. I came to know these people and was soon making new friends all over the world over our mutual love of the show and Lauren Graham's work.

When I was in school the teachers always used to say not to speak to people that you had met online, but online, through this new hobby, I found some of my best friends, including my best friend—my partner in crime, my southern twin—Amy from the UK. We are inseparable. We met via Instagram when she commented on the Lauren hoodie I was wearing in my story. I am so glad she messaged me that day, because we share so many things—a middle name, birth year, family member names, and so much more. We have so many unique similarities and we just love all these small things. Throughout the lockdowns we spent most days on FaceTime all day, just being in each other's virtual company. We became a part of each other's families. She has gotten me through so many struggles, and always knows how to make me smile and cheer me up. I don't have a sister, but I feel like I have one in Amy. We support each other through absolutely everything. We live three hours apart, but we take it in turns to visit and stay with each other and we've met each other's friends and families. It is like we've known each other forever. She's the Sookie to my Lorelai. It just goes to show that you can meet the most amazing people online. I now have someone that will be part of my life forever.

After my Instagram account, my love for *Gilmore Girls* kept developing. I am now the proud owner and creator of 'StarsLorelaiCrafts', A *Gilmore Girls* and Lauren Graham inspired craft store. I originally started on Depop. I had a bit of a rocky start with a few starting problems so then I moved it to Etsy. It has definitely been an adventure. I started my store in December 2020, and was told countless times by friends and family that it wouldn't work out and people wouldn't be interested. Boy, did I prove them wrong.

I initially started out just selling matte stickers with *Gilmore Girls* photos, quotes, and digital art I had done. I remember sharing on my Instagram that I was starting a shop and having sales and orders placed within minutes. It was overwhelming, and emotional. My first sale was, of course, from Amy, who has supported me throughout this journey.

When I started out, I would hand write out all the addresses and a thank you card. Almost 2500 sales later, and I have expanded my product line many times. I now sell stickers, movie prints, art prints, keychains, gift boxes, a *Gilmore Girls* inspired game board kit, mystery sticker packs, apparel and phone cases. It has taken so much time and research, and trial and error to get to this point but the hard work has paid off. Not only has my product line expanded but also the whole branding and aesthetic of my business has grown too. I now have pink poly mailers and pink bubble mailers and I have my logo sticker on my packaging along with small pink stickers that say "thank you for your order", "you have great taste!" and "handmade with love". All my orders get a sprinkle of star confetti wrapped in star tissue paper and all products come in a holographic pouch along with a thank you card and my business card. It has taken some time to get to this point but I am very proud of what I have achieved so far. What amazes me is the journey my products go on to reach their new homes, especially since the majority of my orders go to the USA.

    I cannot thank *Gilmore Girls* and Lauren Graham enough for everything they have done for me.

Candice and Jackie Amundson

Candies Crafties

Gilmore Girls really connects us. We watch it together, and sing the theme song every episode. While going off to college created some distance, and changed the dynamic of our friendship, *Gilmore Girls* was something that we could reconnect over. The show really enriched our friendship, and allowed us to grow into it, even though college kept us physically distant from one another.

One day online, something popped up about the fan festival. At that point, we didn't know anybody who attended but signed up for the Unionville festival and were so excited, especially to meet Scott Patterson.

As the date grew closer, we decided to make some *Gilmore Girls* themed jewellery to wear to the festival. We each have our favourite kind of jewellery to wear—silver, or gold—so we wore necklaces that we made, and shared them on our Facebook profiles. Those early ones said "Gilmore Girls FanFest 2019" and were just for us, but people started messaging us on Facebook, asking to buy one. We started taking orders which could be mailed out, or brought with us to fanfest.

That's when we realised that this was about community. When we were at the airport, we ran into Lisa from Stars Hollow Mercantile, and hung out at fanfest. At fanfest, you end up knowing everyone. Nobody knew our names initially, so they just called us the necklace ladies. It was so amazing to give people their necklaces, and then see them wearing them at the events. The friendships that we have made through *Gilmore Girls* are amazing. We love the *Gilmore Girls* fan community, and feel so grateful for all of the amazing friends we have made. The community that formed at fanfest now exists outside of it. Though we all met in Canada, we have stayed in contact online, and even got together to do the Warner Bros Studio tour, and visit the Greystone Mansion.

When Covid hit, our friendships grew even stronger. On Saturdays a group of us would meet on Zoom. It was just a sanity check, to see how everyone was doing, but that weekly meeting really meant a lot to all of us. We went from not knowing anyone at the fanfest, to knowing everyone. It's a crazy community, but it's one that we have come to consider family. We wouldn't have gotten through the business, or through Covid, without this community.

When the fan festival was over, we didn't want to stop making *Gilmore Girls* inspired jewellery. We started doing new pieces—designing and making fun pieces that *Gilmore Girls* fans would like, and want to wear. Our pieces are something that get people really excited, and that excitement really motivates us to keep working on the business. We loved seeing how much people enjoyed it when they arrived, and wearing them. We enjoy bringing a bit of joy to other *Gilmore Girls* fans.

Being a mother and daughter business team works really well, and mirrors *Gilmore Girls*. A few years ago, we had no idea that our business would evolve like it has. Our relationship has evolved over that time too. Our business is a mother-daughter business, and fanfest is our annual mother-daughter trip. In a way, fanfest, and the family that *Gilmore Girls* created, was what made this all happen. Our business was built from relationships, and the friendships that emerged from other people who loved the show as much as we do.

Now, we make a lot of different things including necklaces, charm bracelets, and earrings. We never expected CandiesCrafties to get as big as it has, but it was a real blessing. It's amazing to think that this all started because we made matching necklaces for ourselves.

Julianne Buonocore

The Rory Gilmore Book Club

In The Rory Gilmore Book Club, where Rory *reads*, we will follow. If you had told me twenty years ago, when *Gilmore Girls* originally aired, that twenty years later, I would be writing about the show on a daily basis, I never would have believed you. This is the story of how one bookish *Gilmore Girls* fan went from a casual observer of the show to a superfan running a themed book club and living in two worlds—one of which is a world of Rory's books.

My name is Julianne Buonocore, and I'm a blogger at The Literary Lifestyle (https://TheLiteraryLifestyle.com), my "little corner of the [digital] world" where books meet lifestyle. My blog helps women looking to find their next great read or to get more from their last great read through related bookish lifestyle pairings.

The Literary Lifestyle currently reaches over one million views per year, and I've been on *The Today Show's* Read with Jenna book club on TV, as well as *Buzzfeed*. As a major component of The Literary Lifestyle blog, I host "The Rory Gilmore Book Club," which you can also find on Instagram @TheRoryGilmoreBookClub.

When *Gilmore Girls* originally aired, I was a fan through osmosis. My younger sister was totally, utterly, and completely infatuated with the show -- to the point where she had the DVDs playing on loops twenty-four hours a day so that it would always be on, whether or not she was actually there to watch it. I remember complaining to my parents about their allowing this costly and omnipresent teenage indulgence, but at the same time, I also couldn't help but watch along and become engaged in the idiosyncratic characters and lighthearted small-town drama.

I found myself stopping to watch and enjoying its quirkiness more and more, from Taylor's preposterous town meeting antics to Rory's getting "hit by a deer," Richard's and Emily's pretentious Friday night dinners, and Lane's humorously overprotective mother.

In 2004, I moved out of our family home to attend school and more or less stopped watching *Gilmore Girls* (and tv in general) while I focused on my studies, except for episodes like the controversial series finale, which several of us school "girls" videotaped to watch after finals (yes, it really was that long ago).

And, by the way, when the movie *Bridesmaids* crushed box office sales in 2011 and the entire world fell head over heels for the comedic timing of Melissa McCarthy, I loved to remind new fans that she was a Gilmore girl first.

I continued to move on with my life and my career, and I didn't think much of *Gilmore Girls* again, until I learned the very sad news of Ed Hermann's untimely death in 2014 and later, the more exciting news of the *Netflix* revival in 2016. When Thanksgiving 2016 came to a close, I, like so many others that holiday weekend, heated up some popcorn and hot chocolate and jumped into bed with a cosy blanket to binge all four "seasons" of the *Netflix* revival. The magic was still there, and it was palpable from the first droplet of snow (I swear, I could "smell" it) to those infamous final four words.

Again, I moved on with my life, got married in Spring 2019, and went on a Summertime European vacation thereafter—not unlike that of Lorelai and Rory. When I returned to the United States, I began to scratch the itch of a creative void that many newly wedded brides feel once months of planning as meticulously as Emily did for Sookie have finally consummated with a wedding.

As I scrolled through all of the notes I had saved on my phone over the Summer, I found that I had compiled a unique mix of thoughtfully researched travel itineraries and book lists for each city we visited. And so, The Literary Lifestyle blog was born as a passion project, pairing books with related lifestyle.

Nearly a year later, as the Gilmore favourite season of fall rolled around once again, it seemed like *everyone* in my social media feeds was talking about re-watching *Gilmore Girls* starting on September 1st. It was the middle of the Coronavirus pandemic when we were all quarantined at home and the outside world was a scary place. The thought of a *Gilmore Girls* rewatch at that time just seemed like such a sweet, simple escape to a much more idealistic world of bountiful New England seasons, quick-witted pop culture references and, of course, lots of coffee.

So, I grabbed my Red Vines and pressed play! I became fully and completely engrossed this time, shedding tears of mixed emotions throughout the finale, and immediately starting a second re-watch. I now had a "Team" (Logan), a favourite "girl" (Emily—a perfectly complex mix of terrible, funny, *and* vulnerable), and my own collection of Luke's Diner merchandise. I also knew, without a doubt, what one local event I would attend if I could (The Bracebridge Dinner), and I had actually cooked, and ate, a Santa burger. It was official -- I was a superfan.

At the same time that I re-watched *Gilmore Girls* after two decades, I was also starting to plan my reading and blogging schedule on The Literary Lifestyle for the coming year. I was thinking about how many classics I still had not read and wanted to read, but how at the same time, I had also missed out on reading more modern "classics" and bestsellers from the first decade of the 2000s, from *The DaVinci Code* to *The Secret Life of Bees* and *The Year of Magical Thinking*, when I was more focused on studying and starting my career.

I recalled that, a few years prior, there had been a popular *Buzzfeed* article floating around the internet listing the books referenced on *Gilmore Girls*, and I thought to myself, "Oy, with the poodles already! That would make the perfect reading challenge for me."

I casually mentioned the idea of reading the *Gilmore Girls* book list on Instagram, and I was flooded with comments and replies from others wanting to join in. In fact, I had never received so much interest and positive feedback. The *Gilmore Girls* fan base is certainly a passionate one.

And there's a real synergy between *Gilmore Girls* and book lovers. After all, Rory is very likely the only television protagonist to ever be called a "book tease" and to exclaim: "I can't believe we get to sit around and talk about books and get graded!"

In other words, Rory is *kind of* a literary superhero. The kind whose habit is taking a book with her everywhere she goes. The kind whose boyfriend is willing to watch her browse bookstores for six or seven hours. The kind who even loves the *smell* of books.

The *Gilmore Girls* book list also happened to perfectly align with the purpose of The Literary Lifestyle—to pair books with lifestyle. So, I began to dive in and research the original *Buzzfeed* book list more thoroughly, adding titles such as those referenced on the *Netflix* revival. When I first posted my own iteration of the *Gilmore Girls* book list, it had 400+ books on it. I have continued to update it over time to include more obscure references, and it currently lists 500+ books. It's a project that I'm not sure will ever be complete because it requires close attention to very little things, like the names and phrases of authors and characters. And as you know, the *Gilmore Girls* talk fast! But, that's what makes our book club especially unique.

Beginning in the year 2021, I gave The Rory Gilmore Book Club its own home @TheRoryGilmoreBookClub on Instagram. Each month, we have a theme (such as "a classic book" or "a book adapted to film"), and members choose any book within that theme from the *Gilmore Girls* book list to read on their own while re-watching the mention of it on the show. Throughout the month, I share my own recommendations for the theme, and I re-share what other club members are reading.

The *Gilmore Girls* book list is incredibly diverse, from ancient literature to twenty-first-century *New York Times* bestsellers and everything in between: classics, plays, short stories, thrillers, non-fiction, religious teachings, contemporary fiction, historical texts, poetry, biographies, and even more. I wasn't kidding when I said that Rory is a literary superhero!

Over the past year and a half, our club members have read such books as:

- *Pride and Prejudice*, which Rory made Dean read;

- *Romeo & Juliet*, which was infamously performed at Chilton;

- *The Godfather*, which Lorelai quoted a zillion times;

- *Encyclopedia Brown: Boy Detective*, which Jess describes as the only book series that Luke owns;

- *Wild*, which was so pivotal and memorable in helping Lorelai cope with her grief; and

- *Anna Karenina*, one of Rory's favourite books, which she also mentions in her very literary valedictorian speech.

I also share *Gilmore Girls* themed blog posts on The Literary Lifestyle, including everything from gift guides to quotes, costume ideas, food references, books reminiscent of *Gilmore Girls*, and even a Spotify playlist of some of the best songs featured on the show.

What's most interesting about it is that, when I talk about The Rory Gilmore Book Club in public now as an adult, the reaction I most often receive is something to the effect of, "I used to watch *Gilmore Girls*, and now my daughter watches it!" Indeed, *Gilmore Girls* has entertained, inspired, and influenced generations of women, and Rory continues to be a wholesome reminder, especially to teenagers, that it's okay to be bookish.

Thanks to Rory Gilmore, there's a virtual place as welcoming as Stars Hollow, Connecticut, for people like us. And, with a 500+ book list and a book club membership that grows beyond all of my expectations on a daily basis, there's so much more in store for The Rory Gilmore Book Club. We're really just getting started reading like a Gilmore, and the show has given us a whole *library* of books to read and discuss.

It's been a two-decade journey for me from a casual observer of *Gilmore Girls* to a superfan blogger at The Literary Lifestyle and a host of The Rory Gilmore Book Club, but, at the end of the day, in the words of Rory herself, "I'm here because I enjoy books, and because I read books."

A. S. Berman

Author of *The Gilmore Girls Companion*

No 'Companion' Without Community

The making of Gilmore's first 'making of' Book

Many *Gilmore Girls* fans remember "the look": that pursed-lip "oh really" stare you received from the uninitiated back in the day whenever you mentioned your unabashed love for all things Gilmore. Some people heard the premise and thought "young mother and daughter who are best friends - oh pleaasssse."

Which is a shame, really, because what they missed out on was something that sets Gilmore apart from nearly everything else on television: an overriding sense of community. What many of us really fell in love with was Stars Hollow. We wanted a Luke's Diner to hang out in, town meetings to wisecrack through; a gentle, slightly odd place to call home.

And in late 2007 or thereabouts I wanted to find out how the people behind *Gilmore Girls* had managed to bring this magical make-believe community to life.

Media coverage of the show at the time didn't reach much beyond the occasional article in *Entertainment Weekly*. Bookshelves were barer still. After several years the only books I could find were one or two novelizations and "Coffee at Luke's," a collection of essays rich in appreciation but silent when it came to how the show was actually made.

Having waited seven years to read a book about the making of *Gilmore Girls* without success, I realised it might only ever happen if I wrote it. After a few email exchanges with the publisher of my first two books, I was given the go-ahead to write *The Gilmore Girls Companion*.

Over the next 2 1/2 years, I tracked down members of the cast and production team one by one and chatted with those I could. The process back then was much as it is now, each interviewee putting me in touch with at least one other person until, before I knew it, I had spoken with more than 40 members of the production.

Many went above and beyond, especially costumer Valerie Campbell, who not only put me in touch with several members of the cast and crew, but also took me on a personal tour of the Warner Brothers lot where Gilmore was filmed. (The Stars Hollow gazebo had been towed off to the side to make way for the filming of *Pretty Little Liars*, but that didn't stop me from getting my picture taken with it.) She also arranged for me to actually hold a Chilton uniform. (Yes, I had my picture taken with that, too.)

One of those she introduced me to was Richard Gilmore himself, Edward Herrmann. I like to think that we instantly bonded over our shared love of old radio shows. (One of his favourites was Bob & Ray.)

All these years later, what I remember most about the actor was his sheer eloquence. He seemed to move from devilishly entertaining to movingly poignant without the slightest effort. When I spoke with his on-screen wife Kelly Bishop later on, I was delighted to discover that they enjoyed a close relationship off-screen, too. Years after his passing he remains the most well-spoken individual I've ever had the privilege to interview; that he agreed to write the foreword to the Companion is something for which I will always be grateful.

Just as important as this community of Gilmore alums was to the writing of the book was another community: those who embraced the project online.

I created a WordPress blog dedicated to the project (gilmoregirlsbook.wordpress.com) which gradually attracted Gilmore fans from all over the world. I shall never forget the enthusiasm I was met with there, particularly after the book was published.

So many people I met in that space encouraged me to continue on those days when I didn't think I could transcribe another interview – far too many to mention here. And they hailed from many lands: Italy, Germany, the Czech Republic. I even had the good fortune to meet a young artist, Eva in Austria, who contributed several illustrations of the cast to the book.

A casual scroll through those posts now reminds me just how much goodwill I received as people spread the word. Seeing pictures of readers holding copies of the book still brings a lump to my throat.

When I first learned of the fan fest, I realised that its organisers had finally brought us all full-circle. Yearning to visit Stars Hollow made us all fans of that show, and now Jennie and Marcus Whitaker, through grit and determination, had somehow found a way to take us there at last in the flesh.

Jess Fellows-Miliner

Oy with the cups already

I started watching *Gilmore Girls* in 2000, when it first premiered on the WB. Being from New England, the show felt extremely special from the very beginning. I loved the fall leaves, and the tight-knit small town. It was everything I loved about where I lived. It wasn't until years later that I decided to revisit Stars Hollow, by rewatching the show on Netflix, and I ended up falling in love with the show, even more than the first time I watched it.

In 2020, when the entire world was shut down, I needed something to bring me joy, to give me a purpose, and I decided to check in with other fans from around the United States. I started out just doing cups, but then expanded into other things. I came up with the idea of themed boxes to coincide with each season of the show. The response was unbelievable. People were telling me how much joy these boxes were bringing them, and how it was helping them cope during the pandemic. Little did they know that it was helping me as well. In 2020 I had lost both of my dogs to heart disease, and I lost my best friend to cancer—all while being stuck at home, and not able to see my friends and family. It felt like the world was standing still, and nothing was ever going to get better. And although I was still stuck inside, I was spending my time crafting and creating these items for fans of the show, and bringing people some much needed happiness, myself included.

Since "cups" is in the name, I make it a point to include a cup with each themed box I put together. I have also built relationships with many small businesses, whose products have been featured in many of our boxes. We have done almost 30 themed boxes now, starting with one for each season of the original run of the show. Season 5 was the most popular (team Logan fans!) We also did a Christmas and Valentine's Day box, which both sold out within an hour. For the Luke's Diner box that we did, I actually had Scott Patterson reach out to see if we wanted to feature his coffee in the box, and we did. We usually do 75-100 boxes, to keep the items special and limited edition. We love that only a small number of people end up with the special items.

Each themed box includes a cup, or drinking item-like a mug, flask, or water bottle. Each box also includes a pin and magnet, along with many other items. Sometimes tote bags and t-shirts, sometimes candles or wax melts. We like to keep it a surprise each month. We also try to make sure we source all of our items in the US, or Canada. We try to work with small businesses as much as possible, if we decide to include an item that we don't make/sell ourselves.

Over the years, *Gilmore Girls* has been a great comfort to me. Whenever I'm having a bad day, I escape to Stars Hollow and forget about everything else. If you were to tell me back in 2000 that *Gilmore Girls* would remain this popular, and bring hundreds of amazing people into my life, I'd never believe you. How could a show do that? But here we are, 22 years later, and every year we all gather together to celebrate the magic of Stars Hollow, and how this little show about a mother and daughter has led to deep, meaningful friendships. This show changed my life, and I am so grateful for that.

Chas Demster

Itsfilmedthere.com

    I would call my location scouting a strong hobby—almost like a second job. When I was a child, the movie *The Blues Brothers* was filmed close to my parents' friend's house. My parents saw the bridge scene from the beginning of the movie, being filmed. After the movie was filmed, my friend's father took me over to see the shooting locations. I was 11 years old, and instantly hooked. I thought it was the coolest thing—to see filming history come alive.

    I got into John Hughes movies, and my Dad (who is no longer with us) and I were really close. He grew up in Chicago and knew the city really well, so I asked him if we could go up to the northern suburbs to see the locations from John Hughes movies. I wanted to see locations like the high school, and Cameron's house from *Ferris Bueller's Day Off*. We went, and I took pictures to show to my friends.

After that we went down to Georgia to see the locations from *My Cousin Vinny.*

After I had collected a lot of pictures and knowledge, people started telling me I should write a book about it. In this industry, I felt that a book would quickly become obsolete. Because there were always going to be more and more filming locations, so any book I wrote would have to lead to further and further editions. It seemed to me that the best idea would be to create a website that could be continually updated.

Gilmore Girls is my all-time favourite show, so I naturally had to find all the locations on that show. I think in a wider sense, I fell in love with Warner Bros—shows like *ER, Moonlight,* etc. I live close to Chicago so I figured I would start with movies filmed in Chicago. One-by-one, I would go after work and hunt down the locations, photographing them as I went. I was single at that time, so I would get off work at 11pm, and work till 3am on the location hunting. Eventually the *Chicago* shows started—*Chicago Fire, Chicago PD* etc. I quickly found out that when you start cataloguing locations on a current show, people become very interested.

I started the locations website in 2010 when *Gilmore Girls* was over, so while I had all the locations, there was nothing new for me to add. When *A Year in the Life* came out, that was a big deal to me, because I had new locations to look for. I had a little bit of inside information when the revival came out, as I had been able to access the permits that had been used by the show to shoot. The small amount of permits used indicated that there were very few locations used outside of the Warner Bros lot, but that the production team had filmed in Malibu Creek State Park, and the Halfway House Cafe. Over the years I have made friends with people in Los Angeles which has been helpful. Since they know the area so well, sometimes if I get stuck they can point me in the right direction.

During the show, I became friends with Dave Berthuiame who was the location manager for *Gilmore Girls*. He was really helpful, and gave me his contact details in case I ever needed help tracking down a location. David told me that the episode where Rory graduates from college was when he knew that Alexis Bledel was done with the show. She was tired, and burned out, and he knew during that shoot that the show would not be able to continue. He told me this before the official announcement was made that the show would not be renewed. I was disappointed because I had arranged to come and watch them film and meet the cast during season 8. I was even offered the opportunity to be an extra, but it wasn't to be.

It's the relationship that makes the show so good, and all the townspeople. I always thought they might spin the show off and call it Stars Hollow. You could do a series just about Jackson and Sookie, or one just about Miss Patty. I think it would have been really successful.

I didn't come to the show right away, because we didn't have the WB channel. I became a fan through the filming locations. My mom and I were really lucky to win a prize to go and watch the taping of *Friends*. That was my first trip to Los Angeles. We got out there, and part of the deal was that we got a free tour of the Warner Bros lot. The tour covered *Gilmore Girls,* which at that stage, I had never heard of. The show was up to filming "A Tisket, A Tasket,". I took pictures of everything, even though it wasn't familiar to me—Luke's Diner, Stars Hollow High etc. The tour guide was talking about how they recently installed a stop light. It was probably a year later when I finally got the channel and I thought I would watch the show to see what it was about. I saw the last few minutes of the town protester episode, where Rory and Lorelai were egging Jess's car. I thought it was really weird and funny, and it was fascinating to watch the filming locations I had seen in person come to life on the show. The next episode—and the first full one I watched—was the Dance Marathon episode. Kirk's character had me hooked.

After that I watched the rest, and on Sundays they would re-run the early episodes so I caught up. Before the opening credits, Lorelai used to narrate a blurb about being a single mom with a daughter, explaining what the show was about before the re-runs would play. Season 4 was the first season where I watched from the start, caught up from the pilot, and looked for locations.

One of the hardest things to work out was how the town of Stars Hollow was set up because they would take turns in their walks and drives and end up in places they aren't supposed to be, according to the layout of the Warner Bros studio. For instance, they would go behind the church, and down the main street, but then end up back behind the church again. I know that set, and Los Angeles so well now that I know how things are laid out. I also now know when I see a location on screen exactly where it is. At the end of season 6 I did another tour, and the backlot was closed because they were making the movie *Norbit*. My sister and I were going together and I was looking forward to going to Midwest St now that I was a *Gilmore Girls* fan. I wanted to go and take pictures, knowing the series so well, but we couldn't and I was so disappointed. We did get to go onto the soundstage where they filmed the internal scenes at Yale. The dining room was the same one they used for Chilton, but had been dressed differently. What was interesting, was that when we were walking along outside, we walked on a rubber pad. This was installed where the sidewalk was supposed to be, so that the footsteps of the extras were quiet while they were walking past buildings, and the foot traffic sound didn't get picked up on the mics. We also got to go inside Logan's apartment at the end of season six when he goes into the elevator to leave for England. That scene is some of the best acting in the show, in my opinion. Those two don't say a word, but the look on his face says everything. We both got to go into the elevator that goes nowhere, and the doors closed, and opened again. It felt surreal to stand in the same place as Logan in that scene.

I have almost 500 autographs from people on *Gilmore Girls*. I have two huge photo albums full of the autographs on index cards. I wrote to different agents to ask for them, and when they sent them to me, I would message those people on Facebook and thank them. Some of those cast members then got in touch with others, and that helped fill some gaps in my collection. Over time, some of those cast members became Facebook friends, and some of them became people I met in person. Every year I go to Los Angeles as part of National Police Week, and sometimes I would meet cast members there, like Granville Van Dusen who played Darren Springsteen in the episode "Application Anxiety". Some of the people I have met have become good friends. Chris Flanders who played Shel in 'Luke Can See Her Face' offered me a tour at Paramount Studios, and John Kapelos who played the Orientation Leader in 'Fight Face' has taken me to dinner a couple of times.

I planned a special proposal for my girlfriend (now wife), and it had a distinct *Gilmore Girls* theme. Emily Kuroda, who plays Mrs Kim is one of the cast members that I have gotten to know. I used to message her once in a while to ask questions about the show, and we would chat. One night, I messaged her with an idea. I had been single for a really long time, and thought of myself as a 'late bloomer'. But, I had met someone. I asked Emily if she would like to take part in a proposal. My plan was that a friend would film it, but at the last minute he ended up working on a commercial and couldn't make it. Emily said that she could arrange a surprise, and she brought along Keiko Agena who plays Lane, and who on this particular day, would play the role of videographer.

When we got down to the park where the proposal would take place, I sent my wife off to get coffee and slipped Emily the ring. Keiko pretended that she just filmed everything, everywhere she went for snapchat, and I told Amanda that we were meeting Emily and Keiko at the park. I asked Emily and Keiko some questions, like what they were currently working on, and we just had a chat. I then asked

Emily if Kim's Antiques sold jewellery as well as furniture. Emily said her store did sometimes stock jewellery, and she happened to have a piece in her purse. She pulled my ring box out of her handbag, with the engagement ring in it, and handed it to me. I got down on one knee, and recited the speech I had prepared:

> *Amanda,*
>
> *I love you very much. People come to this city, from all over the world, chasing their dreams. Today, I am hoping to make one of my dreams come true.*
>
> *Will you marry me?*

I then told her about the set up, and thanked Emily and Keiko for helping me to carry the plan out. In the car, Amanda had a lot of questions about how that was all set up. Amanda called her mom on the way, who I had already asked for permission to marry her. My wife is in the DAR (Daughters of the American Revolution), which has become another funny little Gilmore connection in our lives.

When the revival came out, I had a process that I was already following for all locations. I immediately watched the episodes, and then watched it a second time to take screenshots. I have to watch closely for clues as to where it might be filmed. Street names, numbers, the look and layout of a house, and materials used can all help me figure out where things are filmed. Once I have the location figured out, I go and take photos of the location, and try to get similar angles that are used in the show. I add the photos, the addresses, and the screenshots with timestamps onto the website, which is a time intensive process.

The Wilshire Ebell Theatre in Los Angeles is an interesting location because it was used five times in *Gilmore Girls*. The stairs where Rory and Lorelai argue because Lorelai was kissing Max at

Chilton are at The Wilshire Ebell, and those same stairs are the ones Luke and Lorelai use in the revival to visit the surrogacy office. The debutante ball was filmed there, as was the Chilton dance, the Bangles concert, and Richard and Emily's vow renewal. When Rory is talking to Alex Kingston in *A Year in the Life,* she is out in the courtyard of the Wilshire E Bell. People think it's all different places but it's actually all the same filming location.

When they went to the Harvard alumni family house, it was a couple of blocks away from the Wilshire Ebell, not far from where Amy Sherman-Palladino grew up. Amy knew the people in that house and that's how she got that house for filming.

Greenfield Farms, where Chris and Lorelai have their car date and watch the movie projected onto the barn, is actually just down the road from the location for the Independence Inn. Any time the girls are seen shopping at the mall it is the Burbank Town Center Mall. I went there to take pictures and they got all over my case. I had people running distractions, because of the advertisements in the background.

To me the best looking location in the show is the outside of the Independence Inn. This is first seen in an early episode where there is a wedding of twins marrying twins. Then, Sookie and Jackson get married and they show a lot more of the grounds. That property is beautiful. It took me the longest time to find that place, and it wasn't until I saw the 2001 film *The Animal* that I recognised it. I got hold of the location manager for *The Animal* and confirmed that it was the same location. The back of that property is called Brookfield Farms, and is very popular in commercials and other television shows and movies. It's out in the middle of nowhere in a place called Hidden Valley. You can't even see the house from the road. When I went to that area in 2007, I called the groundskeeper and asked if I could visit and take pictures. One of the great things about the work I do with locations, is that I get to see these places, and to see a little bit more of the Gilmore world.

One of the reasons that the show still has such a following is that everyone is one half of the main relationship that the show presents—they are either mother, or child. Every woman hopes to be in a relationship with their daughter like that, or they have a relationship like Emily and Lorelai. Everyone relates to one of those two relationships. You can watch Emily and Lorelai work their way through it. That's why I think a lot of women like it. I also have female friends who like a lot of the male actors. For me personally, it's the townspeople. The townspeople are awesome in that show. The characters in Stars Hollow —including Lorelai—are tremendously human. They are not perfect. They do things wrong, they are real people.

DeAnn Stansbury

The Furniture Shack
Cloverlane Mercantile & Event Center

I started watching *Gilmore Girls* with my daughter after she received the DVD for Christmas. We devoured every disc during that holiday break and both fell fast and hard for all things Stars Hollow. It's impossible to watch and not love the quirky town and relatable townspeople.

The year we moved to Canada was hard for our family, but one bright light was taking a day trip to Unionville. The pilot was filmed there and we spent a beautiful day in October, walking up and down the main street, checking out all of the small businesses. It was, in a word: magic.

One month before we moved back to the United States I found out the address of the original Gilmore Mansion and after grabbing a Starbucks in Unionville, I stopped by to take photos.

Gilmore Girls and Stars Hollow truly do equal magic for those who know. It isn't a television show. It doesn't have anything to do with regular Hollywood tricks we have grown accustomed to with other shows. It is a beautiful escape from everyday life. It is a place to go when things look grim; friends to visit when we need to laugh or cry.

Since watching those DVD's so many years ago, I was able to bring Stars Hollow to my everyday life and share the magic with friends and fans alike. I opened our furniture store in 2014, and both the business, and my *Gilmore Girls* vision for it has expanded ever since. We started a store and I slowly fit out an area that was themed *Gilmore Girls*. I called this little area, 'Only with my Oxygen'. I created it during the pandemic, knowing that people would come in and see it when they could, but we actually ended up moving buildings first, so the public never got a chance to see that original area.

After some time, I realised that opening it to the fans was going to be delayed due to the pandemic. I had purchased a lot of *Gilmore Girls* inspired merchandise for the room, so I decided to create advent calendars. I love advent calendars so I used the merch we had to make them and they sold out. I made so many friends in the process.

We instead moved to a 4000 square foot space in a new building, 'Clover Lane'. This gave me a much bigger space that could host weddings of up to 300 guests, and brought with it so many opportunities. At the new facility, we can offer Friday night dinners, where people can sit and take pictures. We are working on Lorelai and Luke's wedding area. It's almost like a museum floor, like an exhibition that you can completely immerse yourself in. I love parties and decorating, and it's my dream to be able to offer this space to people who love *Gilmore Girls*. All of the seasons will be represented, and I am even planning a firelight festival. We have weddings, anniversaries, retirement parties scheduled for the next two years.

I just love the show so much that I see it everywhere I go, and the furniture shop reflects that. Once I started envisioning the shop to be a version of Stars hollow, I found things everywhere. The place is loaded with small details including ballerina's above the door, hay bales, and martinis served in a glass with a My Little Pony. I see *Gilmore Girls* everywhere, and associate so many things with it. It has become a part of my everyday life to dwell in the *Gilmore Girls* world, and to bring it to life in the shop.

I pick up the craziest things. There are some things that are mentioned once in the entire show, and I have incorporated them into the shop. For example, Jackson's reference to "Murrays House of Learning". I have a poster of this. It's the smaller things that I pick up on more than the bigger ones. I call them 'Hidden Lorelai's', like the 'Hidden Mickeys' that are planted in Disney movies. I think what I love about incorporating those smaller things is that only the true fans will understand. Casual watchers won't, so you instantly connect with other fans who just 'get it'.

I should be embarrassed at how many times I have watched the show, but having it on in the background is comforting to me. It represents my relationship with my daughter. It gives me great comfort to become a part of the community through the shop I have created, and it is a true joy to have *Gilmore Girls* become a part of my life in this way.

Kendra Westphalen

Oklahoma, USA

I found *Gilmore Girls* very late in its life. I did not watch a single second of the show when it originally aired. During its original airing I was in college, more concerned about classes, grades, friends, and my very active social life than any television show. After college I got married, moved cross country—and back again, all with two children under two. So, I missed a few things like television shows and movies. A few years later, when my kids were growing up, I went back to work, taking a job at a bookstore. My first love, much like Rory, has always been reading. I was in heaven. To top off the sheer joy I felt everyday being surrounded by books, literature, and readers, I made a very dear friend. Haley was my 'ride or die' work friend. She was artsy and interesting. We liked all the same music, shows, and movies, and we both had a penchant for tattoos.

One day during a particularly slow day at work, Haley and I began discussing tattoos and the very intricate work I was having done to complete an entire sleeve. I was toying with the idea of having a quote from one of my favourite books included on my sleeve. Haley had a quote on her arm, but I wasn't sure what it was from. I inquired about it, and she shared with me that it wasn't a complete quote—her mother had the beginning of the quote "Where You Lead"—and Haley had the end—"I Will Follow". I was intrigued.

She shared with me that the quote, in both parts, was taken from her favourite television show of all time—a show Haley and her mother watched together and loved. The show was *Gilmore Girls*. From the moment the first scene began I fell in love and I knew this was my forever show. I would never be able to watch it enough. I binged through the show at lightning speed, just in time for the release of *Gilmore Girls - A Year In the Life*.

At the same time I discovered this amazing show, I began to have health issues, and left my position at the beloved bookstore. I couldn't work outside the home so I began doing a bit of artwork, here and there. The art was mainly fun pop culture inspired pieces that showcased my love of television, shows, books, and movies. I did a few commissions, and shared Gilmore inspired pieces here and there in the *Gilmore Girls* Facebook fan groups. One of those groups was connected to a business called Stars Hollow Monthly. The owner of this *Gilmore Girls* subscription service reached out after I shared a few of my *Gilmore Girls* inspired doodles. She asked if I would be at all interested in doing some artwork for the subscription service, and I immediately accepted her offer. I began creating artwork for Stars Hollow Monthly and a sister sub box, Stars Hollow Book Club.

During this time, *Gilmore Girls* had become the decorating inspiration for my home. I collected prints, knick knacks, elaborate wooden signs—everything I could find that would turn my home into Stars Hollow. I went on wild internet hunts to obtain coveted pieces of items identical to ones used on the show, like the "pornographic monkey lamp", the lite brite lamp, and the flamingo tray also from the Gilmore kitchen. I transformed my kitchen into my version of Luke's Diner.

My collection is quite extensive and I love it so much. Luckily, my husband loves pop culture as much as I do and is okay with me turning part of our house into a shrine of sorts for my beloved show. Our entire home is like a pop culture museum. He has his rooms and his interests are showcased as well. We have a very interesting home to say the least. At one point Peggy—the owner of Stars Hollow Monthly—decided to bow out of the business and sold it to Mary. I was devastated. I enjoyed creating the artwork and I didn't want it to be over. It turned out to be just the beginning. Mary reached out to me and asked if I would like to continue my work, and we became a great team. The business came to be known as Fandom Fix, and my workload increased over time. Though Fandom Fix is no longer operating now, I will be forever grateful to this company for giving me a chance to explore my passion, and try new things. It was an amazing time in my life to get paid to watch shows and create fun art pieces inspired by them. I still watch the show on repeat, for the sheer joy of Stars Hollow.

The show has had a bittersweet connection for me. I am the child of a very young teenage mom, who did not keep me. Sometimes while watching I wonder if she and I could possibly have had a kind of 'Lorelai and Rory' relationship if she had chosen to raise me. After spending many years in the foster system I was adopted by my amazing loving grandparents who gave me everything I could ever have possibly needed or wanted. So that wonder and sadness is short lived.

      I see pieces of myself in so many characters of the show: Kirk when I am awkward, Emily when I am judgemental, Lorelai when I talk faster than others can comprehend or understand, Rory when my love of books and literature leads me, and I see myself reflected in Paris—she is my spirit animal. *Gilmore Girls* is populated by so many characters in whom we can find ourselves. No matter how much time passes, no matter what new shows premiere, *Gilmore Girls* will always be on a constant loop and will have top billing in my home.

PART THREE
CULT FOLLOWERS

It's a Religion

Nicole Gallucci

Connecticut, USA

In the 2000s, an impossibly cool single mother and her introverted, book-obsessed teenage daughter lived together in a picturesque Connecticut town. They both had dark hair, a deep obsession with food, quality taste in pop culture, and they shared a last name that began with the letter G. You might assume I'm referring to the *Gilmore Girls*, Lorelai and Rory, but the duo detailed above is none other than my mom and me, who were known around Trumbull, Connecticut, as the Gallucci Girls.

I've been enthralled by *Gilmore Girls* since the pilot first aired two decades ago, but it wasn't until the series ended in 2007 — the year my parents got divorced — that the show became an immovable part of my identity.

My mom and I had always been close, but with my dad out of the picture we started to rely on each other more frequently for companionship and support. As we developed weekly mother-daughter traditions such as date nights at Old Towne Restaurant (our version of Luke's Diner), Sunday dinners at my nana's house, and cosy nights spent cuddling on the couch in front of the television, our relationship became nearly indistinguishable from Lorelai and Rory's. With each passing year, each new school, each new job, each lost loved one, and each noteworthy milestone, it became clearer and clearer that we had perfected the rare *Gilmore Girls* dynamic. We weren't just mother and daughter, we were best friends.

My mom and Lorelai have quite a bit in common, starting with the fact that they're both incredibly capable, independent women with irresistible charm. They leave an impression on everyone they meet, they're fashionable as hell, and they give invaluable advice about life, friendships, and of course, boys. My favourite trait the two women share, however, is how deeply they care about the people in their lives.

It's worth noting that my mom and Lorelai share more than a few key differences, though. My mom doesn't walk around guzzling coffee by the vat and spouting pop culture references like a sprinkler system, she's always had an extremely respectful relationship with her parents, and she never would have dated my high school English teacher while I was still in his class. Much to my delight, my mom is also a kick-ass cook whose meals would knock Sookie's socks off. But much to my dismay, she *hates* rewatching things.

Like Lorelai, once I've seen a good television episode, series, or movie, it's not uncommon for me to restart it the second the end credits stop rolling. My mom, on the other hand, would be happy watching something once and never again. Her inability to take the same amount of pleasure (if not more) from a rewatch has always baffled me, and it's something we argue about often. Luckily, *Gilmore Girls* is her one exception.

When my parents divorced I had no siblings to lean on or hang out with, so I turned to the most reliable companion I knew for comfort: television. When I wasn't taking solace in on-air shows like *Friday Night Lights*, *The Office*, *Lost*, or *Prison Break*, I was pouring over *Gilmore Girls* reruns to distract myself.

My mom knew that *Gilmore Girls* was one of my all-time favourite series', so when I was in eighth grade she finally decided to watch it with me from the beginning. We've never explicitly discussed this, but I'm confident that she quickly realised my love for the show was an extension of my love for her.

We've gone through the full series at least five times together over the years, though I've lost count of how many times we've rewatched our favourite episodes. Our most recent rewatch took place in quarantine to celebrate the show's 20th anniversary, and I was again reminded of just how much the series bonds us.

Once every few scenes, without fail, my mom will turn to me and say, "That's us." Sometimes the two words come during simple, lighthearted scenes like when Lorelai is painting Rory's toenails, the two are planning elaborate coffee table feasts of junk food and take-out, or they're making their own screeching noises when fleeing the scene of a deviled egg-related crime. Other times she'll drop them during more heartfelt moments, like when Lorelai is pulling an all-nighter to help Rory study, Rory is telling a field of Chilton graduation attendees how much she adores her mother, or the two are comforting each other after heartbreaks. The "that's us" scenes are different with every rewatch, but they are consistent, and they let me know that the show makes us both feel as though we are watching a reflection of our own lives rather than a made-up world.

Reflecting on the impact *Gilmore Girls* has had on my life over the past 20 years has been unexpectedly emotional. I'll always be grateful to Amy Sherman-Palladino for the care she put into crafting such quirky, unconventional, genuinely entertaining characters. I'm endlessly thankful for the laughs, the pop culture references, the lessons in talking fast and exuding wit, and for a show that will always be a delightful escape from reality. But more than that, I'm thankful for the fact that when my world felt like it was falling apart, her fictional world offered me some much-needed positive perspective.

Being a single parent isn't easy, nor is having your parents get divorced when you're a teen, but *Gilmore Girls* made a remarkable effort to depict a single mother raising her daughter as a celebratory situation rather than a shameful one. When I was struggling to adjust to a household of two back in eighth grade, close friends and *Gilmore* fans around the world were marvelling over Lorelai and Rory's setup. Their small, atypical family wasn't seen as lonely or sad; it was one to be desired. They had increased freedom and flexibility, they were experts at finding their own fun, and they knew that as long as they had each other they could survive whatever life threw their way. I had always seen Lorelai and Rory through that same admirable lens, and when I looked at my own life the way I looked at theirs, everything felt better.

Season 1, Episode 14 of *Gilmore Girls* opens with Lorelai and Rory attempting to explain the "incomparable" *Donna Reed Show* to Dean. After hearing their passionate spiel, he has the audacity to say, "So...it's a show?" to which Rory authoritatively replies, "It's a lifestyle." Whenever I'm attempting to explain my love of *Gilmore Girls* to someone, that scene plays on a loop in my mind. For some it's just a show, but for me *Gilmore Girls* will always be a lifestyle.

Laura Sanderfer

Atlanta, USA

My relationship with my mother is very similar to Lorelai and Rory. She is a single mom, we were best friends while I was growing up, and so naturally we watched *Gilmore Girls* together from the beginning. Rory and I are only a year apart, so her life experiences echoed mine, in a way. Since 2000, *Gilmore Girls* has been a constant presence in my life and the background to everything. Now, it is what I put on when I'm anxious and need comforting, or I've had a bad day and need to unwind. I've watched the series hundreds, maybe a thousand times.

Anyway, when I met my husband in 2015, I immediately filled him in on my *Gilmore Girls* obsession. He responded by watching all seven seasons himself, memorising the inside jokes and plotlines, and developing his own opinion about what team he rooted for (he completely bypassed Jess, Dean, and Logan and is firmly Team Richard). I've received a myriad of Gilmore-themed trinkets. Birthday and anniversary gifts are always Gilmore themed. When it came time to propose, he concocted an elaborate ruse.

At the time, I was a freelance writer, so I got this email from a publication needing a weekend write-up about the Smoky Mountains area. I communicated with the editor to choose dates, spoke to the photographer, came up with a whole list of places to visit and things to eat that would be perfect for the tourism magazine. I was supposed to review a bed and breakfast, as well, so the piece would be a full profile on visiting Pigeon Forge/Sevierville for a weekend. We arrived on a Friday afternoon, and I immediately went into work mode. We headed out for a day of interviewing Saturday morning; and went back to the inn around 3:30 to nap, gather notes and do some pre-writing. The minute we walked in the door, Justin got down on one knee and asked me to marry him. The entire lobby was filled with yellow daisies, and Justin was dressed as Luke. He had planned the entire thing - used a fake email address, pretended to be an editor, bought a website, and made sure everyone we spoke to that weekend was in on the surprise. I can also confirm, 1000 yellow daisies in person doesn't fill a room like it did on the show, but they were beautiful and we gave them out to all the guests when we were done.

When our big day arrived, we used understated *Gilmore Girls* details in the wedding. I carried daisies, like Lorelai always talked about. My bridesmaids carried yellow daisies to echo the engagement. My vows echoed Luke's words to Lorelai on their first date:

"I'm in. I'm all in."

Justin ended his vows by calling me his Emily Gilmore and promised me he'll always be my Richard. My mom and I had a mother daughter dance to the theme from the show, and one of our sweet friends created a Sanderfer Bingo card, and handed it out at the ceremony and reception. Naturally *Gilmore Girls* and coffee were squares on it. I walked down the aisle to the song Lorelai and Luke had their first dance to (*Reflecting Light*, by Sam Phillips) and the wedding party was introduced at the reception to the Life and Death Brigade song from the revival. We had two custom drinks at the reception—mine was an old fashioned called, 'The Richard Gilmore'.

Since our wedding, our love for the show has continued to grow. We go to Dragon Con every year, here in Atlanta. We met Sean Gunn (Kirk) at this convention. We told him all about our engagement, and he was so pleased for us. In 2019, Scott Patterson (Luke) came to a store nearby to promote his new coffee line. Justin dressed like Luke, Scott signed one of Kristi Kelly's *Gilmore Girls* cookbooks, a blue hat, and a coffee carafe, and was so kind and gracious when we told him about the whole engagement story.

For most anniversaries and birthdays Justin has given me *Gilmore Girls* inspired items—cards, a toy rocket ship (Logan's love rocket!), 'vicious trollop' lip gloss, various art prints, Pop! Funko figurines, and a few of the *Gilmore Girls* subscription boxes and shirts. For our three year wedding anniversary he found me a signed script of the pilot episode.

Before I met Justin, I patterned my life after Rory's. I wanted to be a writer, went to a private high school, read way too much, took (and loved) Russian literature in college, was best friend's with my mom and got along with my grandparents better than my mom did. When I moved into the college dormitories, it felt like a huge deal. To stay in touch, mom and I watched *Gilmore Girls* together, over the phone, Tuesdays at 8 P.M.

I use *Gilmore Girls* jargon in everyday life. Phrases like 'copper boom', 'coffee coffee coffee', 'oy with the poodles', 'your enthusiasm shocks me', and many more. My big remaining goals are to visit the set out in California and to go to the fan festival one fall. It's so ingrained in my life.

Jennifer Wood

Colorado, USA

I had heard of *Gilmore Girls* for years, but it was on air at a time when I didn't really watch much television. In 2016 my best friend was watching it and suggested it to me. I started watching it and never stopped. It cycles through my home on a constant basis.

From the first episode, I was glued—invested in the characters as if they were my friends. I cried when they cried, I sobbed when they sobbed. I felt their pain and laughed at the hilarious dialogue. I bugged another friend who had watched it for years with all of my thoughts, feelings, and questions.

Then, my daughter started to watch it. At the time she was six years old. Some may think six is too young to watch *Gilmore Girls*, but for us it was perfect. I am a single mom and I related to Lorelai's character. Lorelai Gilmore is my inspiration for everything. She is strong, determined, has big dreams, is a wonderful mother, stubborn, pouts, and loves traditions, and coffee. She goes through her day to day life with humour that I could relate to. I made personal decisions in my life that took years for me to figure out for myself. Lorelai represented this part of me that needed to develop, learn, and process. In an episode where she stayed in bed for days sobbing she became more real than any character ever was to me.

After the show became a staple for my daughter and I, both my sons joined in—following the pop culture references, watching Kirk's antics, and analysing the boyfriends. We never skip an episode, the intro, or the theme song. I even have a part of my room dedicated to the show, with memorabilia and artwork thanks to social media and the passionate fans I have befriended. Watching the show has helped form an additional bond between my three kids and I, that I know they will never forget as they grow older. I believe that the memories of us watching *Gilmore Girls*, talking about *Gilmore Girls*, and looking through my dedicated area in my room every time a new piece is added, are going to be memories we will cherish in years to come. The references made in the show have become natural references we make with each other and I am beyond grateful for that. If I am exhausted, upset, heartbroken, lost, or sick, this show brings me great comfort. The world in which *Gilmore Girls* takes place feels familiar, it feels relatable, it feels hopeful. It has this way of scooping me up when I need it most. In a way, I feel like *Gilmore Girls* rescued me. *Gilmore Girls* changed my life.

Teresa Beracci

Naples, Italy

  I watch *Gilmore Girls* every month of the year because when I watch it the world seems like a better place.

  Lorelai is my favourite character because I am so similar to her. We are both coffee lovers, and music lovers. We want a man that stays forever, and we want to be happy. We smile when things are tough, and we carry on.

  In many ways, I am also Rory. Like Rory, I love books, I love reading tragedies and classics like *Romeo and Juliet,* the poetry of

Emily Dickinson, and also contemporary books that explore the human condition such as *Eat Pray Love* by Elizabeth Gilbert. I read everywhere—in parks, in my bedroom—anywhere. I share my day with books, and the characters, and worlds within them. My next great love is study. I study social relations at The University of Naples Federico II, which is the oldest public university in the world. I study social relations—people, the territory, feelings, media, social media and its effect on people, and the digital world. This contributes to my reading, as I have to read a lot for my exams, and it makes me feel a bit closer to Rory as she goes through her college experience.

However, I also relate to many of the other characters that inhabit the Gilmore world. Like Luke, I hate mobile phones. Like Jess, I make notes in the margins. I love Emily's elegance, Sookie's passion for food, and Lane's taste in music. Paris's perfectionism in her studies is admirable, as is Richard's work ethic. I adore Stars Hollow and its history, but its residents are the best part of its make up. Lorelai is my virtual television sister, and mother. I feel protected in her world, and have more confidence in myself. *Gilmore Girls* is my life, my religion, and a small piece of my heart.

Amanda Ranay Griffey

Georgia, USA

I was introduced to *Gilmore Girls* by my mom when I was about 6 and it was just coming out. Every week we scheduled time together to watch it and it very quickly became our special 'thing'. No matter what was happening in our lives—even if we were in the middle of something—every week as I grew up, we would stop and watch it together.

When my parents got divorced, my mom got me the show on DVD as a birthday present so that I could watch it when I was at my dad's house, when I missed her. Having the seasons on DVD, and being able to watch them when I wasn't with mom made things a little easier when I felt sad. The characters gave me comfort, and cheered me up. I always aspired to be Rory and had even pegged Harvard University as my dream school. I related to her shy introversion, and I resonated with her bookworm nature, because I was one too. I, like Rory, was ambitious. I wanted to excel at my grades and land a job as a judge when I graduated.

Now I'm 26 and while I'm not a judge, and have become more like Lorelai than Rory, the show still takes me back to when my mom and I were best friends and watched it together. I've introduced it to my son to carry on the tradition and love that he will watch it with me every time I turn it on. As he's gotten older I think he starts to see why it's such an important show and a big part of my life.

As I've gotten older I realise that *Gilmore Girls* has gotten me not only through all the tough times I've had in my life, but has also brought out the best in me. Some of the best parts of my life are inspired by the show. The phrase "Coffee in an IV" is how I live my life and being a 'Java Junkie' is how I'm known in my current career. I have an 'Omnia Paratus' tattoo just to remind myself of Logan's advice to really live, and my music taste has increased just by listening to Lane Kim's taste in music. *Gilmore Girls* is a show that has such a strong connection to my life that my son's dad and I use Gilmore references when talking to each other. I strongly believe the show has helped us become better at co parenting. Things are no longer tense thanks to our love of the show. It has also given us the ability to understand, through Lorelei and Christopher's relationship, that sometimes the best relationship for our child is one where their parents aren't married but that the door is always open and that as long as our son is loved by us, then everything is how it's supposed to be.

I cannot overstate how the show has shaped me as a person, and has shaped my relationships with people. I fell in love with the show a long time ago, and now realise that Stars Hollow is the best home I have ever had.

Claudia Schoder

Dresden, Germany

My story starts how a lot of real love stories do: *Gilmore Girls* and I, were introduced through my brother. We had several meetings (on television) before I ultimately fell in love. By the end of season 7, I had taken such a significant journey with the show, that I felt devastated about Rory and Logan saying goodbye. I couldn't believe this was the way my beloved show chose to farewell me, especially since I am a person who craves happy endings. For years I tried to find something new which would catch my heart as much as *Gilmore Girls* did. Some shows came close, but none stayed long.

Nearly a decade later, *Gilmore Girls* and I found each other again. The show planned a revival and I needed cheering up during a period of having been sick at home for several months. In a rewatch of the old episodes we easily fell back into our smart, witty talking, first in my native language German, and shortly after in English. I started to connect on the show's many Facebook fan groups and feverishly joined in the anticipation of seeing my love again to find out what had happened to my Stars Hollow townies in *A Year in the Life*. Just like a high school reunion, I loved it, but not everyone I met had stayed true to my memories or had found the success in life that I had expected. My heart broke as Rory said her final goodbye to the Life and Death Brigade. I wasn't ready for anything—on this matter, *In Omnia Paratus* did not apply to me.

Thankfully life is full of opportunities and, in the words of Lorelai, "as long as everything is exactly the way I want it, I'm totally flexible." I finally found my happy ending in many of the *Gilmore Girls* fan fiction stories that are available online. As I read my way through many of them, I started to discover that the show has more to offer than the usual three teams we attribute to it: Team Dean, Team Jess, and Team Logan. I started reading some fanfiction that depicted a 'Team Finn' and soon moved on to create my own team.

As I watched the show for the first time I liked Dean, then Jess and then Logan, because they were all perfect partners for Rory at various times. Looking back on that first watch through, I remember wishing that Rory would continue to date Robert and leave Logan in my favourite episode "Pulp Friction." As I watched the episode for probably the 100th time, I thought there should be a 'Team Robert' for Rory. He respects Rory's wishes and behaves like a true gentleman on their date. That's when I started to create my own Facebook group, and #TeamRobert was born.

As I started to write the first ever 'Team Robert' fanfiction, I started to think through some of the character development for Robert, and discussed these ideas with a beta reader, Linda. We don't know a lot about Robert, but we know that Amy Sherman-Palladino creates her *Gilmore Girls* characters sometimes a lot like the real actors (anyone who has met Liz Torres who plays Miss Patty knows what I mean). Therefore, I did a bit of research online on the actor who plays Robert, Nick Holmes. To my suprise, I learned that he is an excellent photographer and published poet.

In December of 2017 I was able to announce (in my small little bubble of Team Robert fans) that I was bold enough to buy a fan fest ticket for Kent, Connecticut. I planned to go with Michaela, a lovely Austrian woman I had met online through my fanfiction, but unfortunately she needed to cancel at the last minute. Instead I shared my room with a stranger who turned out to be a charming Australian journalist.

The first day of the fanfest arrived and my wonderful husband who travelled with me to the USA, but didn't join in the event, drove me to Kent in the morning. I wore a Steampunk outfit in honour of the Life and Death Brigade and added a 'Team Robert' shirt to show support for my team. I was standing at registration as my husband sent me a text message with a picture and asked if I perhaps knew the man. The photo showed Nick Holmes. I was speechless that he was wandering around town and my husband had the pleasure of seeing him while I was getting registered for the festival.

Early into the festival, I spotted Nick across the street, perusing a book sale. He turned around and saw me in my outfit, laughed, crossed the street, and took the first steps towards our one-of-a-kind friendship. I was impressed that he remembered me from all my Twitter posts. We had the most precious first meeting. We had a lovely talk while we took some pictures and he signed his poetry book *Time Spent Falling* with a 'Team Robert' message. The week before the event Nick shared on Twitter that he wanted to do a 'pub crawl'. We arranged to meet up after his official meet and greet.

We met each other later and started in the famous Fife 'n Drum Restaurant & Inn. Little did I know at that moment that I would spend about half of my time with a handful of other fans and Nick there, instead of joining in the official fanfest schedule. We never made it to another pub, but I got to know Nick much more in that relaxed environment than I had ever expected. I even saw him spontaneously write a marvellous poem for me in the pub, which is till today one of my favourite gifts ever. He is truly a word artist.

Nick is charming, kind and like I imagined Robert, a true gentleman. All my time spent with him was absolutely magical. On the other hand, the whole weekend was absolutely legendary, with "lots of booze, no food whatsoever." In reality there was, of course, food, but the time was filled with so many highlights, I forgot to eat most of the time. One of these highlights was meeting Stan Zimmerman on Saturday evening, who was a writer in season 5. He approached me to ask me for a picture with him for his nephew. Stan told me he wrote the episode "Pulp Friction" (which is THE Team Robert episode) and named the character Robert after his nephew. Therefore, Stan wanted a picture with me in my Team Robert shirt to show to his nephew. Stan is such a very caring, talented and humble man with so many *Gilmore Girls* stories.

I never expected my 'Team Robert' sub-fandom to become as significant as it is. More than one person cautiously asked me in 2018 at the fan fest in Kent who Robert is. My team group was at this time probably the tiniest *Gilmore Girl*s group on Facebook, but I added several lovely people I met in Kent during the weekend. At no place in the world is it easier to find the best new friends than at a *Gilmore Girls* inspired fan fest, but to me my Team Robert members are always a special kind of people.

As I went to two more fan fests in 2019, again in Kent and Unionville, Canada, nobody asked me anymore who Robert was. Nick was already a fan fest favourite thanks to his relentless niceness to every fan he meets. I also wasn't the only one wearing a Team Robert shirt anymore. My talented friend Lisa created beautiful designs and everywhere I went those weekends, a 'Team Robert' member was never too far away. Even Stan was seen with our team shirt, because the man who was responsible for the episode where Rory had a date with Robert and also named the character, is as important for 'Team Robert' as Nick who played Robert in *Gilmore Girls*.

The last months have been, thanks to the pandemic, difficult for all of us. My 'Team Robert' friends helped me to not only survive, but to have a lot of joyful moments in this crisis. Some examples include getting a surprise Zoom quarantine birthday party and participating together online in a wedding. My team men Nick and Stan, who are my friends now and not just people who worked on my beloved show, shared online fine arts like marvellous poetry and amazing theatre plays. Jennie and Marcus (the organisers of the fan festival) cheered us up with worldwide virtual fan fests, and I became good friends with Shelly Cole (who plays Madeline on *Gilmore Girls*). We always have each other's backs. Last, but not least, festival attendant Ella and her son Ross—my favourite mother-son duo—allowed me to be a virtual honorary family member in their safe social distance family meetings while I couldn't see my own family. Therefore 'Team Robert' is much more than a lifestyle - it's a family. I'm so lucky to have all these amazing *Gilmore Girls* friends in my life and I could shout forever about how kind and supportive 'Team Robert' is through thick and thin. They're my daily ray of sunshine.

Maria Cristina Locuratolo

Rome, Italy

    I discovered *Gilmore Girls* when a friend of mine suggested that I watch it. I like watching shows, but had never seen this one. When I started watching it, it was like love at first sight. I got through all of the seasons in a very short time. After watching it, I went through a difficult period of my life. I broke up with my partner of 13 years, which was really hard. I spent my days crying, and struggling through the work day. What got me through, was coming home to rewatch an episode of *Gilmore Girls*. It was the best part of my day.

Lorelai's character had a kind of magic that felt very reassuring to me. Watching *Gilmore Girls* felt as comforting to me as someone beside me saying, "everything will be all right". In a way, I felt like this show put the pieces of my heart back together.

When *Gilmore Girls: A Year in the Life* came out, it resonated with me immediately. In the time between the first series, and the revival, Lorelai and Rory had grown up, and so had I. It was like meeting an old friend after a long period of time. *Gilmore Girls* is a show that helps me in very difficult periods of my life. It is my happy place—a safe zone where I have found relief and consolation. It's my 'Linus's blanket'.

In 2020, after coronavirus and lockdown, I fell into a depression. I was in a very dark place. One night, I couldn't sleep and I turned on my television. I found an episode of *Gilmore Girls*—the one where Rory attended Yale, and Lorelai and Luke finally expressed their feelings to each other. I felt a sense of consolation and relief. Stars Hollow had once again spread its love and joy in my home, and in my life. This picked me up and prompted me to watch the show again, every day, and eventually, I battled my way out of that dark place I had been in. It is not just a show; I can watch it a thousand times and it will still be like the first time I have watched it. *Gilmore Girls* brings me comfort, and hope. In a way, *Gilmore Girls* saved my life.

Krista Callahan

Pennsylvania, USA

    I will never forget the first time I watched *Gilmore Girls*. Even though it wasn't until November of 2006 that my daughter and I first became acquainted with Stars Hollow—and all of its quirky and colourful characters—our lives were (in the words of Rory) changed impermeably and forever. My daughter and I were living in Germany, stationed there as my husband was in the army. The apartment we lived in had no cable to watch American shows and so our entertainment was made up of watching DVDs of television shows and movies. My mother purchased several complete series' of shows ranging from *Everybody Loves Raymond* to *Seinfeld*. In a way, this aided our sense of normalcy in a foreign country. Among those series was *Gilmore Girls* which fast became my favourite show, and a favourite of my daughter Macy. At first, Macy and I would watch one episode a week, wanting to watch more but wanting to savour it as well. It gave us something to look forward to and something to talk about—wondering what crazy ordeal might ensue next, or what new profession Kirk might have the next evening.

    Macy, who was ten years old at the time, and I bonded even more, not only because she and I were sharing the experience of strange lands and faces together, but because we were sharing in the experiences of Lorelai and Rory and how similar they were to our own lives and relationship. I felt, at the time, as though I was raising Macy alone because her father was in the army. I connected with Lorelai's character, sharing in her anxieties of doing it on her own while embracing the wonderful connection that she and Rory had with my own child. Many evenings Macy and I would plan our own buffet of junk food to enjoy in front of the television while we paid a visit to our gal pals in Stars Hollow.

    Eventually, we became residents of Stars Hollow ourselves. We could put *Gilmore Girls* on anytime, never having to knock on the door, but being welcomed in at Luke's diner, the Independence Inn, the modest home of Lorelai and Rory and even impromptu drop-ins for dinner in Hartford were always fun and appreciated. Macy and I bonded even more when a surprising turn of events took place. I was served divorce papers while my husband was still stationed in Iraq. He had been having an affair with another soldier and wanted to marry her. It became an even harder time for us because we were not at home, and had no family to hug us and wipe away our tears. Macy and

I only had each other and our Stars Hollow family. Our one show a week viewing fast became binge nights where we would watch as many as we wanted, but always together so as not to miss anything or miss the time watching together. It would never have felt right watching it without Macy anyway. *Gilmore Girls* became ours, and it would feel like cheating to watch without her.

I will never forget the day we got to the end of the series. It was Christmas of 2007. Macy and I were still in Germany and it was still just the two of us. I was battling depression over my pending divorce, and spent a lot of my time crying. I remember watching *Gilmore Girls* and crying so hard when Rory and Lorelai came to that tent in the square that Luke had made. I couldn't tell which was my tears and which was the rain on the television—it was as if they were all blending together. The show ended and Macy and I sat on the couch holding each other, crying tears of joy for Rory's new chapter in her life, for Lorelai's accomplishments, strength and struggles, and for all of the love that we shared with the townspeople. The *Gilmore Girls* had become our dear friends, and we celebrated along with the Stars Hollow residents. Macy and I looked at each other and then the tears soon became sadness, as if we were saying goodbye to our best friends for the last time. There was an emptiness that couldn't be matched by a new series. And so….Macy and I decided to rewatch *Gilmore Girls*.

Since then, we have seen the show many times. Macy is now 23 and living on her own. We still watch it together (even on the phone when we are not together) and rewatches are still filled with junk food, laughing and singing. She is my Rory, and I am her Lorelai. Her birth minute is 4:04 a.m. (just one minute off of Rorys 4:03) and I would always wake her up in that minute with a birthday kiss and to tell her how special she is to me. As an adult, she gets a wakeup call and a funny video or snapchat from me. I believe what makes us Gilmores is the way it brought her and I closer together through our experiences, and through Rory and Lorelai's. I eventually went back to college and the day I graduated with my master's degree, Macy threw me a surprise party complete with a tearful speech, much like Rory's own dedication to her mother that I will treasure forever. She is—in the words of Lorelai—my pal, my everything.

Nikki Ella Thomas

Derbyshire, United Kingdom

My first memory of *Gilmore Girls* was when I was around six years old. I had stayed up late past my bedtime and had snuck into our 'snug', The 'snug' was a small room we used to spend time in, where everything just snuggly fit in it. Back then, *Gilmore Girls* was shown at 10pm on Nickelodeon. I have no memory of what episode it was that was playing, but I think it was around the end of season 2. I didn't get to watch much of it before my mum came in and found me. She turned the television off and told me that any programmes showing after 9pm were too adult for me to watch. And that was that—my first, and last encounter with the *Gilmore Girls*, until I turned 19.

In July of 2016 I was scrolling through Netflix trying to decide on my next watch. It came down to either *Pretty Little Liars* or *Gilmore Girls*. Thus, my first watch through of *Gilmore Girls* began. On a Sunday morning, I was part way through season 1, episode 9 when I had to leave for my volunteer shift at the local animal rescue. I paused it just as Rory entered the dance with Dean, and Emily and Lorelai were having it out about eating bananas on toast. It was my plan to spend the rest of my weekend finishing the entirety of season 1, when I came back from my shift.

My volunteer work involved me photographing the animals and making them look cute for the shelter website so that people would want to adopt them. I had been doing this for over a year and had formed a bit of routine. I would photograph the cats, and other small animals first, and leave the dogs for last, so that I got to play with them longer. Over the years I had experienced many encounters with the dogs that had passed through the gates. This included the timid ones that would hide under the bench in the yard (my own dog was one of these, and adopted from the shelter), the dogs that didn't want to be in front of the camera as they were too busy behind it getting cuddles, and the dogs that wanted to stand proud with their toys and show off. At one point I even had a dog that liked me a little too much…if you know what I mean!

I knew from experience that the best way for dogs to greet me and trust me enough to take their photograph was if I was sitting on the floor when they first saw me. This way I was not intimidating to them if they had been brought to the shelter due to abuse or neglect. I would let them sniff my camera and let them get used to me before I even attempted to shove a camera in their face. As I was sitting waiting on the floor for the next dog to be brought into the yard by the staff, I could hear them having a discussion on whether or not to bring in one of the new dogs to be photographed. They were tossing up whether to just get it done and out of the way or not. This dog hadn't been put through the testing system yet, to determine how his temperament was, and how he was with people. Getting the photo taken straight away would mean the dog could be adopted out sooner, rather than later. So, it was decided since he would be on a lead and held by a staff member, that we should get the photo taken.

The dog that came through the gates was extremely thin. His rib cage was showing, and his fur was patchy in places where it would never grow back due to scarring. He didn't see me at first, where I was sitting on the floor, and he was overly excited. I decided to capture his excitement and had my camera to my eye when he turned around and saw me. The next few seconds I do not remember very well, and have only ever relieved through my nightmares and through the account of the staff member that watched in horror. Through the eye piece of my camera I watched as the dog's strength rippled through him and the staff member lost grip on the lead. I heard one single bark that haunts me to this day, before his teeth headed for my face and neck.

As I was already on the floor, I was at a disadvantage and had no way of getting away from the dog. He was larger than I was, and if he stood on his back legs, he would have towered over me in height. I remember the feel of his teeth grazing down the side of my face as I lifted my arm up to try and protect my neck. I don't let myself think about what the outcome could have been if I had been a millisecond late with my reaction speed. Most dogs, when attacking because they are scared, will do one bite and then let go. However, dogs that are reacting out of anger or instinct or because it is what they have been trained to do, will continue to hold on or attack further. The dog wouldn't let go. The dog eventually let go briefly and prepared to go for me again, so I ran. The sound of the dog barking and growling followed me to the gate as I fumbled with the catch. I couldn't move my left arm as it was injured in the attack. Luckily the other staff members were there and opened it for me. I was ushered away and out of the view of the public that had been there viewing dogs for potential adoption.

I sat in the staff kitchen watching as one of the other staff members called an ambulance, one got me something to drink, and one shakily opened up the first aid kit and tried with no luck to stop the blood gushing from my arm. He asked if I was in pain. The poor staff members didn't know what to do with themselves. When the ambulance arrived, I was walking through the shelter, stepping through my own blood on the floor.

I needed surgery on my arm. My muscle was torn in two and my nerve damage was terribly close to being irreversible. By some stroke of luck the dog had not managed to crush the bone in my arm. For two weeks after the incident I was on strong painkillers, and antibiotics. This cocktail made me extremely tired and I don't really remember much from those two weeks. I spent the majority of it on my sofa in front of the television, binge watching *Gilmore Girls* on Netflix.

Eventually, I recovered from my physical injuries, but I never returned to the animal shelter. I started struggling with nightmares, and panic attacks. I couldn't get my head around the fact that if it wasn't for my reaction time that the whole thing could have ended up different. I also couldn't get my head around why the dog would do that to me. All my life I had loved dogs—I grew up with them, and wanted to work with them—and suddenly it was like I was at war with myself. I couldn't make sense of why a dog would want to hurt me and potentially take my life away. The dog had been put to sleep the night of the incident, as they couldn't rehome him after he had attacked a human. I felt remorse at not being able to see the dog again and perhaps have a different interaction with him. I felt that this opportunity for reconciliation had been stolen from me. This also created immense guilt that I couldn't rid myself of. Guilt that the dog had died because of me.

Watching *Gilmore Girls* during my weeks of recovery at home, the show embedded itself in my heart. I had the overwhelming pull to watch the show again. I later learned in therapy that this pull to watch the show is caused by needing comfort. The show provided me comfort during a time I needed it most, even if I didn't remember much of it.

I started rewatching, but when I got to episode 9 of season 1 again, I felt uneasy. As the episode progressed it got harder and harder for me to carry on watching and when the scene of Rory and Dean entering the dance came on the screen I burst into tears. On my first watch of the series just a few months before this was the point that I started watching with my mauled arm and the association with that time pained me. To this day, I can not watch to the end of this episode, but I know what happens from reading about it on the Wikipedia episode guide.

After that episode Lorelei and Rory became the people (in addition to my family and friends) that were always there for me. Lorelai and Rory didn't know about what happened to me. They didn't tiptoe around me trying not to trigger me in any way. They didn't attempt to make me talk about the turmoil in my mind. They simply absorbed me into their wild lives and took me along for their journey too. When I was diagnosed with Post Traumatic Stress Disorder (PTSD) the girls were there making me forget about my own upset as I watched them explore the grounds of Harvard university. When I broke it off with my boyfriend of four years Lorelai was there sharing and understanding my heartbreak. When I sat and cried in therapy, Rory was crying in therapy making me feel less alone. The show itself creates such a sense of safety and comfort, as well as providing an escape to another little corner of the world for a few hours.

It's been years now since the incident happened, and though I no longer need tablets and therapy to get me through a day, I still need Stars Hollow. I still need to wonder where all the anvils have gone to distract me when I wake up from nightmares. In those five years,

Lorelei and Rory not only supported me through my recovery, but they also watched me find the love of my life. They held my hand as I went through a high risk pregnancy which resulted in an emergency C-section, they kept me company on the long newborn nights, and perked me up as I battled with crippling post natal depression. They stood by my side as I went through a second pregnancy and birth completely on my own due to covid regulations, and as I got engaged. The impact the girls have had on my life is evident in almost every aspect of my life—from the one liners I say, to the art work on my walls, even to my bouquet at my wedding, which will be full of yellow daisies.

Ruth and Ellen Bustin

Northamptonshire, United Kingdom

Our story begins back in 1989 when I met my 'Christopher'. We dated in school, went our separate ways, and then eventually got back together again. By 1998, we were happily living our lives when I found out I was pregnant. My 'Christopher' left me all alone to be a mother. Luckily for me, my relationship with my parents is the complete opposite of Lorelai's relationship with Richard and Emily in *Gilmore Girls*. My mum and dad were so understanding and supportive of my decision to go ahead and have my 'Rory'.

One day, when I was surfing through the television channels I found a television show that called out to me. It centred around a fast talking, independent, single mother, and suddenly it was like I had found my place. Lorelai made me feel like I wasn't so alone.

Throughout the show I started to notice that there were more than just a few similarities. When my own 'Rory' was five years old, I met my 'Luke'. We became friends, and he became my rock—always there for me through thick and thin. Like Lorelai, I had a few boyfriends, and my Luke always watched me go through heart breaks, and helped me pick up the pieces and carry on. When I was finally ready to admit my feelings and go get him, he was with another woman, his 'Nicole'. Eventually we found our way back together. Before he came into my life me and my 'Rory' pretty much lived off take out and sweets like they do in the show, but now we have our 'Luke' we get healthy home cooked meals every night.

Everyone in my life couldn't wait for us to get married, and finally when my 'Rory' turned 16, we did. We also went on to have a daughter together. She is everything I hoped for and everything we always wanted Luke and Lorelai to have on *Gilmore Girls*. I lost my dad in 2019 like Lorelai did. We had our ups and downs like Richard and Lorelai but my Dad was my hero and he was always there when and if I needed him. Love you always and forever Dad.

Gilmore Girls became like comfort food for me and my daughter. Whenever one of us is sad or just wanting to reminisce, we cuddle up on the sofa and put it on. It makes us feel like we are watching our life and all the memories we have. We would love to see how *Gilmore Girls: A Year in the Life* would have continued for Rory and Lorelai and hope that they make a follow on from that to see if our lives are still in sync with the show, and the world of Stars Hollow.

Ella Spice

Maryland, USA

I have always been an enormous *Gilmore Girls* fan. This show is really a world that I can always step into—when life is too much, when one foot hesitates to follow the other, when my inner balance is knocked askew by a universe that's got too much grit. I truly believe that *Gilmore Girls* has recalibrating properties. Within minutes, I can escape into the warmth and easy gentle joy of the Gilmore world, and all becomes right again.

Several years ago, my oldest son Ross began joining me to watch (and re-watch) the series. I was over the moon with happiness.

Sharing "my girls" with him was like introducing him to a family he didn't know he had. We laughed together as we watched, eventually saying the lines with the characters, and then even quoting them when we weren't watching. We became fluent in Gilmore. That fluency gave an extra layer of language to our relationship. Sometimes we were exactly mother and child ("Lorelai and Rory"); other times we were old friends ("Sookie and Lorelai", "Lane and Rory"); still others we were wild adventurers ("The Life and Death Brigade" members).

Seeking just such an adventure, two and a half years ago, Ross gave me the most unbelievable Mother's Day present imaginable: he had researched the many real-life inspirations for the town of Stars Hollow and had created an itinerary to go visit them all! We set off for Connecticut in early June of 2018 (*In Omnia Paratus*!), and it was a more magical journey than I could have ever conceived. For three days we traipsed through the gorgeous countryside of Washington Depot, Kent, New Milford, Litchfield, and Bantam Connecticut, exploring coffee shops like Luke's (such as Marty's in Washington Depot), an ice cream shoppe like Taylor's Soda Shoppe (Arethusa Farm in Bantam), markets like Doose's (The Washington Food Market), bookstores like Stars Hollow Books (The Hickory Stick Bookshop), movie theatres like the Black-White-Read Bookstore/movie cinema (The Bank Street Theater in New Milford), the inn that inspired The Dragonfly Inn (The Grace Mayflower Inn), the school that inspired Chilton (Choate Rosemary Hall in Wallingford), and of course several beautiful gazebos (in Kent, New Milford).

We saw town halls and antique stores (like Mrs. Kim's), we stumbled on a community fair and a Strawberry Festival, and we met so many people. We ate (maple cotton candy) and laughed and never slept. We spent so much glorious time in long lazy conversations, learning all about the towns, their traditions, and their festivals. Along the way, we learned that there was in fact an annual *Gilmore Girls* themed festival. We could not believe such a thing existed. It felt as if someone was reading our minds and granting our deepest wishes. We returned home, invigorated and glowing from our incredible weekend, and immediately bought tickets for the fan festival taking place that October.

What followed has been almost uncapturable by words. We have now attended several fan fests and they have changed our lives. We have gotten to meet the celebrities and crew of our fantasy world. They are among the most gracious humans we have ever met. They share their stories, sing and laugh, perform, sit and listen, eat, and love the show with us. They care, and they let us see who they are off the screen. They share pieces of their real selves with us. If other fan festivals allow attendees to see those they admire, the *Gilmore Girls* fan festival creates the space to be seen by them. It feels incredible, as does later re-watching our series, "knowing" the people on and behind the screen as we now do.

The creators of the festival are dream-granting, fairy-tale, magic makers. They are the gate-keepers of a world of sweet nostalgic home-coming. They give us the cast and crew, and they give us each other. We belong together, paying homage to our Girls, and ultimately to each other. Our friendships quickly outgrew the confines of the annual weekend of the festival, and many of us communicate even daily. Being as physically scattered as we are, the festival has become our family reunion, and we look forward to it year round.

I have cherished *Gilmore Girls* for so many reasons. Certainly its quirky, fast-paced, supremely clever, cosy feel-good, comfort-food, qualities, but also, and mostly, for the love of family and friends, of generations, of mothers and daughters. My own mother passed away 15 years ago, and *Gilmore Girls* has a way of bringing her back to me. She is with me in the banter and teasing, in the always enduring connections, in the give and take that is a mother-daughter relationship. I can feel the back-and-forth of life as I watch. I was pregnant with Ross when my mother passed, creating an extra layer within and between the three of us. It feels like the circle of life is embedded within our journey, and our relationships. *Gilmore Girls* in all of its splendour—the show, the community, the shared love—celebrates that mighty circle.

Sarah Putnam

Washington, USA

    One hot summer evening in 2004, while watching a show on the former ABC Family channel, a promotion about a show featuring a mother and daughter who talked fast, drank tons of coffee, had relationship troubles, and lived in a small town came on the screen. I wondered, "Who are these quirky, lovable characters of Stars Hollow? Would Paris always be so vicious toward Rory? Do Lorelai and her parents ever agree on anything?" After watching the first three episodes that aired on ABC Family, I was hooked.

Not long after this show came into my life, there were many hard, life-changing experiences I would face. Most of these experiences involved moving, losing a loved one, or family drama—all while being a college student. Throughout these rough times, the one constant escape I had from reality was *Gilmore Girls*. The quirky characters' intricately intertwined storylines, and the drama, allowed me to experience something relatable to my own problems.

One of the best episode examples is "The Reigning Lorelai" (4.16) in which Richard's mother, Gran, suddenly dies of a heart attack and Emily is in charge of funeral arrangements. My all-time favourite part of this particular episode is when Emily flips out:

> *"Find a box. Throw her in. We're done. Better yet, throw the old harpie's carcass in a ditch. Let a wolverine eat her!!"*

After being treated so crudely by Gran, I don't blame Emily at all for acting in this manner. Quite frankly, I laugh at Emily's entire reaction in this episode because it's uncharacteristic of her, yet I can relate all too well. When my own grandfather passed away suddenly of a heart attack in January 2005, my grandmother became very much like Gran. She was so much like Gran to everyone around her that when I went away to college, I was glad to leave. Though I miss the close bond I had with my grandparents, I don't miss the excess drama that occurred after my grandfather's death.

In August 2016 I learned that *Gilmore Girls* still has a huge international fan base. This journey began by joining a subscription box company, formerly known as Lit-Cube. At the time I had zero *Gilmore Girls* inspired paraphernalia and the subscription box craze was just beginning. Inside my first ever *Gilmore Girls* themed subscription box was an apron, a set of wooden chopsticks, and 2 melamine bowls with "Al's Pancake World" written on the side of them. Yes, I do still have these items tucked away in that very same cardboard box. As I spent more time on the Lit-Cube page, I started to notice the subscription customers were bonding.

As much as the anticipation for the premiere of "A Year in a Life" had all of us fans chatting, the discussions afterward strengthened our relationships even more. Many of us discussed the musical, story lines, the cliffhanger, and how much we loved seeing our favourite actors back in Stars Hollow again. Soon, Lit-Cube's owner created a separate group where our discussions continued. From these various discussions came conversations that extended beyond the *Gilmore Girls* fandom. Over the years, many of us have become best friends who support each other through thick and thin.

Though I could reflect on how we have supported each other through the trials and tribulations of 2020, the story I want to share is from fall 2019, before the COVID-19 catastrophe began.

The day was September fifth, 2019, around 5:30 am. I was starting to get ready for work. As I always do in the morning, I went to Facebook to check for anything of note. On this particular morning, my news feed contained the usual assortment of memes, news station blasts, a few LuLaRoe posts from friends, then I found a disturbing post from my aunt. This post was a missing persons poster of my 37-year-old cousin Cameron. When seeing the post my mind began whirling with disbelief and many questions.

The days turned into weeks and I was glad for the distraction of work and friends. Anger and worry became stronger by the day. Just before what would have been Cameron's 38th birthday, a news article was released from the local paper in the city where he had gone missing. The main synopsis of this article explained the sheriff's office had located his body. Unfortunately, my instinct had predicted this outcome from the beginning. As much as I was hoping he was just injured somewhere in the woods, I am sure he is watching the world now and glad to not be a part of COVID-19.

A few days later, my mom and I would be travelling to Unionville, Canada to attend the *Gilmore Girls* inspired fan festival for the first time. I knew this was an adventure I had to experience. During the following months, I did everything within my power to make this vacation possible including working overtime shifts for most of the summer. Though burn-out was imminent, the outcome was rewarding. When my mom and I arrived in Toronto, Canada on October third, 2019, my excitement finally kicked in. Being in a new place with new people, new scenery, new everything was just what I needed. Though I had seen videos and photos from previous fan fests, being there in person is a million times better.

Upon arriving at the main tent to check-in, there were hundreds of event goers inside. After going through the check-in process, the next step was getting into the line to get tickets for the meet and greet activity with Scott Patterson (Luke) on Saturday morning. While waiting in this long line, I finally saw two familiar faces—Jess and Charlie Miliner from New Hampshire—who until that very moment, I had only known through Facebook. Suddenly, the feeling of being in a dream came over me. As the day went on, this feeling gained strength.

After watching *Gilmore Girls* on television for so long, getting to meet the cast and crew blew my mind. Though the interactions were quick, there are many that stand out. My favourite story to tell is about meeting Nick Holmes (Robert). When the group of us who had participated in the history tour of Main Street Unionville returned to Stiver Mill, my mom noticed a line of people outside the building. She asked me if I knew what was going on. I didn't, though stories from friends who had attended past fan fests indicated that lines were usually for cast or crew members. After standing in line for a few seconds, my eyes caught a glimpse of a bright blue scarf at the front of the line. I remember a sudden feeling of disbelief washing over me. After having worked so hard all year long, and trying to keep myself focused on a goal while struggling through one of the darkest life events, and even questioning for a few minutes if I should follow through with my plans, here I was about to break the "Fourth Wall" (a term used in theatre to describe the imaginary "wall" that exists between actors on stage—in our case the camera lens—and the audience).

When our turn to chat with Nick came, he asked me about the scrapbook I had brought, the sticker I had put on the page, and some other questions that have escaped my memory. After chatting a little bit, he took a couple selfies of us with my cell phone before the next person's turn came. I am a naturally shy person, but as the events of Friday continued, the feeling dissipated. The more activities we participated in, and the more familiar faces I saw, the more of a social butterfly I became.

On Saturday morning, I was so excited to see Jess and Charlie again while waiting to meet Scott Patterson. This time, the three of us got to have a full conversation while standing outside in the cold. After Scott's meet and greet session, my mom and I hiked down to Stiver Mill for a meet–and-greet with Liz Torres (Miss Patty), Emily Kuroda (Mrs Kim), and Biff Yeager (Tom). These next meet and greet lines were just as long, if not longer, than the first line of the day.

Though I saved more faces than names to my memory bank, getting to meet other fans was a lot of fun. Some of us exchanged items we had brought with us to participate in a token exchange. I love all the little enamel pins, pens, key chains, and ornaments I received.

By the time Liz, Emily, and Biff's meet-and-greets were over, my back was so sore from standing and wearing my back pack that I could hardly move. All I wanted to do was sit for a while. Well, Mom had other ideas: Swing Dance Class. Up to the top of Main Street we walked—in my case hobbling—because my pinched nerves were screaming.

We arrived in the ballroom of the Curling Club, late to class. Mom and I quickly partnered up and started catching up on swing moves. After switching partners a couple times, I finally got my rhythm of this dance style. A few minutes later, I was in front and centre with a new partner directly behind Samantha and Nick who were instructing the class.

When dance class finished, the opportunity to sit down in the main tent for a short while finally came while we listened to the panel "From Chilton to Yale: the Rory Crowd" with Shelly Cole (Madeline) and Olivia Hack (Tanna). After their panel, Mom and I attended Valerie Campbell's Cat's EyeScream Social at the curling club.

Shortly thereafter, the evening entertainment commenced in the main tent. There was an intermission at some point so I decided to check out the prices of the food offerings at the food trucks parked outside the tent. Since we were in Canada after all, we needed to try poutine at least once, right? Well, I didn't even reach the entrance of the tent before quickly going back to my seat to grab one of the token exchange postcards I had brought to share.

Seeming as my postcard stash was still plentiful, the effort was made to include the cast and crew in the token exchange. The poutine mission was delayed because I had seen Nick standing outside the tent. What happened in the next few moments is something I will never forget. While handing Nick the postcard, I thanked him for coming to the fan fest. He looked surprised and took the card from me, embracing me in the tightest hug I have ever received.

Not long after returning home from the fan festival, my appreciation for Nick was about to grow stronger. My friend Mary Hoertz, who owned a merchandise company, announced that she would be hosting a Facebook live chat with Nick in a few weeks to discuss his books, *Gilmore Girls*, and other topics. Furthermore, Mary also mentioned in her announcement that Nick had signed 100 copies of his most recent book, *Downpour* and they'd be available for purchase through her website.

The day my copy arrived in the mail, I read a quarter of the book in one sitting! As I continued my reading, various images and emotions came from the pages of this book. The poem on Page 63 struck me like a wrecking ball. This poem was everything I had been thinking about and feeling for weeks. I sat at my desk with the book left open while tears streamed down my face. This was the first time in my life that poetry of any kind had ever struck me so hard.

During the live chat while listening to Nick's stories and answers to our questions, I was slowly gathering the courage to share how much that poem had impacted me. When I did finally send a comment, Nick graciously offered to record himself reading my favourite poem. Since receiving this amazing gift, I've listened to it whenever thinking about those who have gone too soon. To this very day, my eyes well up, just going back to these moments in time.

Nicole Robinson

Arizona, USA

I started watching *Gilmore Girls* when it first aired, and I was in middle school. It was a show that my mom and I bonded over and looked forward to watching together every week. We have always had our own, unique mother-daughter relationship. It isn't like Lorelai and Rory's, or Emily and Lorelai's. It's a special relationship and we are close. It was fun watching a show about a bond between mother and daughter with my own mom. It brought us closer together and reminded us what an important relationship we had.

I was sad when it went off air and I missed it. I didn't have the DVDs, so I couldn't watch it anymore. When online streaming became popular and it was available to watch, I would put it on constantly. When my son got diagnosed with a terminal muscle disease, it became my comfort. I could get lost in the lines that I knew by heart and the characters that felt like family. When my son spent countless days in the hospital, I would hold his hand and watch *Gilmore Girls*. I would pause when doctors or nurses came in the room and then continue to watch it as soon as they left. It made me feel like I was in Stars Hollow instead of the hospital. I would wear all of my *Gilmore Girls* inspired shirts and have conversations with nurses and doctors about our love for the show. One of my best memories was talking with a male doctor and several female nurses about if we were team Dean, Logan, or Jess. The show got me through so many hard times.

When the new series came out in 2016, I stayed up until it was available and watched all of it. I wore dragonfly leggings, an *In Omnia Paratus* shirt and drank out of my Luke's Diner mug. The following weekend, my best friend and I binged the series again. My husband made up burgers, we had candy, wore shirts, and drank out of *Gilmore Girls i*nspired mugs. The show is about mother and daughter relationships, but so much about friendships too. I always want to be an amazing friend like Sookie and Lane. I was so happy I could take some time to watch this with my best friend.

I now have a daughter and I hope we have a close relationship like Lorelai and Rory do. I hope I will support my daughter in her passion like Mrs. Kim supported Lane by setting up a tour for the band. I want to always want the best for my daughter like Emily wanted for Lorelai, even if we don't always see eye to eye. But I know we will have our own unique relationship that I will always treasure. I can't wait until she is older and we can bond over *Gilmore Girls* like I did with my mother. I hope to pass down my love for the show to her. Like any parent, I don't want to ever see her go through hard times, but I know this show can be there for her when she will need it the most.

It has become a running joke with my friends and family that I know every word on this show. My husband hears quotes from it every day. My oldest son made me custom Lego people for each character from the show. When I am sad, he brings me my box set DVDs. It is a funny, witty, fast paced show that is a safe space for so many. Like others, Stars Hollow is my home.

Ashley Tate

California, USA

It's been said that those who have anxiety or worry much, tend to watch the same shows over and over again, as they don't have to fret because they already know what happens. I have had anxiety off and on, and always found comfort in familiarity. I feel the show does such a great job of bringing me to Stars Hollow. Viewers get a feel for the small town, and its colourful characters. I can always bank on Miss Patty saying something risqué, Babette screeching, or Emily rolling her eyes at Lorelai. Those things soothed my need to feel calm, familiar and safe. I could wrap Stars Hollow and its townspeople around me like a hug.

I watched the show from its creation. I actually graduated high school along with Rory in 2003. I laughed, I cried, I became a Gilmore. My high school experience was pretty typical, so I could relate to Rory and her struggles—wanting to succeed in advanced classes, being awkward, and always being the nice one. Like Rory, I was also a big fish in a small pond. Like Rory, I was in for a rude awakening when I got to college and needed to study twice as much, and work equally as hard just to keep afloat. Although I related a lot to Rory, I also related to Lorelai, and her challenges with her family.

I now have three beautiful children. After I had my two boys I found out I was pregnant again. Five weeks later, I wasn't. A year after that, I was pregnant with another boy, and 14 weeks later I lost the baby while out of town for a wedding. I went on a journey of self love and discovery, lost 118 pounds and found out I was pregnant with a baby girl. I was stunned and terrified. I couldn't bear the thought of losing another baby. I was afraid to do anything, move too much, so when I wasn't at work, I was in bed, in my favourite town of Stars Hollow. I dreamed of everything working out, and one day having a friendship with my daughter like Lorelai had with Rory. Through bleeding scares and ambulance rides, I rubbed my belly and talked to Madeline, and found comfort once again in Stars Hollow.

In December, my sister and I took a trip to the Warner Bros Studio for their *Gilmore Girls* holiday experience. It was the trip of a lifetime. We got to take our photo in front of Luke's Diner. and in the Town Square Gazebo, and walk around inside Lorelei's house. This show has brought me so much joy and peace, through all times of my life. I truly cherish it and aspire to 'drink coffee like a Gilmore' and 'talk as fast as I can'.

Trista McMorrow

Florida, USA

My mom, my sister, and I have been fans of *Gilmore Girls* since it aired on television. We are lifelong Gilmore fans. A few years ago, this culminated in me winning the "What's Next?" pitch contest at the fan festival.

In 2018, my mom, sister, and I all happened to be free on fan fest weekend. We had heard about it online, so we signed up and went. Before the weekend, emails had gone out with an itinerary for the event, including the pitch contest, and what to expect. I told Mom and my sister about my own ideas for how the series would end, and what would happen next. They said it was great, and that I had to write it down, so I carved out some time to get it down on paper. It was hard to find the time, and to get my head around the script writing style that would be needed, but once I got going, it didn't take very long for me to get it all out. I sent it to Mom and a friend who both loved it, so I submitted it.

Once I got to the fan festival, there were about ten others who had submitted for the contect, and we each had about three minutes to give our ending as a pitch. Three minutes wasn't very long, so I had to present it at Gilmore speed. I had a great time, and got a lot of good feedback. It was a lot of fun, and winning was a huge bonus! I love public speaking, and being an ideas person, so it really fit my personality, and was a neat experience overall.

At the end of the pitches, the judges went away to deliberate, and then called my name. I went up onto the stage, and was given a Rothy's gift card as a prize, which I spent on shoes. When the finale aired, we threw a graduation party for Rory. I also won the lookalike costume contest for my best impression of Paris. It was the same day as the pitch, so I was wearing my Paris outfit when I gave my pitch.

Though my mom, my sister and I watched the show together, when season 7 aired I was in college, and so was my sister. We had watched the show together, calling to chat about it when I moved away. For the finale of the series, we all came home for it. My mom always makes every event special. She is the kind of person who will bring birthday decorations for the hotel room, if a road trip falls on someone's birthday, and pulls out themed paper plates for every occasion. So, the *Gilmore Girls* finale became an event. My sister and I came home from college, and the boys were kicked out of the house. We had a cake made that said "Congratulations Rory", and wore graduation hats, and watched the final episode while we cried together and ate cake.

My mom and my sister are my best friends. I watched the show at Rory's age, so it followed me throughout high school, and college. My mom is a fairly young mom, so the mother-daughter relationship was key for her, as she resonated with Lorelai, and the close connection that the three of us had. The speed of the Gilmore talk also drew us in. We have always prided ourselves on our ability to talk and hear at the same time. Anytime we get together it's a big talk fest.

Now we live on different sides of the state, but when *A Year in the Life* landed, we got together, rented a hotel room, and did a marathon viewing together. By the time of the reboot I was a mother, and I really felt that transition of having related to Rory, and then to Lorelai. I love it more now. It's the only show I have ever really liked, and that I can pick up anywhere, and anytime. I watch the DVDS in the background while I do laundry, or housework. It never gets old.

I love the quick, quirkiness of the show, and of Stars Hollow. I would love to live there. *Gilmore Girls* was a way my mom, sister and I connected. We are *Gilmore Girls* through and through.

To read Trista's winning fanfest story, see Appendix 1

April Richer

Ontario, Canada

    I was 12 years old when *Gilmore Girls* graced my life and my journey really began. My mom and I would watch every week from the beginning, and what I didn't know at the time, was that the show was shaping me into who I would become. I felt I had a lot of connection with Rory's character. I was shy, but extroverted in my own small group of friends. I wore a uniform that looked a lot like Rory's Chilton uniform.

    The years went on and though many things in life changed (from a tween to a teen, junior high to high school, and different friend groups along the way) one thing remained a constant. My show. My

Gilmore Girls. Of course the show came to an end the year after I graduated high school, but that was okay because I would soon own the entire series on DVD.

I have watched the show, all the way through over a hundred times now—a task which has become easier since Netflix acquired *Gilmore Girls*. I come home from work each day to watch an episode, and on weekends I watch more. Sometimes I start the whole series over and sometimes I just pick a random episode. It's part of my everyday life and it will be forever. Lorelai Gilmore is my spirit animal. She's part of me and who I've grown up to be in so many ways. She has influenced the way I talk, the way I walk, and how I carry myself. She is embedded in my attitude. Relationships I have had seem like direct parallels from the show.

Stars Hollow is my escape and my dream world and I've been immersed for so long that I've become a part of it just as the characters are. The show touches and comforts my soul in a way only a true *Gilmore Girls* fan would understand. It wasn't until the 2019 fan fest that I finally felt at home in my own world. 2019 was my first fan fest because it was in Toronto and I live only a few hours away. I met so many other like minded individuals, that I felt I had gained a new family. Even though the show is over, the fan fest makes it possible for the Gilmore world to live on. For me, the experience of the fan fest was life changing. I found myself tearing up several times each day of the event as I just couldn't believe where I was and what I was doing. The photos, people, actual cast members, and memories from that weekend are something I'll cherish forever. I've made friends all over the world through our love of *Gilmore Girls* and that's truly amazing.

Gilmore Girls also brings me back to a time where things were simpler and reminds me of how lucky I was to grow up in a world of no social media and people spent their time living in the moment. The show has such a home-y feel to it—total comfort and belonging. As snow is a gift to Lorelai, she and the show are a monumental gift to me. I'll be forever grateful for Amy Sherman-Palladino for shaping my life. Like Luke Danes, once *Gilmore Girls* is in your life, it's in your life forever.

Clarissa Jones

Ohio, USA

  I grew up in a very rural town in Ohio. It was a predominantly Amish community and my graduating class was about 75 students. I was always a gifted student and I adored reading. My mom often threatened to take books away if I didn't do chores because I was always reading. I think it was an escape for me. I was accepted into a post secondary program my junior and senior year of high school. This meant I was able to take college courses at a local branch of Kent State University and I adored every minute of it. I was able to read books and have these amazing class discussions. I was introduced to passionate professors who encouraged me to think outside the box. I was introduced to so many more ideas and it just fed my love of learning. At the time, I hated going back to my high school for the few classes I had to take.

I started watching *Gilmore Girls* in high school when I caught a marathon on ABC Family. I instantly fell in love with the characters and the town of Stars Hollow. I resonated so much with Rory in high school. I was a nerd with my nose always in a book and I was very driven in school. I was attending a local branch of a University in my Junior and Senior year hoping to get as many credits out of the way as possible. It was the first show I watched where I felt heard and understood. I think I connected a lot with Rory when she left Stars Hollow High for a more challenging learning environment. The branch was no Chilton by any means but I definitely felt more challenged in those classes.

When I went away to college, I brought the love of the show with me. It was so comforting to watch as I struggled to adjust to college. I was a first generation college student and felt so alone. I dealt with some bouts of depression as I transitioned to a whole other world. I started making friends and then introduced one of my college roommates to the show and they instantly fell in love. My other roommate was already a huge fan. It became our show we watched in our little group. We always joked about which character we best fit. I was always dubbed the Sookie of the group as I worked as a prep cook all through college.

What I loved about *Gilmore Girls* was the way that education was supported and encouraged. I was the first in my immediate family to attend college. I am the middle child of six children and my siblings chose paths that didn't include college. They have created wonderful and successful lives and I am very proud of all of them. However, I often struggled with feeling like the outsider because I chose the route of education. I was told repeatedly that college was a waste of time, and that success is found in other places. I wholeheartedly agree that college isn't for everyone but it often left me feeling ashamed that I chose the college route. *Gilmore Girls* allowed me to escape to a world where education was valued and there was a strong desire to learn. I loved the connection Rory had to her grandfather in their love of books and learning. I had an aunt who is a librarian and with whom I held a strong connection. I loved spending time in her house because we would get into these wonderful debates about politics, current events, or literature. It fed my deprived soul and made me feel less alone.

The episode that always stood out to me was in season one where Rory attended the dance with Dean and she had a book in her purse. That was me—I carried a book everywhere. My backpacks always broke halfway through the year because not only did I have school books, but I also had my "bus books". Watching the show, I felt that someone finally understood me and that I belonged.

When I decided to return to school to become a Social Worker, I met this wonderful group of girls. Ironically, they were *Gilmore Girls* fans and we bonded over this throughout our years in school. We were all working full time and were going to school part time. We would have '*Gilmore Girls*' nights over break, filled with junk food and our favourite episodes. Those nights provided lots of laughs and a much needed break from the demands of grad school and the tough world of social services.

I introduced the show to my husband who would happily watch along and reference the show with me. My husband is 100% Luke and I would always joke with him about this. He is easily annoyed and has some Luke style rants at times. He is an automotive technician and so mechanically minded. He amazed me when we first met in all the ways he could fix things with little to no instruction. He also pined for me a little bit, like Luke did for Lorelai. Underneath that tough grumpy guy is a man with the kindest and most beautiful soul who loves his friends and family fiercely. He is loyal and protective of those he loves. Every time we watch *Gilmore Girls* together we find another likeness and just laugh. He is my Luke and I just don't know how I got so lucky.

When we got married, I actually walked down the aisle to *Reflecting Light*. We threw in a few other *Gilmore Girls* easter eggs into our wedding as well. My bridal party were given Gilmore themed items. I wore a dress that resembled Lorelai's June 3rd dress with a sash, and our venue was decorated with twinkle lights. After our wedding, we had the amazing opportunity to attend the *Gilmore Girls* fan fest in Canada. It felt like family. I loved having a community of people who got the off the wall references and who loved the show as much as I did. My husband and I really felt like we had stepped into Stars Hollow. I very much fangirled out most of the weekend. The overall experience was perfect and probably the best trip we had taken in a long time.

It sounds cheesy perhaps, but at every transition or difficult moment, I have been able to turn to this show for comfort. I have bonded with beautiful people over our love of the show and have had many laughs as a result.

Erica Andrews

West Virginia, USA

My initial introduction to *Gilmore Girls* was the middle of 2006, while I was deployed in Iraq. I was deployed to Fallujah from Feb. 2006 to Feb. 2007, and as a field radio operator, when I was not on convoys or patrols I was doing radio watch on base, which was terminally boring. My friend and rackmate had been a huge fan of

Gilmore Girls since high school. I, on the other hand, had never even heard of it. My family wasn't big on watching television when I was growing up, so I had never really sat down and watched an entire series before. We had access to certain shows in the marines, via intranet and *Gilmore Girls* was one of them. Whenever we had some free time during our deployment, my rackmate and I would sit together and watch *Gilmore Girls* on my laptop. The first thing I did when I got home in early 2007, after buying a car, was go out and buy all the seasons on DVD and get 100% caught up.

While I was stationed, I started a relationship. We clung to each other because we were far away from home—he was from Massachusetts, and I was from West Virginia. I think we both knew that we weren't going to stay together, because once our time in the Marines was over, we had different life goals. We each wanted to go back to our home states, which we knew would cause a huge splinter in our relationship.

After some time, I found myself pregnant. The pregnancy was unplanned, so the surprise of becoming a parent when I wasn't ready was something I related to on *Gilmore Girls.* Neither myself nor my son's dad wanted children at that point, so we had to wrap our heads around how life was going to change. While I hadn't planned to have a child at that time, I was reminded of *Gilmore Girls,* and how Lorelai handled her unexpected pregnancy. One of the things that really resonated with my personality, was something Lorelai said in the second season:

> *"I'm good at doing what I have to do. When I had to get a job, I got it. When I had to find a house for us and a life for us, I got it. When I had to get Rory into Chilton, I did it. But I don't have to leave the Independence Inn. I don't have to go into business for myself." (ep. 8)*

I looked at my pregnancy as something I had to do because that was my responsibility. Once my son was born, that mentality applied more than ever.

I started looking at Lorelai differently and the way she parented. I wanted to be that parent—not just a cool parent, but one that had a child that she respected as an individual and who had a mutual respect for her. Another thing that I tried to emulate was Lorelai's independence. I tried not to ask for help unless I was absolutely drowning.

My son's father and I split up shortly after I gave birth to our son, who was born in June 2008. We never really expected it to go further, but we were both 2000 miles from home and clinging to one another until we both got off active duty. After my son was born, I resented his father. I had his child and was raising him alone. He never called or offered to come visit. Between 2008 and 2013, his dad only came to visit a handful of times. He expected me to bring our son the entire 12 hour trip by myself to visit him. I didn't date while Jack was little, because when Lorelai said that she didn't want men in and out of Rory's life, that was something that I felt I also believed in. I felt like my only focus should be raising my child right. Meanwhile, my son's father was dating, getting good jobs, partying, and having a life while I was raising his child on my own, and committing myself wholeheartedly to that job. I began to form significant hatred in my heart for him, and I didn't know what to do about it.

When I realised I was only hurting myself with my anger, I once again turned to Lorelai. I watched how she handled Christopher. When she told him "I've always had the door to Rory open for you", I realised that's what I needed to do. If he chose not to walk through it, that would be his decision. So that's what I did. I tried to maintain subtle contact (holidays and birthdays), but the rest was up to him.

Eventually, he did use the door. We're friends now. We even went on vacation together a few years back. We both now have other partners, and my son has siblings through his father. Eventually, we both grew into our co-parenting roles, but I think a lot of change came about when our son got older because it became easier for us to travel. Now, he gets to visit his father every school break (fall, spring, and summer) and their relationship has improved vastly.

I am amazingly proud of my son and the person he's becoming. I think, on reflection, if I had never been introduced to *Gilmore Girls*, and the character of Lorelai so many years ago, I might not have made the parenting decisions I did, and be able to parent the way I do now. I wouldn't have the patience or level headedness to deal with a lot of what has happened. So, I'm thankful for the influence of that little corner of the world, and thankful that I get to be a part of it.

Shelly Barnhart

Ohio, USA

I am a more recent fan of *Gilmore Girls*. I watched it straight through for the first time in 2016 after watching *Parenthood* on Netflix. Both *Parenthood* and *Gilmore Girls* were recommended to me through Facebook when I asked for series suggestions. I finished up with the series just in time for *A Year in the Life*. I fell in love with *Gilmore Girls* and have had it on repeat ever since. It is my go to. I find comfort in it when I am stressed. It's like a big hug.

My mom passed away eight years ago when I was almost 32. I had a good relationship with my mom in my adult years, but growing up I was not always the best child and we butted heads a lot. I'm the youngest of four girls and I guess Lorelai and Rory's relationship is the one I wished I had with her.

I was always super close to my Dad, but he got sick in the summer of 2017. I had planned for months to go to the *Gilmore Girls* inspired fan festival in Kent in the fall with my oldest sister, Debbie, who also loves the show. My Dad went into the Veteran's hospital just a couple weeks prior to our trip, but he seemed to be fairly stable and they moved him to a long term facility to await surgery, so we headed off for a few days to go to the festival. On our last day there, we got the news that he had taken a turn for the worse. I drove the nine and a half hours back to Ohio as fast and safely as I could get us there, but it was too late. He had been put on life support after his heart had failed.

The day before, I ran a race dressed as Luke to honour Edward Hermann. We sat and listened to his family talk about his life and how much they missed him. His daughter showed us a film she made in college as a tribute to her dad, and I bawled, feeling guilty for leaving my own. Right after that I spoke to him on the phone for what would be the last time.

It took me a few months to return to the show I love which had always been my comfort, and my companion. After Dad's death, I started associating it with the guilt I felt for leaving my Dad alone in that long-term care facility. Eventually I turned it on again and have been watching it a few times a year since. It has even more significance now. I depend on it, and it feels like going home. I miss both my parents every day and *Gilmore Girls* provides an escape for me and a warmth that I have not found on any other show. I have a teenage son, and now I have a 'Rory' too. She has recognized the theme song since she was a month old. She would turn her little head to the television and then look to me to sing it. I have always had a great relationship with my son, but I hope to nurture a Lorelai-Rory story with my little girl.

Nicole Marreiros

Connecticut, USA

The year is 2011, and my boyfriend has a two year old. He was only 18 when she was born. The relationship had a slow start. We only had her every other weekend, and once during the week. This cute little girl, I could tell, would change my life forever. There were a lot of little moments that led us to the relationship we have now. Things like bringing her to the town fair every year, playing dress up, getting ice cream, and reading books. Dinner at our house consisted of pizza rolls, cinnabuns, or the timeless 'mac n' cheese'. As the years went on I became even closer with her than her Dad. I became the one to give her baths, brush her hair, cook her dinners, and buy her clothes I knew she'd like. My favourite Mother's Day gift to date was a card with Rory's high school graduation quote and a coffee mug that says 'You're the Lorelai to my Rory'.

Flashforward to October 2018. We spent the whole weekend in Kent, at the *Gilmore Girls* inspired fan festival. A whole weekend of bonding over what we love, and what she says is 'our thing'. We met the actors who play Brian, Finn, and Robert. We watched Zach play the guitar, and Caesar did impressions. What a weekend it was. We drank lots of Starbucks and wore matching clothes the entire time.

I am no longer in a relationship with my (step) daughter's father, however I love her more than life itself. We still wear the matching clothes, we still drink all the coffee. She is now 11, going on 25. She is my little built-in best friend. I have a child of my own now with my husband, but there will never be a time I don't consider her my first born.

Zoe Ronchi

Victoria, Australia

I've been a *Gilmore Girls* fan from day one. From a young age I was watching the show with my parents, then when I grew up, watching it on my own. *Gilmore Girls* and I have been together, evolving through the developing media from television, to DVD, and then Netflix.

I know the show line-by-line. It has broadened my vocabulary, and pop culture knowledge, adding words like "redundant" and "existentialist" to my sentences from about the age of 12. *Gilmore Girls* made me smarter. I watched at least two episodes a day from that age, and continue to watch daily now. *Gilmore Girls* is on while I put on my makeup, clean my bedroom, cook, and anywhere that I can zone out and ignore reality for a while.

My love for the show has been with me through multiple health challenges, and life events. When I was 12 years old, I was diagnosed with Epilepsy when I was 12, and about five years ago, Multiple Sclerosis. I remember being in the hospital ward, and having to plug my laptop in to continue watching *Gilmore Girls*. The nurse didn't like me being so invested in watching television while I was a patient, but the show got me through my stay in hospital, and through my MRI results and my confirmed MS diagnosis.

I have so many *Gilmore Girls* inspired clothing it's insane, with some I purchased online, and others I got whilst visiting America at Boxlunch and the Warner Bros store, at Warner Bros studios. I've been to the famous Stars Hollow lot and had my photograph taken under the iconic gazebo, in which I cried tears of happiness. My fiance and I will be returning for our honeymoon to do the tour again, only this time, we're doing the VIP one so we don't miss a thing.

I have an inner forearm tattoo of Rory and Logan, jumping with umbrellas, with the phrase "In Omnia Paratus" written in cursive below it. While this phrase means a lot to me because of the show, it also resonates with me on a deeper level. Living with poor health, and unexpected diagnoses means having to be ready for anything. The *Gilmore Girls* episode, "You Jump, I Jump, Jack" is the first time Rory really starts to come out of her comfort zone, and gains a tougher exterior. I found this really relatable, having had to do this myself.

My Gilmore collection also includes Lauren Graham's books, Milo Ventimiglia's autograph, *Gilmore Girls* socks, keychains, pop vinyls, coffee mugs and more. My collection actually reminds me Lorelai's line to Rory, in "A Tale of Poes and Fire":

> "It means the Harvard Chamber of Commerce made a nice chunk of change from us."

I have a lot of annoying Gilmore habits, which I am sure drive the people in my life nuts. I quote the show daily, often, and with exact dedication to the lines. Even more obnoxiously, I point out facts about the show to people who did not ask to hear them. These are usually abstract things, like talking about the hand that pops out of the side, to stop the door from banging when Sookie opens the barn door to reveal baby clothing and items, or the use of rubber instead of stones outside the Gilmore house so you can't hear the crunching as they walk through. If that wasn't bad enough, I yell while watching other movies and television shows, if I see someone who was in *Gilmore Girls*. This usually begins with a loud declaration,

"THEY'VE BEEN IN GILMORE GIRLS!!"

This is then followed by me whipping out IMDB on my phone to prove it, and finally the aggressive broadcast that:

"I'VE BEEN THERE!!"

This is reserved for when I see places on the lot in a movie or show that I saw on my tour of Warner Bros. My fandom will reach its pinnacle at my upcoming wedding, which is going to take inspiration from the show that means so much to me. I'll be walking down the aisle to a string quartet version of the famous "La La's", and our first dance will be to the song by Sam Phillips, *Reflecting Light*.

It's hard to overstate how much *Gilmore Girls* has shaped my life, from sharing the show with my fiance and many others, to broadening my pop culture knowledge, vocabulary, and sense of humour, and even having *Where You Lead* as my ringtone on my mobile phone. I cherish the times in my life that I watched this hilarious, beautiful, heartwarming show, especially in tough times like in hospital, after an argument, and when I needed to avoid the world. It has been a huge part of my life and I think it always will be. I just hope someday I have a daughter that can truly be the Rory to my Lorelai.

Alicia Reichert

Michigan, USA

When I found out there would be a reboot of a show I really liked—*Gilmore Girls*—I was super pumped about it. I asked my husband if he thought I could watch the whole show (all seven seasons) before the reboot. He said he thought I could do anything I put my mind to. That summer he and I opened our home to my brother, who is also my best friend, and the three of us watched *Gilmore Girls* after work, after baseball with my daughter—any time we could squeeze an episode in. I was so excited to share laughs and experience this show again in a whole new way.

During this rewatch of the original show, I went into planning mode for my binge watch of the upcoming revival episodes for *A Year In The Life*. I bought the *Gilmore Girls* inspired cookbook by Kristi Kelly and tested recipes on my family that I might be able to make for it. I was also hosting Thanksgiving that year and told them I would happily cook for them all day but once I went into Stars Hollow, I was not to be disturbed.

The week of the revival coming out, I was full of excitement. I accepted a new job. I was also taking a few days off for the holiday and to spend it watching the show. We were all in anticipation of the episodes dropping. My brother had been acting strange, tired and distant, but still came up from the basement bedroom to see what was going on in the show. That Tuesday, I talked to him about the Gilmore inspired foods I was making and asked if he was going to join me in my binge. He said, "Yes, I plan to!"

I got up Wednesday like any other day. When I left for work, my brother had already left. He posted a video on Facebook of a car fire that was a little odd. When I texted him to ask about it, and to check that he was still planning on coming over for Thanksgiving dinner the next day, he didn't text back.

That night I texted him again but I knew he had planned to go to his girlfriend's house. The next day it was Thanksgiving, so I got to work on my preparations. The bird went into the oven, and I called my brother to confirm our plans. He didn't answer. I was starting to worry, so I began calling people, but nobody had seen him. After a while, his girlfriend turned up at the house, and that's when I knew something was really wrong.

I called all the hospitals in the area, and finally found him at one. He had overdosed on drugs, and was in the intensive care unit. Four days later, he died.

I couldn't bring myself to watch *A Year In The Life.* for a long time. When I did, I cried…and ate cookies…like a Gilmore.

Over the years I have finally found joy in the reboot but I also have pain when I see Sookie in an episode and remember my brother saying, "she is really pretty" or "the dad is such a good man". *Gilmore Girls* saved me from falling into a deeper depression. It gave my mind something to hold on to while my heart grieved and tried to make sense of a loss that I still cannot believe is true sometimes.

Jamie Lee Marie Naragon

Ohio, USA

Gilmore Girls premiered when I was in college and just starting out professionally, so I didn't discover the show until the later seasons. I found it sweet, but having missed the first few years, I didn't develop a profound love for the show, initially.

That changed when I got divorced. Emotionally, I was deflated. So, I began spending more time with my mom. Mom struggled with complex health problems. When she was younger, she dislocated her knee cap and never got it repaired correctly until years later by which time, it had caused severe damage. Over time, the grinding became unbearable, and she was forced to have surgery. Years of favouring the other knee resulted in her "good" knee also deteriorating. Over the course of about a decade, she had seven major knee surgeries, including multiple replacements, but the damage had already been done. Her limited mobility triggered her depression. This, coupled with Chronic Obstructive Pulmonary Disease (COPD), led to her mobility decreasing. She became bed-ridden, living the last few years of her life in one room. My father and I worked hard, and long hours, to offset the cost of her steadily-increasing medical bills, while television provided an escape for her. I think *Gilmore Girls* resonated with Mom because she had my sister when she was also very young, and for several years, after my sister's father left them, it was just the two of them. When Mom met Dad, that changed, but the bond Mom and my sister had while my sister was in high school was very similar to the close bond of Rory and Lorelai. When we moved to a new state when my sister was in college, they had a falling out similar to Rory and Lorelai's. I think my mom used *Gilmore Girls* to fill that void as well.

While Mom was confined to one room, all we could do was talk and watch shows, so we watched *Gilmore Girls* together, and I began to fall in love with the show. The love and heart of the series also helped me emotionally recover from my own tough year as I watched Lorelai and Rory struggle with their own heartaches and rebound. Sadly, in 2013, my mother lost the battle with her health issues. Sometimes I watch episodes when I miss her, and I remember both her love for the show, and our hours spent in Stars Hollow.

Professionally, I am a high school history teacher in Maumee, Ohio. I attended Bowling Green State University for my bachelor's in education, my master's in criminal justice, and my master's in history. I think working around students, *Gilmore Girls* resonates with me as I see them experiencing many of the same things Rory did—school dances, the difficult college choice, and adjusting to college life. I've had to help students write graduation speeches, had to find ways of getting parents to participate in school groups like Lorelai was tasked by the headmaster to do, and watch students wrestle with whether they should pursue their dreams and goals, or those of their family.

One way that *Gilmore Girls* has influenced my career more directly, is with the Festival of Living Pictures. There have been a number of times where I have used the festival in my classroom. I have had students re-create both famous works of art, as well as put my own unique spin on things and have students pose in tableaux in famous historic images. I also like to think that *Gilmore Girls* shaped my love of coffee. Every time I sit in a local coffee shop where the barista now knows my name, I feel a bit more Lorelai-esque. In addition, *Gilmore Girls* has shaped my life in another way. Whenever I start feeling down, and feeling concerned about my age, or not being married, I think of how happy and successful Lorelai was, and I draw inspiration from that.

Katie Wagner

New Hampshire, USA

I am in the younger generation of *Gilmore Girls* fans. When the show first aired in the year 2000, I was only four years old. I was much too young to understand the witty banter, literary references, and pop culture innuendoes that our beloved *Gilmore Girls* used to speed talk their way into our hearts. I was introduced to the show in 2016 by my cousin, Missy. She grew up watching *Gilmore Girls* with her mother. They have a Lorelei and Rory style relationship—they are mother and daughter, but also best friends.

Missy is seven years older than me and lives over 350 miles away, but she's always been my best friend. Growing up, she was my role model—much in the way that Lorelai is Rory's role model. Even though we could only visit each other a few times a year, we've always been there for each other. We kept in touch by writing letters when I was small, then emails, then texting, and now FaceTime. In 2014, at the age of 18, I was the maid of honour in her wedding, and in 2020, I became the godmother to her son, appropriately named Logan.

When I was in college, I spent the majority of my time in the library studying, or working at one of my jobs. I lived alone in my junior year in 2016, and was focusing on my studies, while also trying to immerse myself in clubs and activities. I had finally jumped on the Netflix bandwagon, and while I typically watched action shows with my friend Ryan in my free time, I felt like I needed something calmer to watch due to my high levels of stress. I texted Missy and asked her for a few feel good comedy shows to watch, and she immediately suggested *Gilmore Girls*.

That year, *Gilmore Girls* helped me through a lot. I watched it every night before bed. It helped me when I was anxious and stressed. It helped me through a strained long distance relationship that eventually ended badly. It helped me through physical health problems when I found out I had chronic appendicitis and needed surgery. In addition to all of this, it gave me another connection to Missy. Because even though she was far away, we had yet another thing to share with each other and talk about. I texted her through every episode I watched and of course, she knew them all by heart and knew exactly which episode I was referring to. During this time, she was also very sick due to her first pregnancy, and watching the show and discussing it together helped both of us to feel better—mentally and physically.

I finished the show for the first time a few weeks before the revival—*A Year In The Life*—premiered on Netflix, in November of

2016. Missy and I weren't able to watch the new episodes together in person, but with both of us watching new episodes at the same time, it was like we had been watching the show together from the start.

Throughout the years, I continued to watch and rewatch the show, and it quickly became known as my 'happy place'. Now, I've graduated from college, have a full time job, and live with my boyfriend, Travis. Though *Gilmore Girls* is Missy's and my show, I've since shared it with Travis as well. From the start of our relationship, Travis knew the best way for me to unwind was to curl up in bed with a cup of chamomile tea, my kitten Lucy, and an episode of *Gilmore Girls*. After three years of dating, when we moved into our apartment, he asked me if he could watch my happy show with me to see why I love it so much. Now, he loves *Gilmore Girls*, too, and watches it with me at night.

Gilmore Girls brings people together. Though Missy and I were always close, we used *Gilmore Girls* as a way to be even closer when we both needed something familiar and fun to focus on, and now I get to share it with my boyfriend as well.

Jessica Weiss

California, USA

I started watching *Gilmore Girls* right from its pilot. Back then, television was my greatest obsession—I never missed premieres of shows that I thought I might like. Television became my replacement for friends. At least with television, we could hang out any time. When I first started watching *Gilmore Girls*, I liked it, but never could have predicted how important it would become in my life. Back in 2000, I was in the eighth grade, and living with my dad after a traumatic custody battle. My mom and I watched *Gilmore Girls* together and we got to finish the series together before she passed away from cancer at the end of 2007. After the show ended, I never stopped watching it, so I've been watching *Gilmore Girls* for 20 years now.

My mom and I were best friends and we even went to college together. I bet Lorelai would have done that, but it would have been tough to get into the same college. However, after community college together, we both got into UC Berkeley. We got an apartment and planned our next couple years, only she never got to attend and 16 months after I started there without her, she passed away. In the months when she had cancer, I remember watching *Gilmore Girls* with her a little more vividly. We watched *Gilmore Girls* so often that our dog Freddie started to recognize the end credits. Later on, I got my grandma and dad to watch every episode and they also both loved it.

Since that time, *Gilmore Girls* has always been the only show I could watch during the worst of times. When I was sick, anything else would make me feel more sick or give me nightmares. When I was sad, there was always the perfect episode to soothe me—though any episode would do. When I've gone through other painful things, *Gilmore Girls* was—and is—the show that I can always turn to. As someone with a good deal of anxiety, I have found it is the best remedy. There is something about a quirky small town with rich characters that makes me feel at home. I even spend most mornings, even when I have a commute, watching a few minutes to help me transition from sleep to reality because it is the most comforting and peaceful thing I could do. But it is also a show with a lot of heart and comedy as well. It has the perfect variety of what I would want in a show. It really is 'a lifestyle…a religion.' It has become a part of my daily routine and important to my emotional health.

When my dog Freddie lost his hearing, he could no longer hear the end credits. He became my best friend after my mother died. He passed away in 2020, and there were a few episodes of *Gilmore Girls* that got me through that time. While connection to people (or animals) is very important, I have learned that *Gilmore Girls* is a constant while people, unfortunately, do pass on. It's the only show that I could watch for 20 years and I will probably end up watching it for the rest of my life even when other shows catch my attention. When I finish the series, I start over. Some of my DVDs no longer work, but thankfully there is Netflix. I don't know what I would do without the show that has been my best friend all of these years.

Datha Caler Curtis

Georgia, USA

Nearly 20 years ago, I remember seeing ads on the WB network for a show with a couple of fast-talking girls who also happened to be mother and daughter. It was called *Gilmore Girls*. I had recently become a mother myself for the first time to my own baby girl. I didn't immediately watch the show, though I was intrigued. This was in the days before the show was available on DVD or Netflix, so I knew I would have to start watching the show after having missed many episodes, so I didn't watch. Then, in 2002, the WB network began to air episodes of the first two seasons on Sundays. They called it *Gilmore Girls: Beginnings*. I watched every episode with bated breath until I was all caught up. Then season 3 began, and I was smitten. I was in love with the idyllic small town, the quirky characters, the witty banter, the literary and pop culture references sprinkled throughout each episode, and, most of all, the relationship between this mother and daughter.

I would go on to have two more daughters and a son, all of whom can sing the theme song by heart and know the show to be nearly synonymous with their mom. My house is filled with *Gilmore Girls* inspired décor such as gnomes, a monkey lamp, a Hallmark cookie jar, Stars Hollow business signs, a crocheted *Gilmore Girls* blanket my own mom spent months making for me, *Gilmore Girls* quilts, countless t-shirts, books, mugs, mementos from the *Gilmore Girls* inspired fan fest, a trivia game, items from *Gilmore Girls* Etsy shops, subscription boxes, and more. This show has become my respite from the world - a place I can visit again and again and find familiarity and comfort. It is a show with humour and intelligence, but it is also a show with lessons about life, love, and relationships.

I have laughed and cried with the *Gilmore Girls*, my children have grown up with *Gilmore Girls*, and I find, at each stage of my life, new meaning in the stories of this show. While my life does not resemble the lives of the characters in many ways, I find myself relating to so much of what they go through.

When the revival came out in 2016, I had built up my expectations and hopes for what would happen to our beloved girls after nine long years. Initially, I was a little disappointed. I wanted a happy ending with a tidy little bow. But as I have watched the revival many times since, I see that the show once again mirrors life in a way, though perhaps with more of a rose-colored tint—and perhaps a little more off-kilter. Life never quite turned out how the *Gilmore Girls* expected, but that did not make their lives any less beautiful or happy.

Stars Hollow isn't just a fictional place on a beloved television show, it's a place we fans hold in our hearts.

Shelby Parker

California, USA

When I was about eight or nine, my parents and I took a tour of Warner Brothers Studio in Burbank, California. Throughout the tour, they made mention of this newer show at the time being filmed on the lot called *Gilmore Girls*. We visited the set of the Gilmore grandparents' home, walked around the town square—otherwise known as Stars Hollow—and saw the focal point of the show, Luke's Diner. We were welcome to take photos in front of the outdoor sets, so my parents encouraged me to pose under the Luke's Diner sign. I rolled my eyes, not wanting to, since I hadn't heard of the show and it had no significance to me at the time. It must have been foreshadowing, because it has now become one of the most significant moments in my life.

The *Gilmore Girl*s have been with me more than half of my life. I started watching reruns on what was then, ABC Family, when I was just 10-years-old. I caught the show after it had already started, when I watched the multiple episodes that aired every afternoon as reruns. It started with a Labor Day marathon of sorts. While I didn't watch from the beginning, I easily found myself getting into the groove and losing myself in Stars Hollow, with its fall vibes and quirky characters. I quickly fell in love with it. In the Christmases, and birthdays that followed, I asked for the seasons on DVD, so I could watch the show from the beginning, and binge seasons at a time.

I loved how close the mother and daughter relationship was, because it wasn't something you'd see too often on television and I related to Rory. She was the quiet girl with her nose always in a book, she was a good student, and of course, she was close with her mom, as am I. As I started watching more and more, my mom also fell in love with it and it became our 'thing', as it has undoubtedly become this for many other mother-daughter duos through the years.

My mom and I have taken the tour of Warner Bros. Studios many times to visit the famous Midwest section, better known as Stars Hollow to Gilmore fans. We've attended the *Gilmore Girls* holiday at the studio every year—it's become our new tradition and something we look forward to doing together now. It really does feel like the Stars Hollow magic comes alive and you're waiting for Luke to walk out of his diner, or Lorelai and Rory to be on one of their long-winded pop culture heavy dialogues, as they walk around the town square.

We were able to meet Lauren Graham at her book signing for *Someday, Someday, Maybe* back in 2013 and tell her how much the show meant to us. She couldn't have been nicer, taking her time to meet and talk with each person. I asked her to sign that same photo that I took under the Luke's Diner sign all those years ago, where I even admitted to her that I hadn't heard of the show at the time, but shared with her what it now meant to my mom and I.

We attended the Entertainment Weekly Pop Fest, before *Gilmore Girls*: *A Year in the Life* came out, where Dan Palladino and Amy Sherman-Palladino made an appearance to talk about the show and give a preview of the Netflix series. Being in the same room as that dynamic duo was a moment I will never forget.

We also met Milo Ventimiglia together last summer, too, which was another bucket list item for me (Team Jess represent!) While we didn't get to spend much time with him and I was struggling to formulate words, he seemed to be such a kind soul, making eye contact with every person and thanking them for coming.

Gilmore Girls has been the thing that bonds us as we constantly drop references in our everyday conversations or attend the events that support the show. Our relationship is a lot like that of Lorelai and Rory—more like sisters than mother-daughter and like them, we are also pop culture junkies.

The show also got me through my awkward junior high years—the loneliness of high school, the questions and doubts of college, and into my adult years. While I related more to Rory at the beginning, I find myself relating more to Lorelai these days. But, through all the highs and lows that life has to offer, I always bring it back to *Gilmore Girls*. I can relate most of my life experiences back to a scene, a bit of dialogue, or a pop culture reference.

The genius of this show is that everytime I watch it, I get something new from it—I notice a new background character, the way a line was said, reactions, connections to another episode, and so on. Amy Sherman-Palladino is the reason I've started pursuing a career in television. It hadn't really occurred to me that it was a possibility for women until seeing her work behind-the-scenes. To be able to create something for someone like what *Gilmore Girls* has meant to me, is my dream.

There will never be another *Gilmore Girls.* It is a timeless story that never goes out of style. And, it's one I will tell my kids about someday.

Valerie Johnston

Ontario, Canada

What drew me to the show *Gilmore Girls* came from the premise; the close bond between mother and daughter. I was very close with my mom. She was a cross between Emily and Mrs. Kim but our relationship was very much like Lorelai and Rory. There were so many times we would spend hours talking and sharing laughs. At the end of each day, good or bad, she welcomed me with open arms and a big smile. A hug was guaranteed. We both loved the *Gilmore Girls,* having watched it from when it first aired back in 2000. My mom was battling breast cancer at the time. She was a fighter, and she was so strong. Unfortunately, the cancer proved to be stronger. In April 2001 in her hospital room, the *Gilmore Girls* played on the television. She was not awake at that time and passed as the credits rolled. I continued to watch the show each year as it brought me comfort and kept me close to her and our shared memories. I have lost track of the amount of times I have played the series and still continue to watch today. It is my feel good show.

In June 2019, I got married. It was a beautiful, sunny, summer day. Our photographer passed a field of canola and thought it would be a perfect place for wedding photos. Without the knowledge of our photographer, this canola field instantly made me think of *Gilmore Girls*. Although this field was not 1000 yellow daisies, the sea of yellow flowers brought me back to the end of the first season. Lorelai sitting amongst the yellow daisies, embedded in the romantic proposal gesture made from Max Medina. The colour yellow was also very significant to me as it was my mom's favourite and it made me feel she was all around me.

In October 2019, I attended my first fan festival in Unionville with my husband Steve. For 20 years I lived very close to where they shot the pilot of the show, and yet I had never been to visit. It was so exciting to meet the cast members from a show I loved so much. Every meet and greet brought such a positive and fun experience. They were all so great and personable. One memorable moment for me was meeting Scott Patterson, who played the beloved character Luke Danes. The excitement was definitely in the air as *Gilmore Girls* fans waited with their cameras. When it was my turn he came to meet me and pose with him for a photo. Scott greeted me with a welcoming hello, warm smile, and open arms. He truly made my day. I could not stop smiling. I posted my experience in some of the Facebook fan groups for fans of the show with the caption, "Meeting Scott Patterson. He was so kind and sweet to me. He made my day." To my surprise and joy he shared my post and responded back in his own social media pages. "Made my day, too, Valerie! Thank you for the kind words, angel." It was an unforgettable and joyful experience.

I had no idea when I started watching *Gilmore Girls*, that it would bring me 20 years of laughter and comfort. Within the *Gilmore Girls* community, I have made some great friends and I know there are many more to meet. "It's a religion, it's a lifestyle" and I am very happy to be a part of it.

Cora Farrish

Michigan, USA

Gilmore Girls was introduced to me by my sister Cathy. Over a span of four to five years, Cathy kept encouraging me to watch it. I was newly widowed, raising my son, and working full time. I didn't feel like I could take time for myself, let alone watch a television program.

Cathy had bought seasons 1 through 6 of the *Gilmore Girls* on DVD and gave them to me, strongly insisting that I watched them. When I asked her why she was so insistent that I must watch it, she stated:

> *"Because it's you! It's about a single mom and her daughter that goes to private school. The only difference is you have a son."*

A few evenings later, I threw in the first DVD, finally deciding to give it a chance. The rest is history.

From the first episode, I became an honorary Gilmore girl. I was hooked. I loved the quick wit, smart humour, and the small town of quirky, loving characters. I watched seasons 1 to 6 from the time I got home from work until sometimes 2 A.M.. After flying through the DVDs, I caught up in time to start watching season 7 on television.

My sister Cathy and I lived in different towns, making it difficult to get together. We didn't have the same interests, or share the same intensity or passion for too many other things. But, over *Gilmore Girls* we bonded. We would call each other and discuss the show and laugh.

Cathy passed away August 19th, 2015. My heart aches daily for her beautiful, happy smile, and warm presence. After Cathy passed, it took a couple years before I could sit and watch *Gilmore Girls* again. I never lost my love for the show, though.

Eventually due to the aching and longing to be close to my sister, I started watching it again. It has helped. It often feels like she's there watching with me.

Gilmore Girls is a generational show that I believe can speak to everyone at each stage of life. The show has provided comfort for me as I navigated through teenage growing pains with my son—adulting, parenting, dating, navigating all relationships—and of loss, all the while keeping a healthy dose of laughter and a few tears. It's a lifestyle. It's a religion.

I'm so glad I chose to listen to my sister, Cathy, whom I love and miss dearly. It took a couple years before I could watch *Gilmore Girls* again. At first, I disconnected from the show as viewing it made me feel the grief worse. I had not lost my love for the show, but I had lost my sister. We had connected with one another through the show. Eventually my feelings shifted. Instead of avoiding the show, I began to watch it again. This time, it felt like Cathy was watching it with me, and it still does.

Karine Michaud

Bron, France

    I am French—like Michel, and *Gilmore Girls* to me is not just a show. It's a religion. A way of life.

    The first time I went to Stars Hollow, I was pregnant with my first child. I had never heard of the show, but watched it quite at random. I immediately fell in love with Lorelai, Sookie, and Luke and the characters of the small Connecticut town. *Gilmore Girls* very quickly became like a drug to me, and I was happy to be an addict.

I didn't know in those early days that I would go on to watch the show every year, that I would memorise the dialogue in both French and English, and that Stars Hollow would become the place I go to feel good. Amy Sherman-Palladino created a magical world where people can be crazy, but where everything is always okay.

The relationship between Emily and Lorelai reminds me a lot of my own relationship with my mother (albeit, with less money in the mix) and at the time I was feeling worried about my relationship with my unborn child. Watching *Gilmore Girls,* and seeing the relationship between Lorelai and Rory gave me a lot of encouragement. Lorelai speaks fast, and often, drinks coffee, and has a pretty good life. I figured if that was what I was in for, then everything was going to be okay. If Lorelai Gilmore can do it, then so can I.

Spending time with the cast of Stars Hollow very quickly became like home. Rory, Kirk, Taylor, Miss Patty, Dean, Jess, Logan, and Michel—It's as if they are real people. They make me smile. Each character is unique, we can easily connect with one of them and they bring an energy to the show. I am a resident of Stars Hollow every time I push play. I enter a world that feels so good, it is difficult to leave.

I want to dance with Miss Patty, chat with Babette, work with Taylor on the town activities, go to Luke's, and eat at the Dragonfly Inn. I want to know what the town loner was protesting, have a drink with Jackson, eat dinner every Friday at the Gilmore's, make a stop at Jojo's, pick up dinner at Al's, listen to Hep Alien, and debate with Paris.

I have two sons now, one called Lucas (after Luke, or 'Lucas according to Mia), and a cat called Paul Anka (Anka for short, and because we realised it was a female). My sons don't speak English, but they can sing "Where You Lead" perfectly. When my first child Romain was born, he cried a lot. I used to put the theme song on to comfort him and its soothing effect on him was incredible.

Gilmore Girls means a lot to me personally. Every time I have struggles in my life, I ask myself, 'WWLD' (What Would Lorelai Do?). I have a bracelet that I wear all the time that says "I'm a Lorelai". It has become a part of my identity.

I am an ordinary woman who lives in two worlds. The first one is the real one. It is full of pain, joy, two wonderful boys, a job I like, coffee, and friends. It is a good reality, and I am happy, but sometimes I feel I need more. That's when I go to my second world. That world is full of books, movies, and historical references. It takes place in a town where each person I see is crazy, fun, and caring. I get to watch them evolve, grow, change, and have happy endings.

Britany Smith

Wisconsin, USA

My *Gilmore Girls* story starts before I was even born. Mom was a teenager—seventeen years old and still in high school when she became pregnant with me. I was born on September 15, 1997, which was the best day of my entire life. It was the day I met my best friend, and the day that our strong bond came to form. Mom raised me as a single parent, with the help of my grandparents. We lived with them for most of my life because she could not afford to live on her own with me. My dad was not in my life very much until recently when he moved to Wisconsin from Virginia. He moved away when I was too young to remember him leaving. My mom did everything she could to provide me with anything and everything I needed. She always put me first and she still does.

Gilmore Girls was a show that Mom and I bonded over. She would be at home, laying on the couch, watching *Gilmore Girls,* and I would join her. My grandpa—I call him Apa—would call us 'The *Gilmore Girls*', because of our shared love for the show. We would watch other shows but *Gilmore Girls* was, and still is, our favourite show. The bond that Lorelai and Rory had is the same bond my mom and I have.

Life often imitates art, and in our case, our lives had a parallel storyline with *Gilmore Girls.* Mom always has, and always will, want the best for me. She enrolled me in dance classes even though I did not like it at times. She knew that in the end I would love it, and it would be a meaningful experience for me. When I was older, Mom impressed upon me the importance of going to college, something she felt was important, because she had not been able to attend at a young age. Unfortunately, I did not listen to her. Similar to how Lorelei and Rory did not talk for a while, my mom and I did not either. I took the side of a boy and we started to become distant. I avoided her. I wish I could take back that time because I missed my best friend. I hurt her and I regret it. She has always been there for me. After I had my son, our bond started to get stronger again.

My mom got married on September 22, 2018 to my now stepdad, Shane. I could not ask for a better stepdad than him. Before the big day, I talked to mom's maid of honour about surprising mum and Shane with a speech. Anyone who knows me, knows that I am very shy and do not like talking in front of a lot of people, so this was a big surprise for everyone. I based the speech on *Gilmore Girls*. I started off with the phrase, "Copper Boom" and I talked about how mom and I shared this incredible bond. I barely made it through the second sentence before crying. I ended my speech with the phrase "Oy with the poodles already." I explained to everyone who came to the wedding the meaning of both phrases. Later on, I found out that I had most of the room crying. I even had Apa crying and he is not one to cry. This was not the purpose of my speech. I wanted to give my best friend the speech she deserved. She was always there for me and I wanted to help make her special day even more special.

I don't know what I would do without my mom. She is my best friend and role model. I hope that one day I have her strength and determination.

Samantha Lloyd

Victoria, Australia

I first watched *Gilmore Girls* when it came on free to air television here in Australia. I spent week after week watching the show as it caught my attention straight away. I loved how fast paced and witty it was, and I loved the characters. I was a teenager, so Rory's good-looking boyfriends drew me in as well. When I met my husband, he helped me purchase the full sets of DVD seasons. Once I had those, I kept working my way from the start, to end of the series. I would put it on in the evening and fall asleep, waking up in the middle of the night to the home menu on the DVD and hear the 'la la la laaa' tune and smile to myself.

I was born with a heart condition known as Tetralogy of Fallot. This means there were four abnormalities within my heart along with a blockage in my pulmonary artery. I first had surgery as a baby. I was 16 months of age and had to be operated on to remove the blockage and sew up some holes in the heart that were present. As a result, I have been medically monitored my whole life. My childhood was filled with medical appointments and tests to see how my heart was handling stress.

When I was 28, I was told that I would have to have my pulmonary valve in my heart replaced. This meant open heart surgery again. On Friday the 4th of November, 2016, I underwent a four hour surgery with one of the best heart surgeons in Victoria. A week later, after I had built up enough of my strength, I got to go home to finish my recovery and rehab at home.

Knowing that I was always going to need more surgery I was never really too worried about it, until the day before my surgery when I was meeting with the surgeon. I had to be at the hospital early the next morning as I was one of the first operations to go ahead that day. I remember being prepped in the operating room by the team of nurses and being asked what I wanted to listen to. I looked at the clock which said 8.30 A.M. That was my last memory before waking up in the intensive care unit. My Mum and husband were there, waiting for me. It was a slow recovery for me as I wasn't allowed out of bed for several days. Finally, they removed all the non-essential tubes from me, and I was able to slowly walk around my ward and do more tasks independently—albeit, slowly.

I was delighted when I finally got told I could go home. At home I spent my days watching television. I spent one day a week in a cardiac rehabilitation class doing simple exercises to build strength and stamina back up. These classes also taught me what to expect post-surgery, and what changes I could make to help my body (and mind) achieve the best outcomes. During this time, *Gilmore Girls: A Year in the Life* was released. I was so excited. One of my best friends had Netflix, so he picked me up and we spent the evenings watching it. I found this gave me something I was very interested in to keep my mind occupied so that I didn't go into a downward spiral during this time.

My husband bought me *Gilmore Girls: A Year in the Life* on DVD, when it came out in 2017. I recently turned one of my co-workers onto the show while she has been stuck at home sick and she binge watched it. She is 20 years old, and it brings me great joy to see the generation below me enjoying it as much as I do.

After my open heart surgery, *Gilmore Girls* kept me sane. It gave my life enjoyment while I was home bound and recovering. It also led me to a new passion—writing fan fiction based on the show. Writing helped keep me mentally busy—stable. After watching *A Year in the Life*, I found—like others—that I was feeling dissatisfied with the ending. I started reading fanfiction, to see how others had perceived the *Gilmore Girls* lives to look like, after the original seven season run. While reading through these, my own imagination started running wild, and I started forming my own ideas of what I thought the *Gilmore Girls* world might have gone on to look like. These ideas developed, and started to include new stories, new characters, and new relationships that were not seen on the show. Through my writing, and love for *Gilmore Girls*, I found some amazing people from around the world that shared my love of the show and for writing. Among these, is one of my best Gilmore friends Tina. Our friendship began when Tina asked me to become a proof-reader for her. During this time, we came up with a number of stories together and helped each other with ideas. Since that humble start we have come to be intercontinental friends that would love to meet some day.

Olivia Roth

New York, USA

My junior year of high school, I discovered *Gilmore Girls*. I saw myself in Rory Gilmore—the 'straight-A' high school student who had ivy league aspirations. In a way, Rory and I grew up together. We sat the PSAT together, and a deer ran into the sides of both of our cars. While her grandfather was in the hospital for a heart attack, so was my dad.

While *Gilmore Girls* provided endless quick, quippy dialogue, they also touched on serious issues. Rory has been a companion throughout some of my most difficult times. When my dad was in the hospital in my junior year, I found solace in the hospitalisation of Rory's grandfather. She verbalised the fears that I didn't have the emotional capacity or distance from the situation to compose. When Rory struggled with finding her path at Yale and took a semester off, I was an unhappy first year student at Haverford College. The show normalised my loneliness and frustration.

I transferred to Yale sophomore year, and *Gilmore Girls* was part of the reason I applied. I have not found the perfect study tree, but it is an incredible school and I've been so grateful for my time there. I attended "The Game" and "Parent's Weekend", ate dining hall food (the pot roast is not all Richard Gilmore talks it up to be) and was even a member of a secret society.

Rory Gilmore taught me to be brave, and strong, and unapologetically smart. I recently graduated from Yale, and for the first time since high school, I will start a chapter of my life where Rory Gilmore will no longer be my guide. While I will not be reporting on a presidential campaign, I will embark on my own adventure, and I will be forever grateful to have grown up with Rory, Lorelai, and the community of Stars Hollow.

Appendix One

"What's Next" Pitch

By: Trista McMorrow

This movie or series picks up right where *A Year in the Life* leaves off.

Season 1

We find out Rory has signed up to be a surrogate for one of Paris's clients. She made the decision in true Gilmore fashion by not wanting to live off her mom and Luke while she completes her book *Gilmore Girls*.

Rory, being pregnant, and editor of the Stars Hollow Gazette, faces a host of challenges. She has discovered how challenging it is to live with her Mom and Luke. Luke lets her use the diner above the apartment, even though she insists on paying rent. It comes to blows when he finds out she's been sneaking money into the register. She convinces him to take the money because she 'needs to make it on her own" just like her mom.

Rory doesn't know how to tell her grandma about her situation. She tries to hide it and avoid the topic all together, until at one Friday night dinner her grandma brings up Logan's upcoming nuptials and passive aggressively attacks Rory for not living up to her full potential. Rory explodes on her grandma saying she doesn't need to explain her life and storms out before she ever tells her grandma about the baby.

Meanwhile, Rory and the couple she is a surrogate for go to weekly doctor visits together. There is clearly something not right with the couple's relationship. They argue, but strangely pretend everything is ok. The doctor tells them all "It's a girl!" The couple seems less than thrilled.

A few months later, Logan shows up. It is two days before his wedding, and he just needed to see Rory. He sees her from across the town square and notices her state of pregnancy and wonders if it could be his. He does not approach her right away so he can have some time to process the prospect of becoming a father. When he finally does approach her, she assures him he is not making a mistake. He should get married and this baby is not his. Logan leaves her with the best of luck and a kiss on the cheek.

In the background, the Stars Hollow doctor is trying to retire but has no successor and brings up a problem that Stars Hollow will not be able to continue to function, as most of the younger generation has moved on to the bigger cities. Rory uses her post at the Stars Hollow Gazette and her connections in journalism to put out an article encouraging professionals to give the small town life a try over the big city.

One episode (scene) can have the town overrun by New Yorkers trying to get jobs and requesting food from Luke's like "avocado toast". Taylor Doose decides to train up a successor who is a strong female character and even Taylor isn't sure he likes her, but when she takes charge of a major event she proves she can do it all and wins him over.

Rory is past-due. Baby will be here any day. Her book is almost done and she is trying to get all the finishing touches complete so it can be sent to publishing before the baby arrives. Paris calls her to unemotionally let her know that the baby's parents have broken up and decided to put the baby up for adoption. She tells Rory not to worry, she has all the legal documents for the adoption ready to go and Rory will still get paid. While Rory is still digesting this information she goes into labor.

Lorelai and Luke rush her to the hospital, only for it to take hours and hours to have the baby. Luke is in the waiting room with his head down trying not to pass out and refusing to leave. Rory tells her mom during a painful contraction that it didn't seem right that the baby was already an orphan. Lorelai says the baby girl will be okay and Paris will take care of everything. Rory admits that she doesn't think she will be able to let that happen, that she already has such a bond with this little girl. Cue another pain, and then time to push.

When the baby arrives the doctor shouts "Congratulations, It's a Boy!"

A BOY?!? They are both shocked. The moment Rory holds the baby it is love at first sight. She knows she has met her son. Paris arrives at the hospital with the paperwork and Rory says she would like to adopt the baby. Paris asks if she is sure and Rory confirms that she is, even if she is not prepared and has nothing to give a baby, she is ready to adopt this child. Paris has Rory sign on the dotted line and it's done. A little later Emily Gilmore enters the hospital room, looks at the baby, and simply asks "So, what's his name?" And Rory replies with "Richard Rory Gilmore, we can call him Rickey". Emily melts as she holds her great-grand-son and all is forgotten.

Season 2

Before leaving the hospital Rory and Lorelai have a meltdown about what they will do with a boy. Will they have to do the sports things? What do boys do? How will they teach him to use tools? They decide Luke is around now and can help with that, but Lorelai can't be "grandma". She insists that it just isn't right. After trying a new 'grandma' name every time she holds the baby she settles on "Lolli- and Pops" for her and Luke – much to his dismay as he is most certainly not a "pops". But the appeal of "Lollypop" isn't lost on Lorelai.

Baby comes home to Rory's apartment where she thinks she will have nothing for the baby, but in true Stars Hollow fashion, her apartment is decked to the brim with baby boy items that her Stars Hollow friends surprised her with.

At the baby's first doctor's appointment she goes in to meet with the doctor to find out the new town doctor is Marty from Yale, her consistent friend whom she never gave a chance to. He is now grown, mature, and hot! She finds out that he decided to come give small town life a try and he is the new doctor.

Rory and Marty run into each other at baby appointments and around town frequently. They have a "Luke and Lorelei" type relationship—a friendship filled with banter that focuses on their history and current professions. They see each other at town festivals and maybe he even accidentally bids on her basket.

In a heartfelt moment Rory finds out that Marty was previously married, but his wife struggled with infertility so they were never able to have children, and then she got cancer and died. That is why he decided to move out of the big city, to run away from the memories of a dying wife that even a doctor husband couldn't help.

They were 'just friends' until one night – when baby Rickey got sick. Marty comes to Rory's apartment and stays up all night watching the baby, going above and beyond the call of a doctor or even a friend. It is clear that he did this not just for baby Rickey—he stayed to comfort Rory and there is no denying it.

Rickey gets better and life moves on. Rory's book is published and is an instant success. We always knew she was an amazing writer. Now she has to go on book tours and even gets picked up to be on the *Ellen* show! She is crazy nervous about leaving Rickey even if it is with Luke and Lorelei his "LollyPop's". Lorelei realizes that changing boy diapers is much different than girl diapers and remembers how much work it is to have a baby around again. Rory and Marty share their first kiss before she leaves.

Rory returns home. Her story has come full circle with a strong finish just like her mom. She is the success story we knew she would be and an amazing mother like her own. She begins writing her second book while sitting at a table at Luke's, and is approached by a director. He asks her if she would consider letting her book be used as a springboard for a television series.

I feel like this story line helps wrap up Rory's happy ending. She becomes the success we knew she could be just like her mother. She fulfilled her own ambitions on her own and in her own time. Her relationship with her son will add a new dynamic to her own story line and may bring a fresh audience. The public will love that she made her own way rather than having her life dictated by mistakes.

Appendix Two

Brooke Criswell, M.A. and Rachel Renbarger, PhD

As postgraduate researchers, we undertook a study that began with an interesting *Gilmore Girls* question: why do people choose to be on Team Dean, Team Jess, or Team Logan? As fans ourselves, we wanted to use a scientific, media psychology approach to better understand fans choosing a romantic team for Rory's main character. Even years after the show has ended, there are dedicated online communities devoted to discussing this topic. From a psychological approach, we began wondering do we project our own romantic preferences to these characters? Is it what we want best for Rory because we believe we know her and she's a friend? Or maybe we identify with Rory ourselves? Is it perhaps we see ourselves in Dean, Jess, or Logan? We conducted a survey with hundreds of participants recruited through various Facebook fan groups to figure this out.

It's essential to explain the theories, and why we asked the questions we did in the survey and discuss the fandom community around *Gilmore Girls*.

Entertainment, such as *Gilmore Girls*, serve as the source of cultural and ritualistic behaviors of fans. Media fandom refers to individuals who collectively and socially unite within a subculture based on a media product's shared appreciation (Tsay-Vogel & Sanders, 2017). Members of fandom groups are typically not just watchers of the show. They are knowledgeable producers of principal cultural characteristics. Jenkins (2000) describes fandom as the "ability to transform personal reaction into social interaction, spectator culture into participatory culture" (p. 451). Often, these subcultures shape social identities, provide a sense of community and social prestige (Tsay-Vogel & Sanders, 2017).

Social media has increased the capabilities of connecting with others who share similar interests and, in this case, the love of *Gilmore Girls*. There are many benefits to being part of an online fandom community. Fans have a shared emotional connection (Tsay-Vogel & Sanders, 2017). Being a fan is a way to engage and connect with others socially. Fandom is primarily predicated on socially ritualized practices, explaining the gravitation toward online communities forming about certain shows (Tsay-Vogel & Sanders, 2017). Possibly, picking a team in a show connects people even further than being a fan of the entire show. When it comes to the media, people are creating a personal media profile to support their identity. In particular, people favor others who like the same media shows because it relates to their idea of similarity in the shared "in-group" mindset that distinguishes them from the "out-group." Social categorization theory (Tajfel & Turner, 1979) could also provide insight into picking a team and then connecting with others to discuss that standpoint. People define categories and schemes to encode and decode messages. People categorize people into groups to simplify understanding the world and structure social interaction (Tajfel & Turner, 1979). Literature supports fandom is facilitated by a meaningful and affective bond between the self and the media world, and the deep connection people share with a community is manifested by central aspects of the fan's identity and the values one holds (Sandvoss, 2013).

To better understand what drives our decision-making in this situation, we looked at Rory's parasocial relationships and with each of the love interests. We also measured character identification with Rory. This provides insight into whether someone who identifies with Rory and picks a team may have different reasoning than someone who does not identify with Rory. The other reason is to determine whether people had a parasocial relationship with Rory and how that could impact their decision making. Let's break that down a little bit further.

People are biologically predisposed to form social relationships and attachment to others (Stever, 2010). Television shows provide audience members with the ability to meet and explore other people they may not get outside of the media. Sometimes, having an attachment and forming a relationship can be to a fictional character. This kind of relationship is called parasocial relationships. The term was first created by Horton and Wohl (1956). Parasocial relationships are usually one-sided. People can form these relationships with celebrities, fictional characters, cartoons, politicians, and anyone else they do not truly know but feel like they do. When people engage in watching *Gilmore Girls,* they may come to know the mannerisms, behaviors, facial expressions, and other personal details learned by being immersed in the show. To have a parasocial relationship, one must feel personally connected to those characters (Horton & Wohl, 1956). This relationship, just like many others, can provide a sort of companionship and become part of the viewer's social world. Relationships are formed throughout time and can also transform over time with ongoing interactions. They can also evoke strong emotional responses.

Parasocial relationships form for various motivations by fans. The three most frequent reasons were task attraction such as they like the celebrity because they are good at what they do, the second is romantic attraction, and third was due to the identification and social attraction which means they like that person because they remind them themselves or who they want to be like (Stever, 2013). Because there are different motivators, there are different types of parasocial relationships, just like people have in real life. They have parasocial friendships, parasocial love interests, and parasocial mentors and heroes. Parasocial romances may provide insight into how one decides whom they want the main character to end up with. In *Gilmore Girls,* one who may have a parasocial romantic relationship with Logan may choose him as their team. It may have nothing to do with the main character and more to do with the options available. Having a romantic parasocial relationship may also help one understand why they are attracted to certain kinds of people versus others and help sort out who they may want to have a real-life relationship potentially. Stever (2013) also points out that people feel attached to characters because they elicit memories or feelings from people they know in real life and the attachment they feel to those individuals. Therefore, parasocial relationships, and primarily when romantic feelings are involved, can provide much insight into the individual's own preferences regarding relationships.

    Identification with characters could also provide insight as to why one picks the team they are on. Whether it is identification with the main character, one chooses the love interest for or identification with the love interest character, or a combination of both, it will be explored through this study. Identification is the idea of feeling and thinking like the character. It involves experiencing what the character is experiencing and understanding them on a deeper, more meaningful level and even living vicariously through them (Oatley, 1999). It also means taking on the protagonist's goals and plans (Oatley, 1999). Cohen (2001) describes identification as a psychological process where people imagine replacing themselves with that character within the context or narrative. Sometimes, one loses awareness of their role as a viewer. It allows a more emotional understanding of their feelings and cognitive understanding of their decisions and actions, which lead to greater enjoyment while watching the show (Tukachinsky & Eyal, 2018).

Several studies (Hoeken et al., 2016) have shown a positive correlation between perceived similarity in a character and identification. Cohen (2006, p. 188) claims that psychological manners, such as having similar attitudes or personality traits, are more critical in identification than demographic similarities such as age and gender. The other characteristics could be having similar life experiences or behavioral tendencies. Another driving force for identification with characters is the character's likeability (Cohen, 2006). For individuals to engage as fans and participate in fandom communities, identification is critical (Tsay-Vogel & Sanders, 2017). These social ties to the fandom community can increase social practices of identification (Tsay-Vogel & Sanders, 2017). Identification can be determined by the viewer's perception of the character. There are many different types of identification as well, and ways one goes about identifying with characters.

The most fundamental dimension of identification is spatiotemporal identification, a process where viewers can adopt the character's physical location in time and space as a vantage (Krieken et al., 2017). Perceptual identification is the second dimension of identification. This happens when viewers adopt the characters' perceptual perspective and mentally represent that the character sees, hears, and physically experiences (Krieken et al., 2017). Next is moral identification, which is conceptualized as a process where the viewer adopts the character's beliefs, goals, moral values, and attitudes (Krieken et al., 2017). Emotional identification occurs when viewers adopt a character's feelings and emotions (Krieken et al., 2017). Cognitive identification happens when the viewer shares the character's mindset. Here, the audience understands the character's thoughts, expectations, aims, and intentions. This also allows people to draw inferences about other characters' thoughts and intentions (Krieken et al., 2017). Last is the embodied identification, which refers to the simulation of performing the character's actions and motions and co-experiencing the character's events (Krieken et al., 2017). When one takes on the identification with Rory, one may be more inclined to pick a romantic partner they wish they could be with because they have taken on the role of being with that person. This idea has been called wishful identification, and it describes the psychological process through individual desires or attempts to be like another person (Hoffner & Buchanan, 2005). Wishful identification is also influenced by the way characters are portrayed (Bandura, 1986). Research has also shown that people evaluate media characters how people evaluate others in their social networks in real life. They assess a character's personality traits and develop impressions that lead to behaviors' expectations (Hoffner & Buchanan, 2005). These theories are the foundation of this study and hopefully provide a greater understanding of fandom, parasocial relationships, and character identification.

Who Took the Survey?

We had 895 people who had responded to the survey when we calculated our results which was a fantastic turnout. We had people take the survey from every continent (with the exception of Antarctica, of course), although most of the people (62%) were from the United States. Over 80% of the people identified as female and White, and about ¾ of the people identified as straight.

Almost everyone who took the survey seemed to be a big fan of the show. In terms of *Gilmore Girls*, the largest group of people began watching the show when it was airing and only about 11% of the participants began watching after the Netflix "A Year in the Life" premiered. Over 80% of the people were a part of at least one of our listed fan groups or pages, with about 30% belonging to three or more groups. Because we recruited people from fan pages, it makes sense that we found dedicated GG fans to participate in our study.

Team Membership

Of course, we asked what "team" people were on- Were they Team Dean, Jess, or Logan, or were they not on any team? In terms of which teams people were on, it was incredibly close and people had many opinions about who Rory should have been with. By a slim margin, the most popular was Team Logan with 42% followed by Team Jess with 38%. Team Dean was the lowest with only 5% of the votes and was even beat by people who were not on any team (12%). When looking at the correlations between team memberships, we saw that there was a much stronger correlation between Team Logan and Team Jess (-0.67) compared to Team Dean and Logan (-0.18) or Jess (-0.17) and these correlations were all negative. These results suggest that people tend to be strongly in either a Logan OR Jess camp and would not feel similarly about the two boyfriends.

We asked people why they were not on any team, and there were three general responses: 1) that each boyfriend played a different role in Rory's life, 2) each boyfriend had all positives and they liked them all, or 3) all of them were terrible and they didn't like any of them.

About 2% said they were neither on a team nor not on a team. These "other" participants were often torn and couldn't just pick one team; often these people were in favor of Logan *and* also another person. Some, though, wrote in other people, such as Tristan (what?!), Marty, or Robert, or said they were on Team Rory.

We then asked a similar question: Who would you want Rory to be with long-term? We received similar results to team membership, but it wasn't identical. Logan was still the first choice (42%) and closely followed by Jess (40%) with few voting for Dean (5%). However, there were fewer people who did not pick any of these three choices. From this, it seems that people did not put themselves on the team of a boyfriend but still thought Rory should end up with one of them, which was interesting.

Still, we wondered if people chose teams based not on who they thought Rory should end up with, but rather who they would have wanted to date. For this reason, we asked if they would date Dean, Jess, or Logan if they were free to do so. Here the results changed. More people said they would rather date Jess (36%) compared to Logan (33%), with almost 10% stating they would date Dean. Over 14% said they would not date any of these men. Generally speaking, people who were on Team Jess were more likely to say they would date Jess whereas people in Teams Dean and Logan were more likely to date other people or not date anyone at all. This helped tell us that team membership was not completely based on who they would date or who they would want Rory to date, and that team membership choices were more complicated. For that reason, we conducted more tests to see what might help us understand why people picked teams.

Identification and Parasocial Relationships

We asked people if they identified with Rory and also if they identified with the boyfriends they picked for their teams. From the correlations, it did not appear that identifying with Rory related to which team the participant chose. However, there were moderate relationships between identifying with Rory and identifying with either Logan (0.48), Jess (.47), or Dean (.40). All of these relationships were statistically significant.

We also asked questions to see if the participants have a parasocial relationship with Rory or the boyfriends they picked for their teams. If a participant identified with Rory, they were much more likely to have higher parasocial relationship scores with Jess (.35) or, to a stronger degree, Logan (.44). This means that those who feel like they identify with Rory tend to also feel like they have a friendship with Logan or Jess. Interestingly, even though there were fewer Team

Dean members, those with higher parasocial relationship scores with Rory were much more likely to have higher parasocial relationship scores with Dean (.76) compared to Jess (.70) or Logan (.70). This means that there is a distinction between people who identify with Rory and those who feel like she is a friend. Those who feel she is a friend were more likely to feel like they have a friend with any of her past boyfriends. Additionally, participants who identified with Rory or one of the boyfriends were more likely to have a higher parasocial relationship score with those characters. As an example, if someone identified as Jess, they were also more likely to feel like they were friends with Jess.

Predicting Teams

Finally, we wanted to know what might help us predict who would be on a certain team. To do this, we conducted multiple regression analyses for each of the teams (Dean/Jess/Logan/no team) with variables such as participants' gender, sexuality, and age as predictors. None of these important demographic variables seemed to matter, so we tried seeing if we could predict team membership based on identification or parasocial relationship scores. Contrary to what we were expecting, only two variables were statistically significant. One finding was not too surprising; people were more likely to choose their team if they also wanted to date them and this was consistent for every boyfriend. In terms of the other statistically significant finding, those who had lower parasocial relationship scores with Rory, they were more likely to pick Team Logan (-.54) or Team Jess (-.48). This means that for people who did not feel like they were friends with Rory tended to be on either Team Logan or Team Jess.

Conclusions

From these results, we know a few key things about fans of *Gilmore Girls*. First of all, Team Dean is a lonely camp—Teams Jess and Logan are much larger. Secondly, team decision making is a complex phenomenon. Fans of the show did not always subscribe to a team and demographic variables and psychological constructs were less powerful in predicting team membership than we expected. When people watch shows and pick teams, sometimes that is because they identify with the character or feel like they have a relationship with them but not always. What we found here was that people tended to pick teams based on whether or not they felt they had a friendship with Rory but not whether they identified with her. This means people had a parasocial relationship with Rory therefore, just like our friends in real life, we want what we think is best for them and not necessarily what we want ourselves. This makes sense because many of the viewers could relate to being someone's friend but many were not women or attracted to men which would limit the ability for someone to identify with them or want to date them. Finally, people can pick teams based on what they relate to or other variables that we did not capture here. More research should add in other variables and test whether these relationships hold up in other shows.

Acknowledgements

As always, my gratitude goes first and foremost to my family, who are always patient and helpful throughout my creative projects. My husband Stephen is a real partner in every facet of life, including my work. He makes himself available to bounce ideas around, reads my writing, sends me relevant resources he finds online, and comforts me during my creative (and uncreative) breakdowns. He really is my rock, and I draw inspiration from him in everything I do. Thank you Stephen for believing that I had another book in me, and for supporting me through yet another large creative undertaking.

Thank you also to my mother Debby, and sister Shaniya-rae. The reason I don't have a large group of friends in my life is because I never find any who are as fabulous as the both of you. Thank you for seeing me through yet another book, and another two years of my life.

Those who know me well know that my life wouldn't mean anything without the inclusion of my miracle baby, and his three chosen siblings. These four beautiful human beings illuminate my life not just because they are beautiful—which they are—but because they are beautiful in every way. Thank you for giving me the space and understanding to write another book. I am incredibly blessed and grateful to be your Mummy.

This book would also not be what it is without the perspicacious advice and assistance of my best friend Erin. What started as an online friendship over our mutual love for the show has grown to mean more and more to me over the years, and I could not have gone on this journey without her. Eventually, her contribution to this project became so significant that she was taken on as a Creative Consultant, and I am forever indebted to her for stepping into that role and supporting me in this process. Thank you for riding the ups and downs of another book journey with me, and for being my best Gilmore friend.

I have to of course, thank the contributors to this book, starting with the cast and crew. Thank you especially to Biff Yeager, who was the first cast member to take a chance on me, and agree to contribute his story to this book. A special thank you is also owed to Valerie Campbell, who put me in touch with a significant number of cast members and crew. The cast and crew section really took off under your influence, and I will be forever grateful for the role you played in making that happen. Thank you to all the cast and crew who gave up their time to speak with me, who shared their personal memories and experiences (sometimes uncomfortable and painful), and for their candour. Not only has it made for an interesting book, but it was an incredibly memorable and humbling experience for me as a fan to get to speak with you all, one on one, about your time on the show.

Thank you to those in the creator section who shared their work, and their love for the show. A special thank you to Chas Demster who also put me in touch with several members of the cast and crew with whom he is connected, and who also shared his own unique story about the show's impact on his life.

Finally, thank you to those who contributed to the fan section of this book. Since this book was originally envisioned as a book of fan stories, these contributors have waited the longest to see publication of this project. Most of the fans and creators submitted written pieces they penned themselves, which have been edited into their final form, and many of them shared emotional experiences that connected their lives to the show. Thank you for your openness, and for trusting me with your Gilmore stories. Your stories highlight the magic of this fan community, and bring the book to life. More than anything, they demonstrate the unique nature of this show in bringing people together.

Taryn

Photo Credits

All photos supplied by those named in each chapter, with the exception of the following:

- Alan Loayza

Photo supplied by Lorna Haigh

The following credits also apply:

- Grant Lee Phillips

Photo by Denise Siegel-Phillips

- Elisabeth Abbot

Photo by Bethany Froelich

- Yuri Lowenthal

Photo by Mikel Healy

- Olivia Roth

Photo by Lev Greenstein

About the Author

Ko Takitumu, ko Hikurangi ōku māunga
Ko Aparima, ko Waiapu ōku awa
Ko Horouta, ko Mataatua ōku waka
Ko Kāi Tahu, ko Ngāti Pōrou, ko Kāti Māmoe ōku iwi
Ko te Aowera, ko Te Aitanga a mate ōku hapū
Nō Otepoti ahau, Kei Tauranga e noho ana
Ko Allen Harris rāua ko Debra Constable ōku mātua
Ko Jonny-ray ratou ko Ciara, ko Nathan, ko Alex aku tamariki
Ko Ciara ratou ko Nathan, ko Alex. He whāngai ratou
Ko Stephen Dryfhout taku hoa rangatira
Ko Taryn Dryfhout tōku ingoa

Taryn is an experienced writer, teacher, theologian, and coffee junkie who lives in New Zealand with her husband and four children.

A Rory-inspired blue-stocking, Taryn is a serial student, earning several diplomas and degrees, and now currently completing a PhD program. She works as a college tutor, and has won awards for her postgraduate research and Māori leadership.

Taryn has written several non-fiction books, tertiary college courses, website content, and more than 400 feature articles, reviews, and columns published in newspapers, websites, and magazines. She has been nominated for "Best Feature Writer" and "Best Columnist", and is a member of Mensa, the NZ Society of Authors, and NZ Christian Writers.

When Taryn is not writing, studying, teaching, or with her kids, she can be found reading books, buying books, or watching her favourite television shows.

www.TarynDryfhout.com